SOCIOLOGY
THROUGH
HUMOR

SOCIOLOGY THROUGH HUMOR

Joseph E. Faulkner
Pennsylvania State University

WEST PUBLISHING COMPANY
St. Paul / New York / Los Angeles / San Francisco

Cover Art: Robert L. Eyster
Cover Design: Lisa Swiatopolk-Mirski
Copyediting: Solveig Tyler-Robinson
Interior Design: Lisa Swiatopolk-Mirski

Library of Congress Cataloging-in-Publication Data
Sociology through humor.
  1. Sociology—Methodology. 2. Wit and humor—
Social aspects. 3. Satirists—United States.
  I. Faulkner, Joseph E.
HM24.S5726   1987   301'.0207   86–26666
ISBN 0–314–28491–5

For Babs
who still brings laughter into my life

Preface

*T*he purpose of this anthology is, first, to introduce a growing interest in sociology: the understanding of the contribution humor makes to interpreting human behavior. Humorists provide, in a delightful manner of course, perspectives beyond those of the social sciences. For example, Arthur Hoppe raises the question of why the upper classes have lower birth rates than the other classes. The answer lies in the upper classes' effective use of geographical birth control:

> The poor, as you know, sleep in double beds. The middle class, in twins. While the rich enjoy separate bedrooms, separate cabanas and separate vacations. This explains why we have so many poor people in the world. And so few rich.... I doubt any more effective method will ever be devised than having to get up on a cold night, fumble in the closet for one's bathrobe and slippers, stumble down a drafty hall and knock three times on a closed door. The very thought quells the spirit of romance. Thus it is no surprise that the Idle Rich, as we call them, average a distinguished 1.2 children. (1968)

Secondly, the anthology organizes a collection of both contemporary and classic selections around the themes covered in introductory sociology classes. It is designed to provide humorous readings which examine the same major concerns as those of sociology. Of course, it is not offered as a substitute for the task of comprehending the social scientific explanation of human behavior. As Feinberg notes, "a man whose reading was limited to satire would have a perverted vision of life." (1967:17) But from the other side of the coin, reading only the social sciences is inadequate, too. Berger, one of the few sociologists who has called attention to "the deeply comic aspect" of our social existence, maintains that "it is quite possible that the total absence of any sense of humor actually interferes with the attempt to give an intellectually adequate picture of society." (1961:67)

Not everyone agrees with those who argue for the inclusion of humor as an aid to studying behavior. Chapman and Foot report that the 1976 International Conference on Humor and Laughter received extensive publicity, but some of it "brought home the fact that 'humor' and 'laughter' are not yet recognized by many as legitimate topics for serious study." (1977:xii) Of course, breaking new ground is never easy. It is hoped that this anthology will help to further our understanding and appreciation of some of the commonalities of interest in humor and sociology. The selections chosen for inclusion are particularly apt illustrations of how humorists examine those areas of life which are of central concern to sociology. They are a pleasure to read, but they are more. They provide the student and instructor alike with an opportunity to go beyond traditional methods of sociological understanding and explore new and challenging ways of interpreting our behavior.

When interpreting behavior, social scientists perceive of themselves as employing the rigors of the scientific method to arrive at conclusions. Sociologists, psychologists, and related practitioners are engaged in a serious business. Definitions of sociology, for example, follow in the vein of this one from a widely used text: "Sociology is the scientific study of human society and social behavior." (Robertson, 1981:3) No nonsense here. Humorists, of course, do not perceive of themselves as social scientists (heaven forbid!), nor are they perceived by anyone else in this fashion. Yet, a careful examination of the work of humorists and social scientists reveals that there is a strong commonality in their efforts to understand human behavior. Humorists, for example, capitalize on one of the major interests of social scientists—social change. How are the changes in our society affecting the social structure of our major institutions? That social scientists explore such a question comes as no surprise to those who have been exposed to the work of sociologists or economists. Humorists also examine the effects of social change. Erma Bombeck states that "it's a frightening thing to wake up one morning and discover th⁻ while you were asleep you went out of style. That's what
        ened to millions of housewives who one day looked into their

mirrors and said: 'I do not feel fulfilled putting toilet seats down all day.' " (1978:58) Changing sex roles, of great concern to sociologists and others, provide the basis for much commentary by contemporary humorists such as Roy Blount, Jr., Art Buchwald, and Russell Baker.

In their writings, humorists examine the basic assumptions underlying what we claim to be the reality of social life. They often engage in what sociologist Peter Berger (1963) describes as one of the functions of sociology: to "debunk," i.e., to get beneath the surface of our behavior and examine why we do what we do. Feinberg argues that the satire of humorists emphasizes "what seems to be real but is not. It ridicules man's naive acceptance of individuals and institutions at face value." (1967:3) Compare this with Berger's assertion that "the first wisdom of sociology is this—things are not what they seem." (1963:23) Humorists add important insights to the findings of social science through their ridicule of basic institutions.

The readings in this book have been carefully tailored to correspond with the many fine introductory texts available in the field. Not every topic covered in introductory texts has a ready parallel in the work of humorists. But all the major concerns of sociology are covered. Part I provides humorous readings which examine the methods of sociological research. The problems of sampling, controlled experimentation, and the sociological perspective are included. Part II deals with the socialization of the individual—how we become social beings. Part III looks at the individual in society, examining the cultural context of behavior. Part IV considers the social structure, including groups and formal organizations, and the problem of deviation from normative structures. Part V examines the existence of social inequality in society by considering social stratification and ethnic and racial groups. The institutional sphere is the theme of Part VI. The family, courtship and marriage, the political order, and religion are examined. In the last section, Part VII, the effects of social change upon our sexual behavior and sex roles is considered, along with the problems of population changes.

The choice of selections for inclusion includes the works of contemporary humorists such as Kurt Vonnegut, Art Buchwald, Russell Baker, Dave Barry, and others. Our classic humorists such as Mark Twain are also included. The focus is primarily on contemporary works, since one of the main characteristics of humor is its timely nature. The humor of even ten years ago is not always funny to this generation. The selections are from novels, magazines, books, and the journalistic columns of Arthur Hoppe, Russell Baker, and others.

Many forms of humor have been omitted. This is not the usual apology in anthologies for what has been excluded. Much humor being written today for both stage and screen is not readily transferable to a reader such as this. I saw an excellent university production of Jules Feiffer's *Little Murders*. The very funny marriage scene is simply not funny when divorced from its total context. This is true of many movie and television scripts. I share the conviction of millions of others that Bill Cosby's mother should be honored for the moment of passion which gave him to us. But his recording of "Noah" has to be heard, not read. The same is true, of course, of today's humorous music. But student and instructor alike will find more than sufficient humor represented in the selections contained in this reader.

REFERENCES

Berger, Peter. *Invitation to Sociology.* Garden City, N.Y.: Doubleday, 1963.

Bombeck, Erma. *If Life Is a Bowl of Cherries, What Am I Doing in the Pits?* New York: Fawcett Crest, 1978.

Chapman, J.J., and Foote, H.C. *It's a Funny Thing, Humor.* Oxford: Pergamon Press, 1977.

Feinberg, Leonard. *Introduction to Satire.* Ames, Iowa: Iowa State University Press, 1967.

Hoppe, Arthur. *The Perfect Solution to Absolutely Everything.* Garden City, N.Y.: Doubleday, 1968.

Robertson, Ian. *Sociology.* New York: Worth Publishing Co., 1981.

Acknowledgments

*A*ll who write know that many people contribute to the success of a book. It is a pleasure for me to recognize the assistance of those who have made this book possible. Clyde Perlee of West Publishing first welcomed the idea and set the whole process in motion. Clark Baxter was the first to read the manuscript in its entirety. Thereafter his enthusiasm and own special brand of wit and humor made this entire project a particular delight. I am grateful for his editorial skills, evaluations, and suggestions.

Other staff members at West Publishing, Rebecca Wee, production editor, and Solveig Tyler-Robinson, copy-editor, helped to smooth out the rough spots in the manuscript. Four reviewers, Stan L. Albrecht, Brigham Young University, Paul J. Baker, Illinois State University, Charles E. Garrison, East Carolina University, and Paul D. Starr, Auburn University, each read the manuscript and offered extremely helpful criticisms. The book has greatly benefited from their perceptive evaluations. Betsy Will, Penn State University, served as my research associate, tracked down all the permissions, typed the manuscript, and performed innumerable other chores to keep me on schedule. I am most grateful for her help.

Finally, those creative geniuses whose works appear in this book receive special accolades for reminding us not to take ourselves too seriously. Their willingness to allow their work to be reprinted here is deeply appreciated.

Contents

PART III / SELF IN SOCIETY / 33

PART IV / THE SOCIAL STRUCTURE AND DEVIANCE / 65

Introduction

C ompared to other areas of interest and research in the social sciences, for example, class and stratification, the investigation of humor has been paltry indeed. Fortunately that condition is changing. A primary reason for this change is the simple recognition that humor is an integral part of all human societies. Berlyne notes that "laughter and play are so widespread in human societies that individuals who abstain from them may be judged abnormal." (1969:795) One sociologist goes so far as to say that one of the major areas of the discipline, symbolic interaction, can be renewed by "making it the only school of sociology that uses *humor* as its principal resource for investigating the social world." (Davis, 1979:106). Not all sociologists will agree with this suggestion, of course, but it is clear that an increasing amount of attention is now being given to a long neglected area of human behavior. Since humor is so extensive in society, efforts are being made to understand its functions, determinants, and techniques or methods. A brief introduction to these concerns is necessary to understand the relationship between sociology and humor as a field of study.

Before examining the functions of humor, it would be helpful to define exactly what it is we are studying. Unfortunately, such an undertaking has no satisfactory conclusion. There are many varieties of behavior which we label humorous, funny, witty, and so on. An early student of humor observed that "hardly a word in the language—and it seems to be exclusively an English word— would be harder to define with scientific precision than this familiar one." (Sully, 1902:297) Goldstein and McGhee note simply that at this stage of investigation "there is no single definition of humor acceptable to all investigators in the area." (1972:xxi)

Such a situation is not that unusual, of course. There are multiple definitions of *attitude* in use by psychologists and social psychologists. Philosophers, after two thousand years, are hard pressed to define *virtue* with precision. And those in biology and medicine struggle to define when *life* ceases and *death* begins. Indeed, on-going research in all fields of scholarly endeavor has as one of its primary goals the increasing clarification of the phenomena under investigation. Notwithstanding definitional problems, humor does have identifiable functions and it is possible to outline some of these generally.

Functions of Humor

Much of the research which has examined humor has concentrated on the social processes of consensus, conflict, and control. Humor is often used to achieve consensus within groups and to enhance group solidarity. Blau's study (1955) of a state employment agency revealed that joke telling among employees served a very specific function of relieving tensions and uniting the group in a pleasant experience, that of laughing together. The nature of work among the employees was highly competitive, and humor served to reduce the dysfunctional aspects of intra group competition by providing release from tension. Coser (1962) found in her study of a general hospital that cohesion and consensus was greatly facilitated by the use of humor among patients. The complaint that "if I don't get out of here I'm going to get sick" was commonplace. Coser concluded that through a "continuous endeavor to overlook or make light of their individual plights, patients were able to bring about a social synthesis of their individual experiences which greatly strengthened ward solidarity." (1962:84)

A particularly vivid illustration of the use of humor to achieve consensus in a situation affecting world history took place at the Yalta conference when Roosevelt, Churchill, and Stalin met to discuss the cooperation of the world powers in the post-World War II era. Perkins describes Roosevelt's use of humor as follows:

On my way to the conference room that morning we caught up with Winston and I had just a moment to say to him, "Winston, I hope you won't be sore at me for what I am going to do."

Winston just shifted his cigar and grunted. I must say he behaved very decently afterward.

I began almost as soon as we got into the conference room. I talked privately with Stalin. I didn't say anything that I hadn't said before, but it appeared quite chummy and confidential, enough so that the other Russians joined us to listen. Still no smile.

Then I said, lifting my hand up to cover a whisper (which of course had to be interpreted) "Winston is cranky this morning, he got up on the wrong side of the bed."

A vague smile passed over Stalin's eyes, and I decided I was on the right track. As soon as I sat down at the conference table, I began to tease Winston about his Britishness, about John Bull, about his cigars, about his habits. It began to register with Stalin, Winston got red and scowled, and the more he did so, the more Stalin smiled. Finally Stalin broke out into a deep hearty guffaw, and for the first time in three days I saw light. I kept it up until Stalin was laughing with me, and it was then that I called him "Uncle Joe." He would have thought me fresh the day before, but that day he laughed and came over and shook my hand.

From that time on our relations were personal, and Stalin himself indulged in an occasional witticism. The ice was broken and we talked like men and brothers. (1946:84, 85)

If a society is to function effectively, consensus must be present. Yet, the opportunities for conflict are seemingly built in to all societies. Humor is one means of reducing social conflict which might otherwise destroy the system. Sometimes a situation is so well defined that one group realizes the futility of open conflict. Then humor may be resorted to as a means of expressing aggression against the oppressor. Such was the case in Czechoslovakia during the time of the German occupation in the Second World War. In this case a particular form of humor arose which Obrdlik (1942) refers to as "Gallows Humor." Gallows humor "arises in connection with a precarious or dangerous situation." In the case of the Czechs, they were awaiting "their 'gallows' as innocent victims of the aggression of the dictators ...." Utilization of humor enabled the Czechs to simultaneously maintain their morale and demoralize their oppressors whom they could not openly attack without disastrous consequences. Obrdlik offers several illustrations of gallows humor, including the following:

To find a Czech who is truly loyal to the Germans is no easy task.
... the Gestapo found one such specimen at long last. He was an
old man walking up and down the street speaking seriously to
himself aloud: "Adolph Hitler is the greatest leader. The Germans
are a noble nation. I would rather work for ten Germans than one
Czech." When asked what was his occupation, this Czech admirer of
Naziism reluctantly confessed that he was a gravedigger.

The use of humor as a tool in racial conflict has been noted
by many (Myrdal, 1944; Dollard, 1937; Davis, Gardner, and
Gardner, 1941). Burma calls attention to the fact that in "any
conflict it is most gratifying to cause one's adversary to appear ludicrous in his own eyes. Where this is not possible, very considerable satisfaction can be secured by making your opponent appear ludicrous in your eyes. It is exactly this which humor does."
(1946:711) Stephenson feels that there is a "particular adaptability of humor as a conflict weapon" since "humor may conceal mal-
ice and allow expression of aggression without the consequences
of other overt behavior." (1951:569) This function of humor has
a long history in black-white relations in this country.

The control functions of humor are widespread:

> As a means of social control, humor may function to express
> approval or disapproval of social form and action, express common
> group sentiments, develop and perpetuate stereotypes, relieve
> awkward or tense situations, and express collective, *sub-rosa*
> approbation of action not explicitly approved. Humor as expressed
> in the controlled laugh or smile may serve as a means of
> communication, signaling the intent and nature of communicating
> parties. (Stephenson, 1951:570)

Bradney (1957) spent some time as a participant observer in a
London department store and found that joking relationships
among employees were quite frequent. Joking was particularly
common when one asked another for help or information.
Through the use of the joking relationship, resentments were
avoided which might otherwise have arisen since the sales staff
worked under great pressures to maximize earnings. Klapp
(1950; 1962) offers very strong evidence for the argument that
humor is imperative in understanding the workings of the social
structure. His studies of the fool type in American society indicate that the fool has a specific role and specified position in society. Fools may depart from norms which are ordinarily held in
high propriety. Their behavior is, of course, ridiculed, and in this
manner fools serve as a negative example for reinforcing the very

propriety which they violate. Klapp discusses several types of fools, three of which have specific control functions: (1) *Discounting types* "take down people who claim too much," (2) *Nonconforming types* ridicule deviants and outsiders; and, (3) *Overconformers* "suffer comic rebuke because they have been too enthusiastic in complying with group standards."

Even though much research has focused on the three functions of humor just discussed, Lindersmith, et al. (1975:160–61) argue that the "only valid generalization about humor we can think of is that it is fun." While few would agree with this limitation, it is a needed addition to the discussion of humor's functions. Surely no one can fail to recognize that people joke, laugh at stand-up comics, read humorous literature, or attend humorous plays and movies simply because it is fun—a source of enjoyment—for them.

Theories of Humor

In addition to understanding humor's functions, much effort has been given to searching for theoretical explanations of humor. Just as there is no single definition of humor, there is no single theory available which can explain humor in all its manifestations. Monro feels that it is possible to summarize all theories with the single concept of "inappropriateness." (1951) However, he reaches his conclusion only after a thoroughgoing analysis of the basic theories of superiority, incongruity, and relief from restraint as explanations of humor.

Superiority theories derive, in one manner or another, from the now classic statement of Hobbes that laughter is occasioned by a "sudden glory arising from some conception of eminency in ourselves; by comparison with the infirmity of others, or with our own formerly." (1650) Comic vice is a ready example of what Hobbes had in mind. The small misfortunes which others experience offer us, also, the opportunity to laugh at "their expense." Children's riddles (which adults often find amusing, too) are further opportunities to assert superiority over those who do not know the answer. Bergson's variation of Hobbes's theory argues that ludicrous situations are characterized by "something mechanical encrusted on the living." (1908) For Bergson the ideal was elasticity, adaptability. The opposite, of course, is inelasticity or rigidity. Hence we find humorous those situations, events, or behaviors which represent rigidity. Superiority theories are sometimes referred to as "moral" theories. We laugh at mores or morals we judge to be inferior to ours.

Incongruity is a widespread explanation of humor. In this view humor arises from tracing connections where none seemed to exist formerly. The disjoined or ill-suited, when paired, form the basis of humor. Schopenhauer (1918) saw laughter as arising from the sudden perception on our part of an incongruity between an object and an abstract concept under which the object has been subsumed. We are surprised. That which is expected is replaced by something else. A visual illustration of incongruity is the well-known *New Yorker* cartoon showing the astonishment of a skier who observes another skier's tracks which approach a tree, part, and then rejoin on the downward slope. Many jokes depend on incongruous endings for their punch lines:

> Fat Ethel sat down at the lunch counter and ordered a whole fruit cake. "Shall I cut it into four or eight pieces?" asked the waitress. "Four," said Ethel. "I'm on a diet."

Of course, not all instances of incongruity cause laughter. This was recognized early by Spencer, who stated that "only when there is a . . . *descending* incongruity" does laughter occur. (1860) In ascending incongruity, when an insignificant entity unexpectedly becomes something great, the resulting emotion is "wonder."

Release or relief from restraint is a third major theory explaining much humor. Freud's contribution is a basic point of departure for these types of theories. According to Freud our natural aggressive and sexual tendencies are repressed and constantly thwarted by the demands of society. Society is a "censor," and wit, a form of humor, enables us to avoid the censor and talk about forbidden topics. Thus, much of our sexual humor derives from the release of suppressed desire. Gregory argues that relief pervades all humor: "Relief is not the whole of laughter, though it is its root and fundamental plan." (1924) In addition to relief from societal demands concerning our aggressive or sexual natures, we also derive relief from the outcome of a struggle, relief from pain, or relief from embarrassing social situations. All provide a common basis for humor.

These theories and others try to explain why we laugh and find particular situations and forms of behavior humorous. Humor is so diverse in its manifestations that no one theory can fit any and all types of humor. Nevertheless, theories do provide a framework for the interpretation of much that we label humorous. Rather than bemoaning the fact that any theory in and of itself is inadequate, it should be, according to Berlyne, "urgently incumbent on us to remedy [it]."

Techniques

Humorists use a variety of methods or techniques to get their message across. Feinberg (1967) points to the wide range of techniques used in satire and which are also applicable to many other forms of humor. These range from simple distortion, minimizing the good qualities and magnifying the bad ones of institutions, groups, and individuals, to exaggeration. Exaggeration is perhaps the most widely used of all techniques, especially within the context of incongruity. An extreme form of exaggeration is *reductio ad absurdum*—beautifully illustrated in Harry Golden's Vertical Integration plan (1967), which was proposed early in the movement to achieve integration for blacks in our society. Since a major problem in integration seemed to be the reluctance of whites to sit by blacks in eating places, schools, and elsewhere, why not, asked Golden, just remove all seats from restaurants and desks from schools? Then whites could simply stand by blacks—a practice apparently acceptable to all. *Understatement* is exaggeration in reverse form. Thurber uses this in his well-known cartoon of two fencers. One has completely severed the head of his opponent. In mid-air the head states, calmly, "Touché." Unexpected honesty is employed by nearly all humorists. In *Catch-22* Yossarian tries to explain to Major Major that he doesn't want to fly any more missions:

> "Why not?" he asked.
> "I'm afraid."
> "That's nothing to be ashamed of," Major Major counseled him kindly. "We're all afraid."
> "I'm not ashamed," Lossarian said, "I'm just afraid."
> (p. 106)

Unexpected honesty is also a staple diet in the highly successful television series, "M*A*S*H."

Techniques associated with superiority theories include derision, insult, and ignorance. A favorite use of ignorance are the college boners collected, periodically, by those in the academic world: "Christianity became popular because it promised immorality to the lower classes. In the Middle Ages all people were middle aged." Disparaging comparisons lend themselves readily to superiority theory: "A professor must have a theory as a dog must have fleas." (Mencken) Relief from tension theories employ several techniques to achieve what Freud called "censor-evasion." Parody is one important technique used here. *Catch-22*'s Milo Minderbinder's antics are justified by "What's good for M and M is good for the country"—a parody of former General Motors president Charles Wilson, who argued that what was good for GM was good for the country. Other techniques highlighted by Feinberg include invective, cliché twisting, surprise, and unexpected logic, as exemplified by the following dialog between a mental patient looking over the wall of the hospital at a fisherman:

Been there long?
All day.
Catch anything?
Nope.
Come inside.

A final point for consideration is the role of the humorist in our society. Do humorists seek to act as agents of change, as reformers? Political cartoonists and humorists such as Art Buchwald or Russell Baker, some argue, exaggerate the political foibles of our day to effect change. After a particularly brilliant series of spoofs on the MX missile by Russell Baker in his *New York Times* column, a letter to the editor stated that "it is comforting to think that wit and humor can sometimes protect us from our solemnly thought-through errors.... We owe much to the hard work of those who make fun seriously." (*New York Times*, Oct. 23, 1981) Later events, of course, dispel the accuracy of this letter. Blair and Hill argue that humor in the colonial era "preaches much of the time." (1978) But this has changed. Twain's constant attacks on all forms of social injustice in his times might suggest that reform was his intent, but such was not the case. The consensus would appear to be that entertainment, not reform, is the business of the humorist. That which is entertaining can also be informative, of course. If entertainment results in enlightenment along the way, for those who use this book, well and good.

REFERENCES

Berger, Peter. *The Precarious Vision.* Garden City, N.Y.: Doubleday, 1961.

Bergson, H. *Laughter: An Essay on the Meaning of the Comic.* New York: Macmillan, 1911.

Berlyne, D.W. "Laughter, Humor and Play," in Lindzey, G., and Aronson, E., *Handbook of Social Psychology,* 2d ed. Reading, Mass.: Addison, Wesley Publishing Co., 1969.

Blair, W., and Hill, H. *America's Humor.* New York: Oxford Press, 1978.

Blau, Peter. *The Dynamics of Bureaucracy.* Chicago: Univ. of Chicago Press, 1955.

Bradney, P. "The Joking Relationship in Industry." *Human Relations* 10 (1957), 179–87.

Burma, J.H. "Humor as a Tool in Race Conflict" *American Sociological Review* 11 (1946) 710–15.

Coser, R.L. *Life in the Ward.* E. Lansing, Mich.: Michigan State Univ. Press, 1962.

Davis, A., Gardner, B., and Gardner, M. *Deep South.* Chicago: Univ. of Chicago Press, 1941.

Davis, Muray S. "Sociology Through Humor." *Symbolic Interaction* 21, 1, Spring, 1979, 105–10.

Dollard, J. *Caste and Class in a Southern Town.* New Haven: Yale Univ. Press, 1937.

Golden, Harry. *The Best of Harry Golden.* Cleveland: World Publishing, 1967.

Goldstein, J.H., and McGhee, P.E. *The Psychology of Humor.* New York: Academic Press, 1972.

Gregory, J.C. *The Nature of Laughter.* London: Kegan Paul, 1924.

Hobbes, T. *Leviathan.* 1651.

Klapp, O. "The Fool as a Social Type." *American Journal of Sociology* 55 (1950), 157–62.

———— *Heroes, Villains, and Fools.* Englewood Cliffs, N.J.: Prentice-Hall, 1962.

Lindersmith, A., Strauss, A.L., and Denzin, N.K. *Social Psychology,* 4th ed. Hinsdale, Ill.: Dryden Press, 1975.

Monro, D.H. *Argument of Laughter.* Melbourne: Melbourne Univ. Press, 1951.

Myrdal, G. *An American Dilemma.* New York: Harper, 1944.

Obrdlik, A.J. "Gallows Humor: A Sociological Phenomenon." *American Journal of Sociology* 47 (1942), 709–16.

Perkins, F.W. *The Roosevelt I Knew.* New York: Viking Press, 1946.

Schopenhauer, A. *Die Welt als Wille und Vorstellung.* Leipzig: Brockhaus, 1819.

Spencer, H.   "The Physiology of Laughter."   *Macmillan's Magazine* 1
    (1860), 395–402.

Stephenson, R.M.   "Conflict and Control Functions of Humor."   *American Journal of Sociology* 56 (1951), 569–74.

Sully, J.   *Essay on Laughter.*   London: Longmans, Green, 1902.

I

STUDYING SOCIETY

Chapter One

The Sociological Perspective

E ach of the social sciences employs a specific method of investigation and has a given perspective which is applied in the effort to understand human behavior. The sociological perspective is not always easy for the beginning student to understand. Having lived for the past 18 years or so in our society, students often assume that they know just what is going on. Such is seldom the case. Exactly what constitutes a *society* and how sociologists analyze it presents an intellectual challenge for students and sociologists alike. The sociological perspective focuses on behavior in groups, the way we interact in the groups in which we participate, and how our behavior is shaped by this interaction. Behavior is not random; it quickly becomes structured. When change occurs, we seek to understand what brought about the change and how it affects the total pattern of behaviors which we call society. The sociological perspective differs from that of an economist, a psychologist, or an historian in that it concentrates on the nature of the social relationships which characterize our behavior in the many groups of which we are a part. A basic contention of sociology is that how we perceive the world is in large part, a function, of the groups in which we spend our daily lives.

In its search for understanding, sociology utilizes the scientific method. Some critics of sociology argue that it is not a "true" science—implying, usually, that sociology cannot exercise the same degree of precision in its work which is possible in the physical sciences such as physics or chemistry. The complexities of this argument are beyond the scope of this chapter, but it is clear that all the social sciences have modeled their research procedures after those utilized in older sciences such as physics. The results have been impressive, and current trends suggest increasing success in sociology's efforts to understand behavior.

Sociologists use a variety of research methods. Basically, there are three major techniques for gathering and analyzing data. When possible, the *experimental design* is employed. Two groups are matched and measured on properties which are under investigation. A stimulus is introduced to one group, called the experimental group, and withheld from the other, called the control group. Following the stimulus introduction, measures are taken a second time. Any observed differences between the

4

control and experimental group are attributed to the stimulus. Studies concerned with the effect of viewing violence on television may use the experimental design.

A second technique is *observational* studies. The researcher may be either a participant or non-participant observer. Detailed knowledge of how individuals and groups behave can be gathered in this fashion. One sociologist (Sudnow, 1967) worked for a year and a half in two hospitals, observing and recording the social organization of how people die. While this topic may, at first glance, seem somewhat weird, death is a social fact, and how we respond to our inevitable fate is of extreme importance to families, doctors, ministers, and the legal profession.

The third research technique is the most widely known among the lay public and is widely used by sociologists. Prior to the study of sociology the student is quite likely to be familiar with the use of *surveys*. When using the survey technique one of the first questions which must be addressed is the size of the population to be studied. If the population is sufficiently small it may be possible to include everyone in the study. As the population increases to perhaps hundreds of thousands of people, it is neither necessary nor desirable (due, among other things, to cost) to include everyone. Thus, a representative *sample* of the population will be chosen. Data from the representative sample can then be used to make inferences about the total population. The United States Census regularly employs sample surveys in its highly accurate work. The Gallup and Harris poll organizations are now household phrases in the United States. These organizations regularly poll a sample of the nation's population on issues of public concern. Candidates for political office employ polling organizations in their bid for election. Each of these methodological techniques—experimental, observational, and survey—has advantages and disadvantages, but all are used to further the goal of understanding how humans perceive the world in which they exist and how they behave in the groups in which they participate.

The readings in Chapter 1 address some of the concerns which sociologists themselves have about the sociological perspective and the use of methodological techniques. The "Little Miss Muffet" selection by Russell Baker is a parody of the sociological perspective. It is, also, an exaggeration of the use of jargon by sociologists—a common charge that sociology rephrases the everyday language to render it obscure. The ending is another common critique of sociology—that it is nothing but common sense, that which any child in his or her wisdom knows.

The article by Dave Barry, "When The *Times* Hears the Nation, Dave Barry Doesn't," examines the practice by journalists of reporting on what the "nation" knows or feels about given issues of great public interest. Journalists are similar to sociologists in that they, too, seek to understand how and why we behave. Indeed, journalistic stories are often reported as if they had used careful sampling techniques to reach their conclusions. What Barry is discussing here is the very important matter of how representative of the total population are conclusions which are presented as applying to the nation.

The final selection, by Lee J. Haggerty, reports on an experiment designed to test the effects of marijuana upon human behavior. Carrying out such research is difficult in the social sciences since humans are not always readily available for testing—especially in an area such as drug usage. Resort to rat studies is common, since for most scientists no ethical considerations are involved and control of the subjects is as thorough as need be. While some debate whether or not results from such studies can be generalized to human populations, Haggerty points out that the "validity of the experimental findings does not rest upon rats being human, but only on the similarity in basic physiology and the ability of rats to engage in problem solving and other general types of mental behavior."

The three selections in Chapter 1 are indeed caricatures of types of sociological research and the sociological perspective. By highlighting the humorous they call attention to the need for careful work as sociologists seek to understand the many facets of behavior.

 **RUSSELL BAKER**

Little Miss Muffet

Little Miss Muffet, as everyone knows, sat on a tuffet eating her curds and whey when along came a spider who sat down beside her and frightened Miss Muffet away. While everyone knows this, the significance of the event had never been analyzed until a conference of thinkers recently brought their special insights to bear upon it. Following are excerpts from the transcript of their discussion:

Sociologist: We are clearly dealing here with a prototypical illustration of a highly tensile social structure's tendency to dis- or perhaps even de-structure itself under the pressures created when optimum minimums do not obtain among the disadvantaged. Miss Muffet is nutritionally underprivileged, as evidenced by the subminimal diet of curds and whey upon which she is forced to subsist, while the spider's cultural disadvantage is evidenced by such phenomena as legs exceeding standard norms, odd mating habits, and so forth.

In this instance, spider expectations lead the culturally disadvantaged to assert demands to share the tuffet with the nutritionally underprivileged. Due to a communications failure, Miss Muffet assumes without evidence that the spider will not be satisfied to share her tuffet, but will also insist on eating her curds and perhaps even her whey. Thus, the failure to preestablish selectively optimum norm structures diverts potentially optimal minimums from the expectation levels assumed to . . .

Militarist: Second-strike capability, sir! That's what was lacking. If Miss Muffet had developed a second-strike capability instead of squandering her resources on curds and whey, no spider on earth would have dared launch a first strike capable of carrying him right to the heart of her tuffet. I am confident that Miss Muffet had adequate notice from experts that she could not afford both curds and whey and, at the same time, support an early-spider-warning system. Yet curds alone were not good enough for Miss Muffet. She had to have whey, too. Tuffet security must be the first responsibility of every diner . . .

Book Reviewer: Written on several levels, this searing and sensitive exploration of the arachnid heart illuminates the agony and splendor of Jewish family life with a candor that is at once breathtaking in its simplicity and soul-shattering in its implied ambiguity. Some will doubtless be shocked to see such subjects as tuffets and whey discussed without flinching, but hereafter writers too timid to call a curd a curd will no longer . . .

Editorial Writer: Why has the Government not seen fit to tell the public all it knows about the so-called curds-and-whey affair? It is not enough to suggest that this was merely a random incident involving a lonely spider and a young diner. In today's world, poised as it is on the knife edge of . . .

Psychiatrist: Little Miss Muffet is, of course, neither little nor a miss. These are obviously the self she has created in her own fantasies to escape the reality that she is a gross divorcee whose superego makes it impossible for her to sustain a normal relationship with any man, symbolized by the spider, who, of course, has no existence outside her fantasies. Little Miss Muffet may, in fact, be a man with deeply repressed Oedipal impulses, who sees in the spider the father he would like to kill, and very well may some day unless he admits that what he believes to be a tuffet is, in fact, probably the dining room chandelier, and that the whey he thinks he is eating is, in fact, probably . . .

Flower Child: Like this beautiful kid is on a bad trip, dig? Like . . .

Student Demonstrator: Little Miss Muffet, tuffets, curds, whey and spiders are what's wrong with education today. They're all irrelevant. Tuffets are irrelevant. Curds are irrelevant. Whey is irrelevant. Meaningful experience! How can you have relevance without meaningful experience? And how can there ever be meaningful experience without understanding? With understanding and meaningfulness and relevance, there can be love and good and deep seriousness and education today will be freed of slavery and Little Miss Muffet, and life will become meaningful and . . .

Child: This is about a little girl who gets scared by a spider. (The child was sent home when the conference broke for lunch. It was agreed that he was too immature to subtract anything from the sum of human understanding.)

 DAVE BARRY

When The Times *Hears the Nation, Dave Barry Doesn't*

A while back, the *New York Times* (a competing newspaper) published an editorial that began:

"The nation cheered last March when President Reagan declared himself eager to reduce dependence on imported minerals."

Now the *New York Times* is a fine newspaper, containing many facts and an excellent crossword puzzle. But let's be realistic here: The nation did *not* cheer when President Reagan declared himself eager to reduce dependence on imported minerals. I was in the nation at the time, and I didn't hear a peep out of it. Perhaps the *Times* editorial writer heard a loud noise outside his office window, but I doubt it was the nation cheering about imported minerals. More likely it was a group of New Yorkers gathering to watch a pedestrian beat a taxi driver to death with an umbrella.

What the editorial writer actually meant, of course, was that *he* cheered when President Reagan declared his feelings about imported minerals. If the writer had been honest, he'd have written: "I and a few close friends here at the *Times* cheered when President Reagan declared himself etc." But that would have sounded silly, so instead he had the entire nation cheer.

I don't mean to single out the *New York Times*. This is merely one example of something journalists do all the time, namely, pretend that just because *they* feel a certain way about some issue, then *everybody* feels that way about it. Suppose, for example, an editor wakes up one morning and, while he's shaving, starts to feel gravely concerned about possible CIA involvement in Nicaragua. He'll send a reporter and a photographer out to a shopping mall, and they'll stop shoppers at random and interview them like this:

> Reporter: Excuse me, but I'm a reporter with the *Daily Sentinel Standard Reporter Journal Tribune Courier Express*, and I'd like to know whether you're concerned about possible CIA involvement in Nicaragua.
> Shopper: In what?
> Reporter: Nicaragua. It's a country. Well? Are you concerned?
> Shopper: Well, I imagine so, yes.
> Reporter: Gravely? Would you say you are gravely concerned?
> Shopper: Sure. I would say gravely is correct.
> Reporter: Thank you.
> Shopper: Do I get any free samples or anything?

After a few more interviews, the reporter will write a story that runs under the headline:

AREA RESIDENTS GRAVELY CONCERNED
ABOUT CIA INVOLVEMENT IN NICARAGUA

which looks a lot more impressive than

EDITOR WORRIES ABOUT
NICARAGUA WHILE SHAVING

It's not just journalists who claim to speak for everybody. Politicians do it all the time. Let's say a congressman wants the government to fork over $463 million to dredge a harbor in his district. You'll never hear him say: "This project is good for 325 dock workers and maybe a half-dozen people in the shipping business who contributed a lot of money to my campaign." Instead, he'll say: "The American people believe that dredged harbors are vital to the very survival of the nation." And when the government forks over the money, the local newspaper will report that the public is extremely pleased. In fact, the public is probably at work, or out drinking beer and playing Space Invaders, and harbor dredging is the farthest thing from its mind.

Lately, President Reagan has been going around saying that the American people support his economic program, and Democratic leaders have been going around saying that the American people oppose it. You'll notice that neither side ever names any actual American people. I strongly suspect that many American persons would like both the President and the Democratic leaders to shut up and go away, but I don't presume to speak for them.

I think it might be a good idea if we passed an amendment to the Constitution that said:

> "No government official shall be allowed to use the words 'public,' 'people' or 'nation' to support or oppose anything without providing a list of the people he or she is talking about. The people on this list will bear the cost of whatever it is the public official claims they want to do."

So if, for example, Secretary of State Alexander Haig suddenly decides that the "nation" wants to give $43 million worth of nuclear helicopters to the government of El Salvador, he would have to tell us exactly which members of the nation he is referring to. Suppose he came up with a list of 86,000 people. The Defense Department could then send each of them a bill for $500, and when they had all paid, Al could buy his helicopters.

Or suppose some official of the National Endowment for the Arts wants to provide "public" support for the arts by commissioning an artist to paint a modernistic painting, the kind that costs $5,000 and looks as though your kid drew it in five minutes with felt markers, only not as attractive. The arts official would have to list the, say, 25 people who actually *like* such paintings, and the government would bill them $200 apiece.

I think this would be a terrific amendment, and I'm sure I speak for the American people when I say so.

LEE J. HAGGERTY *

An Experimental Design in the Study of the Effects of Marijuana Upon Human Behavior

Methodological problems with existing experimental and non-experimental designs in assessing the effect of marijuana upon human subjects are reviewed and a design innovation is proposed and implemented to overcome these problems.

Introduction to the Problem

In legislative hearings associated with bills for the legalization of marijuana, major concern has centered around experimental evidence on the effects of the drug upon mental and motor response. The high degree of validity associated with experimental findings, as opposed to survey methods of polling human respondents, lies in the ability of experimental designs to control possible confounding factors and thereby rule out alternative explanations for findings. Major difficulties with the survey method in evaluating the effects of marijuana include: 1) unrepresentative samples due to the illegal nature of marijuana use, 2) bias in responses related to respondent's values, and 3) unreliable measuring instruments which reflect biases of the investigator in the way questions are worded and the way responses are categorized.

As a means of eliminating these and other alternative explanations of the effects of marijuana, and at the same time eliminating the ethical problems of experimentation with human subjects, researchers have relied heavily upon experimental designs utilizing rats in laboratory settings.

While it may at first blush appear that the baby has been thrown out with the bath in turning to observation of rat behavior to tell us something about human behavior, this is most certainly not the case. What is lost in organismic dissimilarity between rat and human physiology is gained in efficiency of design. If we bear in mind that

* I should like to express my feelings about the assistance given me in the preparation of this paper by Joseph F. Jones. Without him the paper would have been finished approximately one and a half years ago.

the crucial questions being addressed deal with the effects of marijuana upon human motor and mental response, we see that only two aspects of human behavior have been abstracted from the multidimensional construct of "being human." It would of course be foolish to argue that rats have "life styles" similar to humans but that is irrelevant. The validity of the experimental findings does not rest upon rats being human, but only on the similarity in basic physiology and the ability of rats to engage in problem solving and other general types of mental behavior.

If the experimental evidence to date were sufficient, however, there would be no need for the present paper. While experimental research on human subjects has shown quite conclusively that marijuana has very little, if any, physiologically measurable effect, research concerning the effect upon mental response is found lacking in several respects. The most crucial problem here centers around our inability to directly observe cognitive behavior and the consequent necessity of inferring cognitive response from observable behavioral modifications induced by marijuana. Since we cannot actually observe image formation "inside the heads" so to speak of rats (or humans for that matter) findings concerning mental response can only be as valid as the isomorphism between the actual mental activity and the experimental apparatus designed to reflect such activity. The major contribution of the research reported in this paper is a design modification which greatly increases the isomorphism between cognitive processes "inside the head" and the subsequent interpretation of these processes by the researcher. In addition, the research reported herein takes particular care in establishing baseline behavior prior to the administration of marijuana so as not to lack the credibility which is lacking in previous research.

Experimental Design

The experimental design involved the use of a standard Harlow-Wexler rat maze with 16 problem corridors. The basic methodology involved observation of 15 one hour trials, each involving 3 rats, under normal conditions. On each trial, the rats were placed at the entrance to the maze and a timing bell set for one hour. These 15 one hour trials under normal conditions were the most difficult portion of the experiment to conduct but were necessary in order to establish a reliable baseline. Since each trial involved the behavior of the same rats in an attempt to run the same maze, the observation became extremely tedious and boring. We mention this here to suggest why baselines have been given short shrift by previous researchers. Nevertheless, observations were carefully recorded concerning timing, mistakes, and pattern of problem solving activity for each rat for each trial. Since conditions were nearly identical for each trial under normal conditions, there is nothing of interest for the findings to report at this stage. The experimental treatment was then administered in the form of 70 ml of THC, and the timing bell was set for one hour.

Findings

For the first 2 minutes and 34 seconds after administration of the THC there was no noticable deviation from baseline activity. Then rat #3, which had an exceptionally rich whiteness to its coat, became especially interesting. While his activity prior to this point had appeared quite normal it now began to take on interesting new dimensions. Rather than appearing merely perplexed at arriving at his second dead end in the maze, he seemed to reflect a more general displeasure with the lack of sensory input in his surroundings. And, with nothing better to do in his relatively sterile environment, began to nose around to examine the texture of the maze itself. With apparent suddenness, my attention was shifted to a different rat who was moving stealthfully through the maze but with incredible slowness. It seemed an hour passed while he moved through but two corridors of the maze, never hesitating, never looking back, with a sincerity of purpose resident, I am sure, in only the highest quality of laboratory rat. This was indeed a beautiful rat. That rats could have come to represent the most repulsive of nature's rodents became a perplexing mystery. Hoards of rats swarming over Europe captured my imagination as I remained fixated on this particular rat. How large would the population of the world be now if it hadn't been for the rat. Without the plague man would no doubt have reached already the carrying capacity of the earth, and be either embroiled in an apocalyptic conflict of all against all or organized in an entirely different manner than the current organization of nation states would even suggest. It is indeed strange that the nature of human social organization assumes the degree of reality accorded it by the human psyche, when with this experiment itself it becomes obvious that the nature of reality is quite variable from the perspective of a single individual under differing conditions. If the same individual can come to structure reality under different conditions in quite different ways, is it not reasonable that different individuals would come to structure reality in ways at least, if not more, different than one another even when external physical objects stand in the same relationship to the different individuals?

At this point while it seemed that the experiment had hardly begun the timing indicator bell rang signaling the end of the experimental trial. My physical alertness at this point was overcome with immobility while my mind continued to examine, with visual brilliance and auditory clarity, the nature of reality and the relative nature of our feeble attempts to verbally structure it within scientific paradigms. My assistant, I was able to determine later, returned the rats to their cages and turned out the lights so as not to disturb my apparent slumber.

Conclusions

The experiment itself proved highly pleasurable. The design modification incorporated here proved extremely useful in increasing the isomorphism between mental activity and the researcher's ability to interpret it. It is recommended that subsequent research conducted on the effects of marijuana upon human subjects also incorporate this design modification. By administering the treatment (normally 30 to 70 ml of THC) to the researcher, rather than to the subjects being observed, important insights may be made in understanding behavior. As previously indicated, however, the real questions have to do with the effect of marijuana with respect to human subjects and this research should be seen as only a beginning in that direction. By showing how the behavior of rats observed under the influence of marijuana can cut through all the preconceived structuring of the setting we suggest that the substitution of human subjects within this experimental design would prove even more rewarding. This design modification can be carried out without knowledge of the subjects, and without having any adverse effect on them, merely by administering the treatment and then going to a party or attending a meeting. These specific suggestions are to be taken only as examples of the rich mines of experimental settings which are readily available to the imaginative researcher.

Permission to reprint granted by THE JOURNAL OF IRREPRODUCIBLE RESULTS. Article first published in Vol. 27, Issue #3/1981.

QUESTIONS FOR DISCUSSION

1. The different perspectives which Baker discusses in "Little Miss Muffet" are a caricature not only of sociology but of each of the other perspectives as well. If a sociologist were investigating a serious matter, such as the government's foreign policy in Central America, do you think his or her perspective would be different from that of the military? How? While student demonstrations about our government's foreign policy are not as prevalent today as they were in the 1960s, what difference in perspective would draft-age students today be expected to have from that of the federal government? Are these perspectives a result of the groups in which students participate?

2. Seeing a given phenomenon from different perspectives can be most helpful. If a prostitute and her customer were arrested by the police, what differences do you think would be present in each of their interpretations of the activity? If you brought a priest into this situation, how do you think his interpretation would differ from the others? How would a sociologist perceive the entire incident of prostitution, arrest, and priestly counseling? Does the sociological perspective offer insights here which none of the other views possesses? What are they?

3. Sociology is sometimes accused of being an elaboration of the obvious—"everybody knows that." Are many young couples living together today without being married? Of course. Is this widespread? Of course. But *of all* couples living together, what percentage are unmarried? The correct answer is far from obvious, and illustrates that often what people *think* is common knowledge, is not.

4. Sociologists and journalists often report on what the "American public" believes, thinks, or feels about particular issues. What is the difference in the way sociologists and journalists derive their respective information?

5. If a member of Congress hired a polling organization to use correct sampling techniques and find out how the people of his or her home district felt about a public issue, would the member of Congress then be justified in saying that "the peo-

ple of this country" are for (or against) proposition X? Why? Why not?

6. Is it possible to have an intuitive but accurate feeling about "the nation's" attitude toward pornography or television violence without taking a carefully chosen national sample? Do you think you know how "we" feel about violence on TV? What is the basis of your position? Would a sociologist be happy with how you arrived at your conclusion?

7. Haggerty suggests that there would be *ethical* problems in using human beings in experimentation. Yet this is done quite frequently in medicine with volunteers. Why should the situation be different in sociology?

8. In a study of the "Tearoom Trade" (oral sex in public restrooms), Laud Humphreys (1970) observed men engaging in oral sex without their knowing that he was doing a study of their behavior. Critics, both outside sociology and within the discipline, accused him of unethical behavior. In a sense Humphreys did "use" these men as subjects for research. What are the pros and cons of the ethical nature of such research activity in sociology?

9. Haggerty says that "the nature of reality is quite variable from the perspective of a single individual under differing conditions." Users of drugs have often reported that they "see" another reality or that they "take a trip" into another world. Is this simple hallucinatory behavior on their part? Under what circumstances are you likely to see the world differently than you see it as a student? From which perspective are you seeing the "real" world?

10. If reality varies for the individual "under differing conditions," does this help to explain how different groups occupying distinct positions have sometimes completely opposing views of reality? How do the rich explain why some people are poor? Is this explanation likely to differ from that of the poor?

11. Haggerty feels that "it is indeed strange that the nature of human social organization assumes the degree of reality accorded it by the human psyche. . . ." Relate this to the belief in God, or witches, by some people but not by others.

REFERENCES

Humphreys, Laud. "Tearoom Trade: Impersonal Sex in Public Places." *Transaction* 7, 3 (1970), 10–14.

Sudnow, David. *Passing On: The Social Organization of Dying.* Englewood Cliffs, N.J.: Prentice Hall, 1967.

II

SELF AND SOCIETY: BECOMING A SOCIAL BEING

Chapter Two

The Socialization Process

READINGS

D avid Reisman asks the question: "How is it that every society seems to get, more or less, the social character it needs?" (1961:5) The answer is by training, or socializing, the young to the values and norms of the society. Such training is usually thought of in terms of formal education. But training begins in infancy—long before the onset of formal education. Each family seeks to put its imprint upon the child. The child learns very early what the family, and that part of the society which his or her family represents, thinks is important. This early training is both a conscious and unconscious effort on the part of parents. It is what sociologists refer to as *socialization*: the interaction with others in society which leads to the development and formation of the individual personality.

Interaction with others is crucial to the maturation of the child. Reports of feral children, children alleged to have been reared by wild animals, have long been a part of popular mythology. In India in 1961, an abandoned child, estimated to be about nine years old, was found in a railway depot in Lucknow. He could not walk or talk and did not have control over the excretion functions of his body. It was reported that he ate raw meat. Many Indians believed that he had been reared by wolves. He was kept in a hospital for several years and efforts were made to socialize him—with minimal results. He died in the hospital when he was about 22 years old. All such reports of feral children lack careful scientific substantiation. It is probable that most of these children were simply abandoned by their parents at an early age and were thus not subject to normal socialization practices.

Other cases of children reared in isolation from normal human contact (cf. Davis, 1940, 1947) and later subject to direct attempts to socialize them have met with varying degrees of success. In a study comparing children reared in institutions with those reared by their own parents, Spitz (1945) reports that the institutionalized children suffered emotional stress which, in many cases, led to mental retardation. Harry Harlow's study (1958) of rhesus monkeys deliberately raised in isolation from their parents revealed that they acted in ways uncharacteristic of monkey behavior. They were apathetic, would not mate with each other, and were generally hostile to fellow monkeys. There is always a problem of generalizing from animal studies to human behavior, but it seems clear that infants—animal or human—need the love and care ordinarily associated with families for proper development.

The family, of course, is not the only agency of socialization. At an early age the child's formal educational training is begun. In the school the teacher becomes an important influence shaping the personality of the child. By the time of high school the child's peers, particularly in our society, have become a very important socializing agency. Tastes in music, clothing, recreation, and other important areas of a child's life are heavily influenced by one's peers. The socialization process continues throughout life. Occupational groups, religious groups, and various other organizations in which we participate help to mold and shape our personalities.

The process of socialization is not always as smooth as we might expect. Societies may, as Reisman notes, get more or less the type of individuals they need, but Dennis Wrong (1961) has pointed out that we are sometimes forced to do things we may not want to do. Furthermore, the various groups which socialize us may have differing and, at times, conflicting ideas about what is proper behavior. Religious groups may desire one form of behavior while peer groups insist upon an opposing form. Parental desires often conflict with peer group pressures. And, even though socialized to a given perspective upon life, some individuals may deviate and do their own thing. It remains true, however, that societies continue to function effectively because most of us are socialized to their norms and values.

The selections in Chapter 2 examine particular aspects of the socialization process. Since we know that children must be trained to take over various responsibilities in the society, an ever present concern of those who teach children involves the most effective means of education. The first selection, *Raising the Perfect Child*, calls attention to the "constant stream of articles, books, and even adult education courses on how to raise the perfect child." Today's methods vary greatly from those of prior eras when children were to "be seen and not heard."

In *Parental Guidance* Fran Lebowitz notes that, even though childless herself, she is "possessed of some fairly strong opinions on the subject of rearing the young." Using unexpected logic, she offers advice on training the young in specific norms and values in current society—use of money, sexual activity, television viewing, music lessons, and the like. Example: "Do not allow your children to mix drinks. It is unseemly and they use too much vermouth."

Russell Baker, admitting his lack of "fluency in the sociological tongue, a language almost as difficult as Basque," nevertheless addresses an important sociological concern with *Role Models*. The question he raises, should schools permit teachers who are homosexual, is an extremely sensitive issue in our society. While homosexuals may be found in many occupations in our society, their presence in the school system is still subject to intense debate. Baker's conclusions about the probable effects of homosexual teachers are not based on sociological studies, but are worthy of consideration.

 ARTHUR HOPPE

Raising the Perfect Child

For millions of years, untrained, unskilled, amateur parents have been raising their children without the faintest idea of how to go about it. All they knew was to yell and scream and occasionally belt them one willy-nilly. Consequently, their children grew up to be parents who yelled and screamed and occasionally belted their offspring when circumstances and frayed nerves demanded. But in recent times all that has begun to change. Now there is a constant stream of articles, books, and even adult education courses on how to raise the perfect child. When I think of this radical departure from the past, I think of my friend Philo Gompers. Philo, the father of an amateur child named Irwin, not only underwent Parent Effectiveness Training, but he enrolled in a Responsive Parent Improvement Program and joined a study group entitled "Children: The Challenge"—which they certainly are. Like any well-trained parent, Philo exhibited the required amount of delight on bumping into Irwin on the sidewalk outside Irwin's school:

"Good morning, Irwin," said Philo, extending his hand, "and who do you think is going to win the race for alderman? I ask you this as all my instructors agree I must stop treating you as a puppy who needs to be housebroken and start treating you with the respect and courtesy I afford human beings of the adult persuasion."

"Oh," said Irwin, "it's you."

"Let us talk about topics of mutual interest in order to establish and maintain a helping relationship," said Philo. "What are you doing?"

"I'm setting fire to the school," said Irwin.

"I won't ask why because that would invite you to blame others, offer excuses, and dwell on feelings, rather than behavior," said Philo. "Instead, I will merely be prepared to offer my aid if needed."

"Okay," said Irwin. "Got a match?"

"But in a friendly, nonjudgmental way, let me suggest that you evaluate your behavior yourself," said Philo. "Is what you are doing helpful to you?"

"Yeah," said Irwin. "It'll help keep me from flunking today's quiz in Interpersonal Relationships."

"Let me assist you in constructing more responsible behavior," said Philo. "Without my experienced counsel, you may evolve a plan that is overly ambitious. Perhaps you should consider smaller, more realistic goals so you can enjoy success and thereby build the self-confidence you will need in facing life."

"Okay," said Irwin. "I'll just burn down the Interpersonal Relationships classroom."

"Allow me to reward your good thinking with high praise," said Philo. "And should your plan fail, rest assured that I won't punish you as punishment creates isolation and hostility."

"Swell," said Irwin. "Where's the match?"

"First, in order to strengthen your motivation and increase your involvement with me as a parent, I'd like you to make a solemn commitment to your plan," said Philo. "Which would you prefer, a handshake, a verbal agreement, or a written contract?"

"Put her there," said Irwin. "Now do I get the match?"

But the moment of denouement was too much for Philo, and rationality took over. "Absolutely not," he said firmly. "But in treating you as I would any mature, responsible adult, I'll see you get ten to twenty instead for attempted arson. Officers, do your duty!"

FRAN LEBOWITZ

Parental Guidance

As the title suggests, this piece is intended for those among us who have taken on the job of human reproduction. And while I am not unmindful of the fact that many of my readers are familiar with the act of reproduction only insofar as it applies to a too-recently fabricated Louis XV armoire, I nevertheless feel that certain things cannot be left unsaid. For although distinctly childless myself, I find that I am possessed of some fairly strong opinions on the subject of the rearing of the young. The reasons for this are varied, not to say rococo, and range from genuine concern for the future of mankind to simple, cosmetic disdain.

Being a good deal less villainous than is popularly supposed, I do not hold small children entirely accountable for their own behavior. By and large, I feel that this burden must be borne by their elders. Therefore, in an effort to make knowledge power, I offer the following suggestions:

Your responsibility as a parent is not as great as you might imagine. You need not supply the world with the next conqueror of disease or major motion-picture star. If your child simply grows up to be someone who does not use the word "collectible" as a noun, you can consider yourself an unqualified success.

———

Children do not really need money. After all, they don't have to pay rent or send mailgrams. Therefore their allowance should be just large enough to cover chewing gum and an occasional pack of cigarettes. A child with his own savings account and/or tax shelter is not going to be a child who scares easy.

———

A child who is not rigorously instructed in the matter of table manners is a child whose future is being dealt with cavalierly. A person who makes an admiral's hat out of a linen napkin is not going to be in wild social demand.

———

The term "child actor" is redundant. He should not be further incited.

Do not have your child's hair cut by a real hairdresser in a real hairdressing salon. He is, at this point, far too short to be exposed to contempt.

Do not, on a rainy day, ask your child what he feels like doing, because I assure you that what he feels like doing, you won't feel like watching.

Educational television should be absolutely forbidden. It can only lead to unreasonable expectations and eventual disappointment when your child discovers that the letters of the alphabet do not leap up out of books and dance around the room with royal-blue chickens.

If you are truly serious about preparing your child for the future, don't teach him to subtract—teach him to deduct.

Make every effort to avoid ostentatiously Biblical names. Nothing will show your hand more.

Do not send your child to the sort of progressive school that permits writing on the walls unless you want him to grow up to be TAKI 183.

If you must give your child lessons, send him to driving school. He is far more likely to end up owning a Datsun than he is a Stradivarius.

Designer clothes worn by children are like snowsuits worn by adults. Few can carry it off successfully.

Never allow your child to call you by your first name. He hasn't known you long enough.

Do not encourage your child to express himself artistically unless you are George Balanchine's mother.

———

Do not elicit your child's political opinions. He doesn't know any more than you do.

———

Do not allow your children to mix drinks. It is unseemly and they use too much vermouth.

———

Letting your child choose his own bedroom furniture is like letting your dog choose his own veterinarian.

———

Your child is watching too much television if there exists the possibility that he might melt down.

———

Don't bother discussing sex with small children. They rarely have anything to add.

———

Never, for effect, pull a gun on a small child. He won't get it.

———

Ask your child what he wants for dinner only if he's buying.

———

From SOCIAL STUDIES by Fran Lebowitz. Copyright (c) 1981 by Fran Lebowitz. Reprinted by permission of Random House, Inc.

 **RUSSELL BAKER**

Role Models

Anita Bryant's triumph over homosexuality in Miami reminded me of schoolteachers. There was a lot of discussion in that dispute about teachers and whether their sexual proclivities do or do not influence children and, if they do, whether homosexual teachers can divert the young from the heterosexual path.

People who took Miss Bryant's view that they may talked about teachers as "role models." Lacking fluency in the sociological tongue, a language almost as difficult as Basque, I am unclear what a "role model" is, but those who used the term seemed to be saying that teachers are people children tend to emulate. In any event, many Miamians must have thought their children would become homosexual if subjected to homosexual teachers.

That prompted me to ponder teachers I haven't seen, and scarcely thought about, for decades, and for the first time I reflected on how their sex lives had affected my own. My first thought was that it was curious, perhaps perverse, that I have not turned out to be a spinster.

Nowadays, I know, spinsters have been eliminated from society by the lexicographers of the feminist movement, but there were still quite a few 40 years ago, and most of them seemed to gravitate to school-teaching. Until eighth grade, I did not realize that males were permitted to teach school, and my impression was that married females were almost as unwelcome in the trade.

If the teacher was a "role model," parents were obviously unaware of it, for most of them surely did not want their children to grow up to be spinsters. Yet, despite almost constant tutelage by spinsters, I never felt the smallest temptation to indulge in spinsterism. When a group of us classmates sneaked off to somebody's cellar to play, we didn't play "spinster." We played "doctor," despite the fact that in those days you never found a medical man teaching elementary school.

Looking back, it seems we were always at least dimly aware of the sexuality of teachers, or in most cases, the absence of it. Even at an age foolishly thought to be innocent, one made certain assumptions about most of those teachers, and one of the firmest was that they had no sex life whatever. The idea of a teacher in the coils of rapture was as inconceivable as the idea of Herbert Hoover in Bermuda shorts. Yet very, very few of us, I suspect, were seduced by these "role models" into the juiceless life of celibacy.

At age 11, I and the other males in my class were stirred by the spectacle of a teacher who, though unmarried, was definitely not a spinster. Definitely not. She wore no girdle in the battle against ignorance. I—and, I am sure, 15 other men my age—still remember her voluptuous chalk movements at the blackboard as she struggled to help us grasp the distinction between a sentence's subject (one chalk line underneath) and its predicate (two lines underneath). Until then I had never seen a teacher fight ignorance without her armor on.

Was she a "role model"? Perhaps. To this day I enjoy lecturing helpless children on the finer points' of English grammar, which is almost as difficult as Basque grammar and may, therefore, suggest that that teacher led me down the path to sadism.

High school—it was an all-male establishment—exposed me to masculinity at the blackboard. The teachers wore three-piece suits and smelled of forbidden cigarettes which they were allowed to puff unseen between classes in private hideaways. One assumed them to be married and, therefore, beyond sex. Being for the most part dull, they made marriage seem dull and sexless, yet I already knew that I would someday marry, and knew with equal certainty that even though married I would not turn my back on sex. Sex was what the football captain was up to and, though not yet ready for operations at that rarified level, I was confident that once I was, I would not wither away as teachers did.

I had at least two homosexual teachers in that school. They didn't tell us they were, but we all knew it. I learned to jeer about them when they were out of earshot and to laugh about "queers," but I learned it from my "role models" in the schoolyard, and not from them.

One of them was largely responsible for encouraging a class-mate to pursue a form of art at which he is now one of the world's best practitioners, besides being a family man. The other woke me to the amazing fact that in life there was also wit. The teacher I most wanted to emulate, however, was single, drank wine and had been gassed in World War I. Of his three admirable traits, there was only one I wanted to copy, and sure enough, to this day I love the sound of a popping cork.

QUESTIONS FOR DISCUSSION

1. Books, manuals, and seminars on how to raise children are common in contemporary society. One widely used guide (Brazelton, 1974) describes a mother's efforts to feed a child who throws spoons, pushes away his favorite ice cream, and,

in general, refuses to eat. What conclusions about this behavior does the mother reach? "Mrs. Lang was sure he was ill." How else might such behavior be interpreted? Would such an interpretation be akin to Philo Gompers' conclusion about Irwin's behavior?

2. Socialization usually refers to adult training of children. In the following episode from Brazelton, who is socializing whom? "When father began to draw the water for his tub, Greg watched in anguish, saying, 'no, no, no.' Mr. Lang then ran through the rituals they had developed together to overcome his anxiety. They tried a toy, a truck, a finger, a toe, a leg, an arm, and finally his bottom ... Only with this playful routine could Greg make it into the tub." (1974:117) Is this actually adult socialization to childhood needs? Who is in charge of adult socialization?

3. Children learn from others: "We develop our initial appreciation of most norms by watching others perform." (Shibutani: 1986: 156) If this is the case, from whom did Irwin learn to burn down school buildings? Since schools and other buildings are burned down by teenagers in this society, from whom are they learning this behavior?

4. Lebowitz suggests that one's responsibility as a parent "is not as great as you might imagine. You need not supply the world with the next conqueror of disease or major motion-picture star." Is this a fairly typical parental idea about their children's anticipated future? What evidence can you offer that parents do feel that their sons or daughters must be doctors, lawyers, or engineers?

5. The list of suggestions by Lebowitz includes among other items advice on money, television, drinking, and sex. Is there a subtle class bias in the areas of socialization on which Lebowitz offers advice?

6. Lebowitz, though childless, wants to help in the socialization of children. The number of never married males and females and the number of voluntary childless couples is increasing in the United States. Should couples without children, or the never married, have any say in how children are socialized? Such individuals pay school taxes, even though childless. Should they have a say in the educational curriculum of

schools in their communities? Is socialization of the next generation the responsibility only, or even primarily, of the biological parents?

7. Baker is concerned with children's being socialized to sexual awareness. How do children learn about any activity, including sex? Shibutani says, "In most instances we learn by becoming involved with people who are more experienced." (1986:156) Which experiences is the teacher in the classroom most likely to impart to children? Why do some parents, and others, think that a school teacher, if homosexual, is likely to foster this experience upon the child?

8. Baker says the fact that most of his teachers were spinsters leaves him wondering why he did not turn out to be a spinster, too. How would a sociologist explain to Mr. Baker, or anyone, that this aspect of a teacher's life is not a determinant in the student's life? Would understanding the nature of dominant roles be helpful here?

REFERENCES

Brazelton, T. Berry. *Toddlers and Parents.* New York: Dell Publishing Co., 1974.

Davis, Kingsley. "Extreme Social Isolation of a Child." *American Journal of Sociology* 45 (1940), 554–64.

———— "Final Note on a Case of Extreme Isolation." *American Journal of Sociology* 50 (1947), 432–37.

Harlow, Harry. "The Nature of Love." *American Psychologist* 13 (1958), 673–85.

Reisman, David, et. al. *The Lonely Crowd.* New Haven: Yale Univ. Press, 1961.

Shibutani, Tamotsu. *Social Processes. An Introduction to Sociology.* Berkeley: Univ. of California Press, 1986.

Spitz, Rene. "Hospitalization: An Inquiry into the Genesis of Psychiatric Conditions in Early Childhood," in Freud, Anna, et. al., ed. *The Psychoanalytic Study of the Child.* New York: International Universities Press, 1945.

Wrong, Dennis. "The Oversocialized Conception of Man in Modern Sociology." *American Sociological Review* 26 (1961), 183–93.

III

SELF IN SOCIETY

Chapter Three

Culture

C ulture is a term with multiple meanings. It is often used in the sense of refinement, meaning "high culture"—i.e., the arts. France has a minister of culture who is responsible for the government's concern with the nation's music, painting, opera, and the like. We sometimes use the phrase, "She's a very cultured person." Biologists use *culture* to refer to the propagation of microorganisms. *Agriculture* refers to the practice of farming in its broadest sense. Each of these meanings is a restricted use of the term. Anthropologists and sociologists employ the term to refer to the total way of life of a given people. Thus it is appropriate to refer to the "French culture," but this would involve far more than just reference to the fine arts, including every material and nonmaterial aspect of French life.

Some cultures, including ours, are characterized by the fact that they give extreme importance to the material objects which are produced. These objects range all the way from highly sophisticated computers to the electric can opener to the omnipresent television set. Others see our culture, sometimes disparagingly, as a "materialistic" one. But all cultures produce material objects which are essential to their way of life. We do seem to take inordinate pride in the fact that we are capable of producing vast quantities of such material.

On the other hand, the nonmaterial aspects of culture refer to the language, ideas, beliefs, values, and symbols in terms of which we interact with one another. It is important to understand how these nonmaterial aspects of a culture are an integral part of a people's total way of life.

Language is, of course, a form of communication and perhaps the basic component of culture. Language readily identifies one as belonging to a particular culture. It can also brand one as an "outsider" if one speaks a language other than the dominant one in the culture. Groups develop their own language habits within the larger culture. Teenagers employ words and phrases which are not always readily translatable by adults.

Immigrants to a new culture must learn the language if they are to adapt fully. In the United States today there is an ongoing debate over bilingual education. Controversy centers around the schools' responsibility for helping newcomers preserve and use their native tongues to continue their cultural heritage. One group

argues that new arrivals must learn English at the outset.
Opposing groups argue that this defames their culture origins.
The controversy testifies to the powerful relationship between
language and culture.

Norms are cultural prescriptions for behavior. They range in
importance from folkways to laws. Folkways are everyday habits
which are the preferred ways of doing things. Mores are norms
which are related to our ideas of what is right and wrong, and the
violation of mores can bring strict sanctions. Laws, in many cases,
are the codification of mores and thus are formal rules about what
we may or may not do. Violation of the laws may result in
imprisonment and, in extreme cases, death. All of our norms tell
us how we are to behave in given situations.

There is great normative variation among groups within a
society. Criminal elements in a society have norms which are
binding upon the criminal but which are a violation of the law of
the larger society. Religious orders have specific norms which the
larger society tolerates but feels no obligation to follow. There are
norms which are appropriate in one place but which may be
totally inappropriate in another. Shouting and drinking may be
tolerated at a football game but are unacceptable behavior in the
classroom. Overall our behavior conforms to the norms of the
society. (Deviation from the norms is considered in Chapter 5.)
We behave as we do because "that is the way it is done" in our
culture.

The *values* of a society are closely related to the norms.
Briefly, values are the ideas and beliefs which people consider
very important. While we have many values in our society,
sociologist Robin Williams (1970) lists equality, freedom, and
democracy as those about which there is basic consensus. We also
value individualism, humanitarianism, and success. A society's
values ultimately find expression in its norms. If we value success
then it becomes normative to work hard. If we value health then
normative prescriptions suggest activities which promote well-
being. The ongoing debate over abortion is a function of how we
value life and when we say that life begins. The opposing groups
in this debate illustrate the important fact that not all groups in
the society share the same values equally.

Culture variation is the last aspect of the culture concept which
we will discuss. One of the most fascinating things we learn about
culture is that it is unique to a given society. Other cultures may
not share our particular values and norms. Young American

females appear on the beach in attire which exposes all but a very
small portion of their bodies to the sun. Such attire would be
unthinkable in Muslim countries and is equally incomprehensible
to older females in our society. The American drive for success at
any cost would be incomprehensible to many peasants in
developing countries. The use of hard drugs is illegal in the
United States, but many primitive tribes use them routinely in
their way of life. Whatever comprises the culture of a people, it is
the guiding principle for their life-style.

The selections about culture in this chapter begin with a
discussion of a prominent aspect of our culture's way of life:
professional football. In "He Didn't Watch the Game," Art
Buchwald raises the question of whether or not one can be a
"genuine" American if he or she violates one of our most sacred
folkways—watching the Super Bowl. Millions do watch the Super
Bowl, of course, and in this delightful account of one man who
didn't, Buchwald discusses the consequences of an individual
departing from this normative behavior.

The next selection examines the cultural component of
language. Language is the basis of communication, but our
language *symbols* must be shared if we are to communicate with
one another. Woody Allen's plea to speak "A Little Louder,
Please" should be read keeping in mind George H. Mead's
seminal work (1934) on the importance of gestures in human
communication. Mimes use only gestures to communicate. Allen
feels culturally incomplete because he cannot follow the symbolic
meanings of the mime.

Culture norms are the subject of Roy Blount's selection,
"How to Visit the Sick." What is appropriate behavior when
visiting patients in a hospital? Virtually the only rules posted by
hospitals are visiting hours and signs designating restricted areas.
Blount offers several more helpful things you should know when
visiting patients. The second selection dealing with normative
behavior is a catalog of desirable behavior traits for "The Modern
Real Man." All cultures have ideal images of what a real man or
real woman should do. Feirstein's listing of what real men should
do and know in today's society should be of immense value to
college students as they prepare to take their place in the world
beyond college.

In "The Whore of Mensa," Woody Allen offers a parody of
our concern with the intellectual life in America. Hofstadter
(1966) documents a long-standing anti-intellectual strain in

American life which is still with us. In one of his most delightful essays, Allen offers an unexpected analogy through his comic comparison of prostitutes hired for intellectual rather than sexual purposes.

Good health is one of the values in our society. Dave Barry calls into question one of the means millions are employing to attain good health—jogging. In "Jogging for President," Barry suggests that jogging is actually dysfunctional—indeed, that it destroys brain cells and has other injurious consequences.

The final selection "Woman, God Bless Her!," points to cultural variations in dress. Mark Twain compares the dress of the Fans, an African tribe, with that of women in our "high modern civilization." In reading this one should bear in mind that Twain wrote in 1882, before the contemporary woman's liberation movement. Twain calls attention to the fact that the Fan woman wears no clothing, and thus "When you call on a Fan lady and send up your card, the hired girl never says, 'Please take a seat, madame is dressing; she'll be down in three quarters of an hour.' "

 ART BUCHWALD

"He Didn't Watch the Game"

A bunch of us were standing around the bar on Monday talking about Super Bowl Sunday, and what a dandy day it had been. We all had that warm feeling you get when you have shared a great common experience. I was telling everyone how I had watched the game on a large super screen which my friend Stevens had bought just for the occasion. Next to being at the game itself, this gave me quite a bit of clout.

I noticed that the only one who wasn't enjoying the scene was Apple. With good humor I said, "Where did you see the Super Bowl, Apple?"

"I didn't," he replied.

There was a hush in the bar.

"Did someone die in your family?" Nelson asked.

"No," Apple said.

"I know," Bailey interjected, "you were on an airplane, flying back from a business trip."

Apple shook his head. "I wasn't on an airplane and no one died in my family and no one got sick. I was home."

"Your television set was broken?" someone suggested.

"My television set was perfect. As a matter of fact, my wife and I watched *To Kill a Mockingbird* with Gregory Peck. It was an excellent movie."

"What were you doing watching a movie instead of the Super Bowl?" I wanted to know.

"I don't believe in the Super Bowl," Apple replied, "and neither does my wife."

Ogilvy slammed down his beer. "What the hell do you mean— you don't believe in the Super Bowl? Are you some kind of atheist nut or something?"

Apple was really cool. "I believe in God, but I don't believe in football."

I thought Woodstock was going to slug him. "Super Bowl Sunday is the holiest day of the year. One hundred million Americans observe it, believe in it, live for it. And you're trying to say it don't do nothing to you?"

"It may have religious significance for some people. But it doesn't have meaning for my family. I have no objection to other folks believing that the day has some super power as long as they don't try to inflict their beliefs on me."

The bar was tensing up. I tried to be the peacemaker.

"Apple may have a point," I said. "After all, what makes America the greatest country in the world is not that you have to watch 'The Game,' but that you DON'T have to watch it if you don't want to."

"If you don't like it here," Ogilvy spat out at Apple, "why don't you go back where you came from?"

"Ogilvy's right," Nelson said. "Millions of dollars were spent to give us the Super Bowl. The two greatest teams in American football played their hearts out, and many fell on the field of combat."

"They put on a half-time show that would put the Roman circuses to shame. American advertisers spent every nickel they had to bring us a day we will remember for the rest of our lives. Only a pervert would be tuned in to *To Kill a Mockingbird*."

"I'm sorry you all feel this way," Apple said, "but we do have separation of state and sports in this country. Besides, I believe the Super Bowl has been hyped up to the point where it has lost all sportsmanlike meaning. It is now nothing but junk food."

I wish Apple hadn't said that. But our lawyers tell us that, no matter how much Apple sues us for assaulting him, no jury of 12 just men is going to award him a dime when they find out he doesn't believe in Super Bowl Sunday.

Reprinted with permission of the author.

WOODY ALLEN

A Little Louder, Please

It began one day last January when I was standing in McGinnis' Bar on Broadway, engulfing a slab of the world's richest cheesecake and suffering the guilty, cholesterolish hallucination that I could hear my aorta congealing into a hockey puck. Standing next to me was a nerve-shattering blonde, who waxed and waned under a black chemise with enough provocation to induce lycanthropy into a Boy Scout. For the previous fifteen minutes, my "pass the relish" had been the central theme of our relationship, despite several attempts on my part to generate a little action. As it was, she *had* passed the relish, and I was forced to ladle a small amount on my cheesecake as witness to the integrity of my request.

"I understand egg futures are up," I ventured finally, feigning the insouciance of a man who merged corporations as a sideline. Unaware that her stevedore boy friend had entered, with Laurel and Hardy timing, and was standing right behind me, I gave her a lean, hungry look and can remember cracking wise about Krafft-Ebing just before losing consciousness. The next thing I recall was running down the street to avoid the ire of what appeared to be a Sicilian cousin's club bent on avenging the girl's honor. I sought refuge in the cool dark of a newsreel theatre, where a tour de force by Bugs Bunny and three Librium restored my nervous system to its usual timbre. The main feature came on and turned out to be a travelogue on the New Guinea bush—a topic rivalling "Moss Formations" and "How Penguins Live" for my attention span. "Throwbacks," droned the narrator, "living today not a whit differently from man millions of years ago, slay the wild boar [whose standard of living didn't appear to be up perceptibly, either] and sit around the fire at night acting out the day's kill in pantomime." Pantomime. It hit me with sinus-clearing clarity. Here was a chink in my cultural armor—the only chink, to be sure, but one that has plagued me ever since childhood, when a dumb-show production of Gogol's *The Overcoat* eluded my grasp entirely and had me convinced I was simply watching fourteen Russians doing calisthenics. Always, pantomime was a mystery to me—one that I chose to forget about because of the embarrassment it caused me. But here was that failing again and, to my chagrin, just as bad as ever. I did not understand the frenetic gesticulations of the leading New Guinea aborigine any more than I have ever understood Marcel Marceau in any of those little skits that fill multitudes with such unbounded adulation. I writhed in my seat as the amateur jungle thespian mutely titillated his fellow-primitives, finally garnering hefty mitt with money notices from the tribal elders, and then I slunk, dejected, from the theatre.

At home that evening, I became obsessed with my shortcoming. It was cruelly true: despite my canine celerity in other areas of artistic endeavor, all that was needed was one evening of mime to limn me clearly as Markham's hoe man—stolid, stunned, and a brother to the ox in spades. I began to rage impotently, but the back of my thigh tightened and I was forced to sit. After all, I reasoned, what more elemental form of communication is there? Why was this universal art form patent in meaning to all but me? I tried raging impotently again, and this time brought it off, but mine is a quiet neighborhood, and several minutes later two rednecked spokesmen for the Nineteenth Precinct dropped by to inform me that raging impotently could mean a five-hundred-dollar fine, six months' imprisonment, or both. I thanked them and made a beeline for the sheets, where my struggle to sleep off my monstrous imperfection resulted in eight hours of nocturnal anxiety I wouldn't wish on Macbeth.

A further bone-chilling example of my mimetic shortcomings materialized only a few weeks later, when two free tickets to the theatre turned up at my door—the result of my correctly identifying the singing voice of Mama Yancey on a radio program a fortnight prior. First prize was a Bentley, and in my excitement to get my call in to the disc jockey promptly I had bolted naked from the tub.

Seizing the telephone with one wet hand while attempting to turn off the radio with the other, I ricocheted off the ceiling, while lights dimmed for miles around, as they did when Lepke got the chair. My second orbit around the chandelier was interrupted by the open drawer of a Louis Quinze desk, which I met head on, catching an ormolu mount across the mouth. A florid insignia on my face, which now looked as if it had been stamped by a rococo cookie cutter, plus a knot on my head the size of an auk egg, affected my lucidity, causing me to place second to Mrs. Sleet Mazursky, and, scotching my dreams of the Bentley, I settled for a pair of freebees to an evening of Off Broadway theatrics. That a famed international pantomimist was on the bill cooled my ardor to the temperature of a polar cap, but, hoping to break the jinx, I decided to attend. I was unable to get a date on only six weeks' notice, so I used the extra ticket to tip my window-washer, Lars, a lethargic menial with all the sensitivity of the Berlin Wall. At first, he thought the little orange pasteboard was edible, but when I explained that it was good for an evening of pantomime—one of the only spectator events outside of a fire that he could hope to understand—he thanked me profusely.

On the night of the performance, the two of us—I in my opera cape and Lars with his pail—split with aplomb from the confines of a Checker cab and, entering the theatre, strode imperiously to our seats, where I studied the program and learned, with some nervousness, that the curtain-raiser was a little silent entertainment entitled *Going to a Picnic*. It began when a wisp of a man walked onstage in kitchen-white makeup and a tight black leotard. Standard picnic dress—I wore it myself to a picnic in Central Park last year, and, with the exception of a few adolescent malcontents who took it as a signal to re-edit my salients, it went unnoticed. The mime now proceeded to spread a picnic blanket, and, instantly, my old confusion set in. He was either spreading a picnic blanket or milking a small goat. Next, he elaborately removed his shoes, except that I'm not positive they were his shoes, because he drank one of them and mailed the other to Pittsburgh. I say "Pittsburgh," but actually it is hard to mime the concept of Pittsburgh, and as I look back on it, I now think what he was miming was not Pittsburgh at all but a man driving a golf cart through a revolving door—or possibly two men dismantling a printing press. How this pertains to a picnic escapes me. The pantomimist then began sorting an invisible collection of rectangular objects, undoubtedly heavy, like a complete set of the *Encyclopaedia Britannica*, which I suspect he was removing from his picnic basket, although from the way he held them they could also have been the Budapest String Quartet, bound and gagged.

By this time, to the surprise of those sitting next to me, I found myself trying, as usual, to help the mime clarify the details of his scene by guessing aloud exactly what he was doing. "Pillow . . . big pillow. Cushion? *Looks* like cushion . . ." This well-meaning participation often upsets the true lover of silent theatre, and I have noticed a tendency on such occasions for those sitting next to me to express uneasiness in various forms, ranging from significant throat-clearings to a lion's-paw swipe on the back of the head, which I once received from a member of a Manhasset housewives' theatre party. On this occasion, a dowager resembling Ichabod Crane snapped her lorgnette quirtlike across my knuckles, with the admonition "Cool it, stud." Then, warming to me, she explained, with the patiently slow enunciation of one addressing a shell-shocked infantryman, that the mime was now dealing humorously with the various elements that traditionally confound the picnic-goer—ants, rain, and the always-good-for-a-laugh forgotten bottle opener. Temporarily enlightened, I rocked with laughter at the notion of a man harassed by the absence of a bottle opener, and marvelled at its limitless possibilities.

Finally, the mime began blowing glass. Either blowing glass or tattooing the student body of Northwestern University, but it could have been the men's choir—or a diathermy machine—or any large, extinct quadruped, often amphibious and usually herbivorous, the fossilized remains of which have been found as far north as the Arctic. By now, the audience was doubled up with laughter over the hijinks on the stage. Even the obtuse Lars was wiping tears of joy from his face with his squeegee. But for me it was hopeless; the more I tried, the less I understood. A defeated weariness stole over me, and I slipped off my loafers and called it a day. The next thing I knew, a couple of charwomen at work in the balcony were batting around the pros and cons of bursitis. Gathering my senses by the dim glow of the theatre work light, I straightened my tie and departed for Riker's, where a hamburger and a chocolate malted gave me no trouble whatever as to their meaning, and, for the first time that evening, I threw off my guilty burden. To this day, I remain incomplete culturally, but I'm working on it. If you ever see an aesthete at a pantomime squinting, writhing, and muttering to himself, come up and say hello—but catch me early in the performance; I don't like to be bothered once I'm asleep.

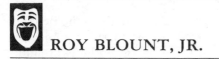

ROY BLOUNT, JR.

How to Visit the Sick

Bounding into the room is wrong. Hospitalized people do not like to be bounded in upon. The first thing visitors should see as they step off the elevator is the following sign.

PLEASE DO NOT

TRY OUR PATIENTS BY

1. **Bounding in upon them.**

2. **Creeping in upon them.**

3. **Being festive.**

4. **Being grave.**

5. **Saying, "You look *fabulous!*"**

6. **Saying (if the patient's name is Vern McGiver), "Oh! Excuse me! I was looking for Vern McGiver's room. I ... Vern! *Is that ... you!?*"**

7. **Telling obvious jokes. For instance, if the patient has had an operation on his or her colon, you may be sure that he or she has heard all the punctuation jokes by now.**

But there is no way to squeeze onto one sign all the things that hospital visitors should bear in mind. Some people assume that just by visiting someone who is sick, they are doing a heartwarming thing. That is like assuming that just because you are walking out onto a stage, you are doing an entertaining thing. A person in a hospital bed is often tempted to take advantage of his position (whose advantages are few enough) by cutting into visitors' conversation sharply with: "If somebody doesn't say something *interesting* pretty soon I'm going to hemorrhage."

But he doesn't want to deprive his visitors—call them the Bengt-sons—of the chance to feel warmhearted. So he doesn't complain.[1] He just lies there, biding his time until the day when he is up and around and the Bengtsons aren't, and he can visit *them* in a hospital and spill their ice water on their pillows. And the Bengtsons, of course, will have to say, "Oh that's all right! Don't worry!"

One of the burdens of the hospitalized person is that he is, in a sense, the host, and must be gracious to the well. Even though the well often go too far in playing down the seriousness of the patient's complaint: "What you've been through is nothing! My sister had *both* of hers taken out *with no anesthetic.*"

Or they play it up too much: "You poor thing. I could no more have borne up under this terrible thing the way you have than . . . Of course, I don't think the full impact of it has hit you yet."

Or they claim too much expertise with regard to the patient's complaint: "Oh, no, no, that's not right at all. What you've actually had removed is *urethral* stones. My aunt had the same thing and I did some research on it to fill her in. You see, your trouble is too many cola drinks. Probably been going on for years. So that a kind of fine brown sediment . . ."

Or they are too innocent: "Where exactly *is* the prostate, any-way?"

What are some guidelines to appropriate visitor behavior?

Be sensitive, but not to a fault. Say you are telling a story about frogs. It is better to go ahead and use the word "croak" than to stop at "croa—" and bolt from the room.

Bring gossip. Preferably gossip about people other than the patient. But do not preface such gossip with something like, "Be grateful you're in here. If you were able to work you'd probably be getting fired like Morris Zumer."

Bring anecdotes that make interns and nurses look foolish. Once, in an emergency ward, an intern was trying to deal with a

---

1.   The careful reader will note that sometimes my pronouns imply that every person in the world is male, and sometimes that he isn't. When I go out of my way to avoid saying something like, "The trouble with nuclear conflagration is that it will leave man with no sense of his sociometric place" (by saying, "The trouble with nuclear conflagration is that it will leave a person with no sense of his socio-metric place, or hers either"), it is because I am suffering from Pronoun Guilt. The question of sexism in pronouns is one that deeply concerns me, since that is the kind of guy I am. I have invented new pronouns, none of which I will cite here be-cause there is nothing quite so funny-looking as a new pronoun. I have devised hermaphroditic characters named Heshie and Sheehy, who have failed to find favor as pronoun replacements. Man has yet to deliver himself from Pronoun Guilt.

patient who had delirium tremens. "It's your imagination!" the intern insisted. The patient seized him by the necktie so ferociously that the intern could neither breathe nor break the patient's grip. The intern cried out for a nurse, who arrived. "Get ... scissors ... cut ... tie," the intern gasped. The nurse briskly left the room, returned with scissors, pounced, and snipped off the intern's tie—the loose end.

That is a story someone told me in a hospital once, and I enjoyed it. It may not be perfect for every patient. Some patients may prefer quieter stories. Others may have delirium tremens, in which case entertainment is the last thing they need. Every patient is different. But there are three rules that apply to visitors in every case:

- Don't bring hand puppets.

- Don't, even as a "hoot," serve a subpoena.

- Don't get up under the bed and bump around for any reason.

Are you reading this in someone's hospital room? Can it possibly have been left, on purpose, where you would find it? If by any chance you found it under the patient's bed, please get out from under there.

And now please let the patient watch "Family Feud" in peace.

 BRUCE FEIRSTEIN

The Modern Real Man

In the past, it was easy to be a Real Man. All you had to do was abuse women, steal land from Indians, and find some place to dump the toxic waste.

But not anymore.

Society is much more complex today. We live with different threats and terrors. Robots are challenging us for spots on GM assembly lines. Women are demanding things like equality and respect. And instead of merely having to protect themselves against gunslingers and poker cheats, men today face a far more sinister crowd of predators: IRS agents, uninsured motorists, meter maids, carcinogenic food additives, and electronic banking machines.

So what, then, makes someone a Real Man today?

What sets him apart from the average Joe who can't find his car in the shopping-mall parking lot? Or the joker who takes his girl out on her dream date—only to have the computer reject his credit card at the end of the meal?

How does he prove himself, now that things like barroom brawling, waging war, and baby-seal killing are frowned upon by polite society?

The answer is simple.

A Real Man today is someone who can triumph over the challenges of modern society.

Real Men, for example, do not cower and shake in the face of double-digit inflation.

Real Men do not worry about the diminishing ozone layer.

Real Men are not intimidated by microwave radiation; they're not afraid to fly DC–10s, drive Corvairs, or invest in the city of St. Louis municipal bonds.

In short, strength and bravery are still the hallmark of today's Real Man; but he's just found modern ways to show it.

Real Men carry cash. Never the American Express card.

Real Men don't buy flight insurance.

Real Men don't smoke low-tar cigarettes.

Real Men are not afraid of the communist threat.

Real Men don't take guff from French maître d's.

Real Men don't cry during the "Mary Tyler Moore Show."

Going further, today's Real Man is still interested in the Spartan, simple life. He still believes in "roughing it"; he doesn't own a shower massage, remote-control TV, or an electric blanket.

Real Men don't floss.

Real Men don't use ZIP codes.

Real Men don't have telephones in the shape of Snoopy.

Real Men don't drive Volvos because they're supposedly safer; they don't have special jogging shoes or telephone answering machines. (Real Men, after all, are secure enough to know that if it's important, people will call back.)

Real Men don't itemize their tax deductions.

Real Men still pass in the no-passing lane.

A Real Man would never use a designated hitter.

But this is only the tip of the modern Real Man's psyche.

Today's Real Man is intelligent and astute; he's nobody's fool.

Real Men know that things don't really go better with Coke; he's not really in good hands with Allstate; and weekends were—in fact—not made for Michelob.

Real Men understand that using a Jimmy Connors tennis racquet will not improve a weak backhand; they realize that designer jeans, Paco Rabane and Riunite on ice will not help seduce any woman whose IQ is higher than the average number of a UHF television station.

Basically, today's Real Man is unaffected by fads or fashion.

Real Men don't disco.

Real Men don't eat brunch.

Real Men don't have their hair styled.

Real Men don't meditate, golf, practice Tai Chi, or use hair thickeners.

Real Men don't advertise in the Personals section of the *Village Voice* for female companionship.

Real Men don't play games with wine in restaurants; they don't sniff the cork and say things like "It's a small, unpretentious, fruity red, with ambitious overtones of Bordeaux" about a four-dollar bottle of Ripple.

Real Men don't need water beds, lava lights, musk oil, mirrors on the ceiling, X-rated videocassettes, or Ravel's *Bolero*.

Real Men don't want Bo Derek.

Real Men don't use black condoms.

Real Men stop reading—and writing—letters to *Penthouse* when they're sixteen.

Real Men are secure enough to admit they buy *Playboy* for the women.

Politically, Real Men today are, well, realistic.

They don't trust the French.

They don't rely on NATO.

They don't contribute to PBS.

They don't believe in bilingual education.

They don't belong to the National Rifle Association.

And Real Men don't believe in the United Nations.

("After thirty-five years," say Real Men, "all they've proved capable of doing is producing a marginally attractive Christmas card.")

Unlike his predecessors, today's Real Man actually can feel things like sorrow, pity, love, warmth, and sincerity; but he'd never be so vulnerable as to admit them.

All told, today's Real Man is probably closest to Spencer Tracy or Gary Cooper in spirit; he realizes that while birds, flowers, poetry, and small children do not add to the quality of life in quite the same manner as a Super Bowl and six-pack of Bud, he's learned to appreciate them anyway.

But perhaps there's one phrase that sums up his very existence, a simple declaration that he finds symbolic of everything in today's world that's phony, affected, limp, or without merit:

Real Men don't eat quiche.

Admittedly, this may seem—if you'll forgive the pun—a bit hard to swallow at first.

But think about it.

Could John Wayne ever have taken Normandy, Iwo Jima, Korea, the Gulf of Tonkin, and the entire Wild West on a diet of quiche and salad?

 WOODY ALLEN

The Whore of Mensa

One thing about being a private investigator, you've got to learn to go with your hunches. That's why when a quivering pat of butter named Word Babcock walked into my office and laid his cards on the table, I should have trusted the cold chill that shot up my spine.

"Kaiser?" he said, "Kaiser Lupowitz?"

"That's what it says on my license," I owned up.

"You've got to help me. I'm being blackmailed. Please!"

He was shaking like the lead singer in a rumba band. I pushed a glass across the desk top and a bottle of rye I keep handy for nonmedicinal purposes. "Suppose you relax and tell me all about it."

"You ... you won't tell my wife?"

"Level with me, Word. I can't make any promises."

He tried pouring a drink, but you could hear the clicking sound across the street, and most of the stuff wound up in his shoes.

"I'm a working guy," he said. "Mechanical maintenance. I build and service joy buzzers. You know—those little fun gimmicks that give people a shock when they shake hands?"

"So?"

"A lot of your executives like 'em. Particularly down on Wall Street."

"Get to the point."

"I'm on the road a lot. You know how it is—lonely. Oh, not what you're thinking. See, Kaiser, I'm basically an intellectual. Sure, a guy can meet all the bimbos he wants. But the really brainy women—they're not so easy to find on short notice."

"Keep talking."

"Well, I heard of this young girl. Eighteen years old. A Yassar student. For a price, she'll come over and discuss any subject—Proust, Yeats, anthropology. Exchange of ideas. You see what I'm driving at?"

"Not exactly."

"I mean, my wife is great, don't get me wrong. But she won't discuss Pound with me. Or Eliot. I didn't know that when I married her. See, I need a woman who's mentally stimulating, Kaiser. And I'm willing to pay for it. I don't want an involvement—I want a quick intellectual experience, then I want the girl to leave. Christ, Kaiser, I'm a happily married man."

"How long has this been going on?"

"Six months. Whenever I have that craving, I call Flossie. She's a madam, with a master's in comparative lit. She sends me over an intellectual, see?"

So he was one of those guys whose weakness was really bright women. I felt sorry for the poor sap. I figured there must be a lot of jokers in his position, who were starved for a little intellectual communication with the opposite sex and would pay through the nose for it.

"Now she's threatening to tell my wife," he said.

"Who is?"

"Flossie. They bugged the motel room. They got tapes of me discussing *The Waste Land* and *Styles of Radical Will*, and, well, really getting into some issues. They want ten grand or they go to Carla. Kaiser, you've got to help me! Carla would die if she knew she didn't turn me on up here."

The old call-girl racket. I had heard rumors that the boys at headquarters were on to something involving a group of educated women, but so far they were stymied.

"Get Flossie on the phone for me."

"What?"

"I'll take your case, Word. But I get fifty dollars a day, plus expenses. You'll have to repair a lot of joy buzzers."

"It won't be ten Gs' worth, I'm sure of that," he said with a grin, and picked up the phone and dialed a number. I took it from him and winked. I was beginning to like him.

Seconds later, a silky voice answered, and I told her what was on my mind. "I understand you can help me set up an hour of good chat," I said.

"Sure, honey. What do you have in mind?"

"I'd like to discuss Melville."

"*Moby Dick* or the shorter novels?"

"What's the difference?"

"The price. That's all. Symbolism's extra."

"What'll it run me?"

"Fifty, maybe a hundred for *Moby Dick*. You want a comparative discussion—Melville and Hawthorne? That could be arranged for a hundred."

"The dough's fine," I told her and gave her the number of a room at the Plaza.

"You want a blonde or a brunette?"

"Surprise me," I said, and hung up.

I shaved and grabbed some black coffee while I checked over the Monarch College Outline series. Hardly an hour had passed before there was a knock on my door. I opened it, and standing there was a young redhead who was packed into her slacks like two big scoops of vanilla ice cream.

"Hi, I'm Sherry."

They really knew how to appeal to your fantasies. Long straight hair, leather bag, silver earrings, no make-up.

"I'm surprised you weren't stopped, walking into the hotel dressed like that," I said. "The house dick can usually spot an intellectual."

"A five-spot cools him."

"Shall we begin?" I said, motioning her to the couch.

She lit a cigarette and got right to it. "I think we could start by approaching *Billy Budd* as Melville's justification of the ways of God to man, *n'est-ce pas?*"

"Interestingly, though, not in a Miltonian sense." I was bluffing. I wanted to see if she'd go for it.

"No. *Paradise Lost* lacked the substructure of pessimism." She did.

"Right, right. God, you're right," I murmured.

"I think Melville reaffirmed the virtues of innocence in a naïve yet sophisticated sense—don't you agree?"

I let her go on. She was barely nineteen years old, but already she had developed the hardened facility of the pseudo-intellectual. She rattled off her ideas glibly, but it was all mechanical. Whenever I offered an insight, she faked a response: "Oh, yes, Kaiser. Yes, baby, that's deep. A platonic comprehension of Christianity—why didn't I see it before?"

We talked for about an hour and then she said she had to go. She stood up and I laid a C-note on her.

"Thanks, honey."

"There's plenty more where that came from."

"What are you trying to say?"

I had piqued her curiosity. She sat down again.

"Suppose I wanted to—have a party?" I said.

"Like, what kind of party?"

"Suppose I wanted Noam Chomsky explained to me by two girls?"

"Oh, wow."

"If you'd rather forget it . . ."

"You'd have to speak with Flossie," she said. "It'd cost you."

Now was the time to tighten the screws. I flashed my private-investigator's badge and informed her it was a bust.

"What!"

"I'm fuzz, sugar, and discussing Melville for money is an 802. You can do time."

"You louse!"

"Better come clean, baby. Unless you want to tell your story down at Alfred Kazin's office, and I don't think he'd be too happy to hear it."

She began to cry. "Don't turn me in, Kaiser," she said. "I needed the money to complete my master's. I've been turned down for a grant. *Twice.* Oh, Christ."

It all poured out—the whole story. Central Park West upbringing, Socialist summer camps, Brandeis. She was every dame you saw waiting in line at the Elgin or the Thalia, or penciling the words

"Yes, very true" into the margin of some book on Kant. Only somewhere along the line she had made a wrong turn.

"I needed cash. A girl friend said she knew a married guy whose wife wasn't very profound. He was into Blake. She couldn't hack it. I said sure, for a price I'd talk Blake with him. I was nervous at first. I faked a lot of it. He didn't care. My friend said there were others. Oh, I've been busted before. I got caught reading *Commentary* in a parked car, and I was once stopped and frisked at Tanglewood. Once more and I'm a three-time loser."

"Then take me to Flossie."

She bit her lip and said, "The Hunter College Book Store is a front."

"Yes?"

"Like those bookie joints that have barbershops outside for show. You'll see."

I made a quick call to headquarters and then said to her, "Okay, sugar. You're off the hook. But don't leave town."

She tilted her face up toward mine gratefully. "I can get you photographs of Dwight Macdonald reading," she said.

"Some other time."

I walked into the Hunter College Book Store. The salesman, a young man with sensitive eyes, came up to me. "Can I help you?" he said.

"I'm looking for a special edition of *Advertisements for Myself*. I understand the author had several thousand gold-leaf copies printed up for friends."

"I'll have to check," he said. "We have a WATS line to Mailer's house."

I fixed him with a look. "Sherry sent me," I said.

"Oh, in that case, go on back," he said. He pressed a button. A wall of books opened, and I walked like a lamb into that bustling pleasure palace known as Flossie's.

Red flocked wallpaper and a Victorian décor set the tone. Pale, nervous girls with black-rimmed glasses and blunt-cut hair lolled around on sofas, riffling Penguin Classics provocatively. A blonde with a big smile winked at me, nodded toward a room upstairs, and said, "Wallace Stevens, eh?" But it wasn't just intellectual experiences—they were peddling emotional ones, too. For fifty bucks, I learned, you could "relate without getting close." For a hundred, a girl would lend you her Bartók records, have dinner, and then let you watch while she had an anxiety attack. For one-fifty, you could listen to FM radio with twins. For three bills, you got the works: A thin Jewish brunette would pretend to pick you up at the Museum of Modern Art, let you read her master's, get you involved in a screaming quarrel at Elaine's over Freud's conception of women, and then fake a suicide of your choosing—the perfect evening, for some guys. Nice racket. Great town, New York.

"Like what you see?" a voice said behind me. I turned and suddenly found myself standing face to face with the business end of a .38. I'm a guy with a strong stomach, but this time it did a back flip. It was Flossie, all right. The voice was the same, but Flossie was a man. His face was hidden by a mask.

"You'll never believe this," he said, "but I don't even have a college degree. I was thrown out for low grades."

"Is that why you wear that mask?"

"I devised a complicated scheme to take over *The New York Review of Books*, but it meant I had to pass for Lionel Trilling. I went to Mexico for an operation. There's a doctor in Juarez who gives people Trilling's features—for a price. Something went wrong. I came out looking like Auden, with Mary McCarthy's voice. That's when I started working the other side of the law."

Quickly, before he could tighten his finger on the trigger, I went into action. Heaving forward, I snapped my elbow across his jaw and grabbed the gun as he fell back. He hit the ground like a ton of bricks. He was still whimpering when the police showed up.

"Nice work, Kaiser," Sergeant Holmes said. "When we're through with this guy, the F.B.I. wants to have a talk with him. A little matter involving some gamblers and an annotated copy of Dante's *Inferno*. Take him away, boys."

Later that night, I looked up an old account of mine named Gloria. She was blond. She had graduated *cum laude*. The difference was she majored in physical education. It felt good.

DAVE BARRY

Jogging for President

Lately, I have noticed large numbers of people staggering along the sides of major highways, trying to get in shape. I think they have the right idea: most of us Americans are out of shape. I know for a fact that I am.

When I was in high school, my friends and I were in terrific shape. Our bodies were fine-tuned machines. We would routinely drink quarts of warmish beer, then perform feats of great physical prowess. For example, during the Halloween Dance we carried a 1962 Volkswagen all the way up the front steps of Pleasantville High School, right into the lobby. I bet we couldn't do that today. I bet you couldn't, either.

Now I grant you that most of us no longer feel any great *need* to drink warm beer and carry Volkswagens into high schools, but the point is that if some emergency arose, if for some reason involving national security we *had* to carry a Volkswagen into a high school, we couldn't do it. We'd go a few steps, then we'd drop the Volkswagen and collapse on the ground, gasping and heaving, and that would be the end of our national security. So I figure it's time to get in shape.

But jogging is not the way to do it. For one thing, jogging kills your brain cells. The Army has known this for years; it forces recruits to jog every day, on the theory that some of them will lose so many brain cells that they will eventually reenlist. Your really dedicated joggers know it, too; in fact, it's one of the main reasons they jog. The idea is that if you're troubled about your job or world affairs, you go out and jog until you've killed whatever brain cells are responsible for those thoughts. The problem is that you may also kill the brain cells that remember your name and address, in which case you keep right on jogging, sometimes for days. This is what has happened to the people you see jogging along major highways, the ones with vacant expressions on their faces: they left home as nuclear physicists, heart surgeons, corporation presidents, and so on, but after a few hours most of them have library paste for brains.

Remember Jimmy Carter? Every day at the White House he used to wake up at the crack of dawn, develop some brilliant plan to save the economy, then head out for his morning jog. His aides would find him stumbling around hours later, sweaty and confused, his economic plan gone forever. Jimmy might have stood a chance in the 1980 elections if he had run against another jogger, but instead he faced Ronald Reagan. Ron has his horses jog for him and thus is able to preserve what brain cells he has, although I suspect his horses are fairly stupid.

My other objection to jogging is that even if you manage to jog yourself into shape, you still don't *look* all that great. I mean, look at marathon runners: they appear gaunt and desperately hungry, like refugees wearing numbers. They're always snatching scraps of food from spectators and stuffing them (the scraps of food) into their mouths. If you were to toss, say, a side of raw beef into their path, they'd all dive for it, teeth bared, and that would be the end of the marathon.

So I have rejected jogging as a way to get in shape. In fact, I was about to give up altogether when I discovered body-building magazines. Body-building magazines are published for people, mostly male, whose idea of being in shape is to have muscles the size of lawn tractors. You've probably seen these magazines: they're full of pictures of people who have smeared Vaseline all over their bodies and are wearing bathing suits no larger than a child's watchband; they are trying to smile in a relaxed manner but end up with more of an intense grin, because they have enormous muscles lunging out from all over their bodies, and Lord only knows how many bizarre chemical substances coursing through their veins.

These people obviously do not jog—I doubt they ever leave their gymnasiums, for fear their muscles will lunge out and kill innocent bystanders—but they are obviously in *terrific* shape. At least they *look* as if they're in terrific shape, which is the important thing. If Jimmy Carter had spent his time body-building instead of jogging, he would be president today. His aides would have carried him into the presidential debates and propped him up against his lectern, and when it was time for him to make his opening statement, he would have just stood there, Vaseline shimmering on his muscles, grinning intensely at the audience. Who would have dared to vote against him?

So I've been reading body-building magazines, hoping to pick up some tips on getting in shape. The idea seems to be to lift a lot of heavy objects until you get dense. Density is much sought-after in the body-building world. For example, *Muscle Digest* magazine, in its October issue, refers to one promising body builder as "one of the most dense bodybuilders in senior level competition." Evidently this is considered high praise.

So I plan to lift heavy objects, starting with my typewriter and working up to a 1962 Volkswagen, until I get fairly dense, after which I intend to smear Vaseline on my body and maybe run for president.

 MARK TWAIN

Woman, God Bless Her! *

The toast includes the sex, universally; it is to Woman comprehensively, wheresoever she may be found. Let us consider her ways. First comes the matter of dress. This is a most important consideration, and must be disposed of before we can intelligently proceed to examine the profounder depths of the theme. For text let us take the dress of two antipodal types—the savage woman of Central Africa and the cultivated daughter of our high modern civilization. Among the Fans, a great negro tribe, a woman when dressed for home, or to go out shopping or calling, doesn't wear anything at all but just her complexion. That is all; it is her entire outfit. It is the lightest costume in the world, but is made of the darkest material. It has often been mistaken for mourning. It is the trimmest, and neatest, and gracefulest costume that is now in fashion; it wears well, is fast colors, doesn't show dirt, you don't have to send it down-town to wash, and have some of it come back scorched with the flat-iron, and some of it with the buttons ironed off, and some of it petrified with starch, and some of it chewed by the calf, and some of it rotted with acids, and some of it exchanged for other customers' things that haven't any virtue but holiness, and ten-twelfths of the pieces overcharged for and the rest of the dozen "mislaid." And it always

* A speech delivered before the New England Society in the City of New York, December 22, 1882.

fits; it is the perfection of a fit. And it is the handiest dress in the whole realm of fashion. It is always ready, always "done up." When you call on a Fan lady and send up your card, the hired girl never says, "Please take a seat, madame is dressing; she'll be down in three-quarters of an hour." No, madame is always dressed, always ready to receive; and before you can get the door-mat before your eyes she is in your midst. Then, again, the Fan ladies don't go to church to see what each other has got on; and they don't go back home and describe it and slander it.

Such is the dark child of savagery, as to every-day toilet; and thus, curiously enough, she finds a point of contact with the fair daughter of civilization and high fashion—who often has "nothing to wear"; and thus these widely-separated types of the sex meet upon common ground. Yes, such is the Fan woman as she appears in her simple, unostentatious, every-day toilet; but on state occasions she is more dressy. At a banquet she wears bracelets; at a lecture she wears earrings and a belt; at a ball she wears stockings— and, with true feminine fondness for display, she wears them on her arms; at a funeral she wears a jacket of tar and ashes; at a wedding the bride who can afford it puts on pantaloons. Thus the dark child of savagery and the fair daughter of civilization meet once more upon common ground, and these two touches of nature make their whole world kin.

Now we will consider the dress of our other type. A large part of the daughter of civilization is her dress—as it should be. Some civilized women would lose half their charm without dress; and some would lose all of it. The daughter of modern civilization dressed at her utmost best, is a marvel of exquisite and beautiful art and expense. All the lands, all the climes, and all the arts are laid under tribute to furnish her forth. Her linen is from Belfast, her robe is from Paris, her lace is from Venice, or Spain, or France; her feathers are from the remote regions of Southern Africa, her furs from the remoter home of the iceberg and the aurora, her fan from Japan, her diamonds from Brazil, her bracelets from California, her pearls from Ceylon, her cameos from Rome; she has gems and trinkets from buried Pompeii, and others that graced comely Egyptian forms that have been dust and ashes now for forty centuries; her watch is from Geneva, her card-case is from China, her hair is from—from—I don't know where her hair is from; I never could find out. That is, her other hair—her public hair, her Sunday hair; I don't mean the hair she goes to bed with. Why, you ought to know the hair I mean; it's that thing which she calls a switch, and which resembles a switch as much as it resembles a brickbat or a shotgun, or any other thing which you correct people with. It's that thing which she twists and then coils round and round her head, beehive fashion, and then tucks the end in under the hive and harpoons it with a hairpin. And that reminds me of a trifle: any time you want to, you can glance around the carpet of a Pullman car, and go and pick up a hairpin; but not to save your life can you get any woman in that car to acknowledge that hairpin. Now, isn't that strange? But it's true. The woman who has never swerved from cast-iron veracity and fidelity in her whole life will, when confronted with this crucial test, deny her hairpin. She will deny that hairpin before a hundred witnesses. I have stupidly got into more trouble and more hot water trying to hunt up the owner of a hairpin in a Pullman car than by any other indiscretion of my life.

Well, you see what the daughter of civilization is when she is dressed, and you have seen what the daughter of savagery is when she isn't. Such is woman, as to costume. I come now to consider her in her higher and nobler aspects—as mother, wife, widow, grass-widow, mother-in-law, hired girl, telegraph operator, telephone hel-loer, queen, book-agent, wet-nurse, stepmother, boss, professional fat woman, professional double-headed woman, professional beau-ty, and so forth and so on.

We will simply discuss these few—let the rest of the sex tarry in Jericho till we come again. First in the list of right, and first in our gratitude, comes a woman who—why, dear me, I've been talking three-quarters of an hour! I beg a thousand pardons. But you see, yourselves, that I had a large contract. I have accomplished some-thing, anyway. I have introduced my subject. And if I had till next Forefathers' Day, I am satisfied that I could discuss it as adequately and appreciatively as so gracious and noble a theme deserves. But as the matter stands now, let us finish as we began—and say, without jesting, but with all sincerity, "Woman—God bless her!"

QUESTIONS FOR DISCUSSION

---

1. Prebish, discussing the parallels between sport and religion, says that "*sport is religion* for growing numbers of Americans ... the yearly Super Bowl is no less a religious holiday than Easter." (1984) Is this what Buchwald seems to be saying in a

humorous fashion? When Apple says that he doesn't believe in the Super Bowl, Ogilvy asks: "Are you some kind of atheist nut or something?" Is football now one of our sacred norms such that nonparticipants are seen as atheists?

2. One sports analyst says that "by the end of the 1960s ... religion was a spectator sport while professional and college athletic contests were the only events Americans held sacred." (Lipsyte, 1975) What is the meaning of these terms commonly used to describe the activities of athletes: *dedication, suffering, sacrifice*? Do they have religious meanings, also?

3. One indicator of the importance of a phenomenon is the number of people who support it. Some 100 million people regularly watch the Super Bowl and we assume, accordingly, its importance in our national life. Every Sunday some 70 million Americans worship in the churches of the land. Does this suggest that traditional religious expressions are as important as football to many millions?

4. Woody Allen cannot understand the gestures of a mime and says that to this day he remains "incomplete culturally." If you did not understand some commonly used gestures would this make it difficult for you to adjust in our culture? Example: You are driving on the highway and a man with a wide-brimmed hat in a grey uniform holds his hand up—palm facing you. What do you do?

5. Could you identify the antics of the mime who spread out an imaginary tablecloth and took imaginary items out of a picnic basket? Where and how did you learn the meaning of such gestures? Most of our communication is verbal, of course, but does Allens' predicament suggest that nonverbal communication is more important than we ordinarily think?

6. Do we tend to speak more softly in a hospital room than in a classroom? Why? Do we, as Blount suggests, avoid certain words in a hospital room? Who teaches us this behavior?

7. Some hospitals will not allow children under a certain age to visit patients. Relate this to normative behavior of children. If Blount is right, are some adults more likely than children to engage in abnormal behavior?

8. Blount says that one thing which should not be said to the patient is: "Of course, I don't think the full impact of it has hit you yet." Is there a norm governing what medical doctors should say to a person who has experienced a life-threatening situation? Is it similar to this?

9. Males may, or may not, agree with Feirstein's approved behavior for the modern real man. How might females view these desirable traits of the real man?

10. Feirstein says that "strength and bravery are still the hallmark of today's Real Man; but he's just found modern ways to show it." Other than the items in his list, what are the culturally approved traits demonstrating male strength and bravery in today's society? Are they really different from those of earlier years? How?

11. What is the image of women which Allen is satirizing in the "Whore of Mensa"? Do men tend to see women primarily as sex objects—as many women argue? How many women, or men, could engage in a "comparative discussion" of Melville and Hawthorne? Do *you* see *Billy Budd* "as Melville's justification of the ways of God to man"? Are women today any less likely than men to fit the image which Allen portrays here of the intellectual depth of conversation among men and women?

12. Feirstein doesn't say whether or not real men jog. Is jogging an activity you would expect of the real man?

13. Does jogging seem to be associated more with middle class than working class men and women? If so, why do you think this is the case?

14. Jogging can result in a lean, lithe look. Our society frowns upon fat persons and tends to idealize the lean, slender body shape. Is jogging, then, more than a concern with health? Is it a reflection of our value structure which idealizes particular body types?

15. Twain suggests that "some civilized women would lose half their charm without dress; and some would lose all of it." Would this be more true of female college students than upper class women with many social commitments? Are college females likely to change their current ideas about the impor-

tance of proper dress when they enter the business or social world? Why?

16. Twain, as previously noted, wrote "Woman, God Bless Her!" in 1882. How do you think the editors of *Ms.* magazine would respond to such an article published today? Examine any current issue of *Ms*, and look at the dress of the women appearing in the advertisements. Do Twain's comments still have a right of validity?

REFERENCES

Hofstadter, Richard. *Anti-Intellectualism in American Life.* New York: Vintage Books, 1966.

Lipsyte, Robert. *SPORTSWORLD: An American Dreamland.* New York: The New York Times Book Company, 1975.

Mead, G. H. *Mind, Self, and Society: From the Standpoint of a Social Behaviorist.* C. W. Morris, ed. Chicago: Univ. of Chicago Press, 1934.

Prebish, Charles. " 'heavenly father, divine goalie': sport and religion." *The Antioch Review* 42, 3 (1984), 306–18.

Williams, Robin. *American Society: A Sociological Interpretation.* New York: Alfred Knopf, 1970.

THE SOCIAL STRUCTURE AND DEVIANCE

Chapter Four

Forms of Human Organization

S ociologists are interested in how people behave in groups. Professors often go to great lengths to stress the importance of how much our behavior is a function of the groups in which we participate. Students can be put to sleep by such discussions (I speak from personal experience), but they could be awakened quickly if the university were to decide, for example, that a given fraternity, sorority, or religious group could no longer have a chapter on campus. Although many people do not belong to or participate in social or religious groups on campus, if the university were to rule that no such groups could be organized even nonparticipants might join in the argument that people have a right to belong to such a group if they so choose. Some people are shocked to know that there are people in this society who join together to form political organizations such as the Nazi party or the Ku Klux Klan. You may never want to be a part of either of these political parties, but our society guarantees the right of participation in political parties even though they are not compatible with our concept of democracy. Sleepy students pretty soon realize that understanding all we can about the groups we live in and among is not just an intellectual pastime.

Groups may be defined as "two or more people who interact in patterned ways, share beliefs, values, and goals, and have a sense of membership." (Rose, et. al., 1982:17) It is obvious that groups are closely related to the cultural norms and values discussed in Chapter 3. One of the distinctive things about groups is that they often develop a language which tends to identify themselves as the *in-group*—all others are *out-groups*. This language can become so specialized that even though the language used by both groups is English, out-group members may not understand what is being said. Try this: "You can improve performance characteristics of this program substantially through execution of a compiled code as opposed to use of an interpreting system." Some of you reading this will know what is being referred to since you are members of the in-group. Those of you in the out-group will not, at this time, understand what is being said.

Within groups, we occupy a specific social position which we call a *status*. As a student your status is different from that of the professor or the maintenance crew member at the university. Within your family your status is that of daughter or son and, perhaps, of sister or brother. Status is important in that it allows us to identify where individuals fit into the larger group. Statuses are often ranked so that we are able to predict the nature of social relationships within a given group. Office clerks may never interact with the president of the company, but sales managers may have daily or weekly contacts with the top status individuals within the firm. In the society at large, status has another but related meaning. We tend to evaluate certain social positions and accord them a higher ranking than others. While both a bricklayer and a banker occupy a status, we accord more distinction to that of the banker than the bricklayer. We are not, of course, discussing the worthfulness of bricklayers versus bankers, but simply acknowledging that various statuses are accorded different evaluations in society.

Some statuses are *ascribed* to us at birth and persist throughout our lifetime. Age, sex, ethnicity, race, and family are examples of ascribed statuses. These can influence which statuses we later *achieve*. No woman has yet become president of the United States; blacks, until recently, have not entered the race to be a presidential candidate. Of course, both these consequences of ascribed statuses are changing in the last quarter of the twentieth century. Age is a particularly interesting aspect of statuses, since we ordinarily do not think of age as a status. Yet being a child (minor) or a senior citizen very definitely carries expected role behavior.

Statuses are closely associated with *roles*—the manner in which we are expected to behave in our given status. Sociologists speak of *playing* roles. The president of the company behaves in a manner quite different from that of the office clerk. All company presidents have the same status, but how they fulfill their roles may vary from highly efficient to just average. What we do in our roles is determined by the expectations of others. Company presidents who play their roles in an average fashion may find that the members of the company's board are expecting a very high level of performance. If it is not forthcoming the president may find himself or herself replaced. Students who do not play their roles according to professors' expectations may find their status as a student terminated. And, of course, professors themselves are not exempt. Their status, too, can be terminated due to poor role performance.

Of the many groups in which we have a status and play out our roles, some are organized into a larger entity called *formal organizations.* In such organizations the statuses and roles of all members are clearly defined with definite guidelines as to how each person is to operate so that the organization may achieve its goals. Large formal organizations tend to become bureaucratically structured. They develop a hierarchy of statuses which become highly specialized to accomplish specific organizational tasks. Any student is aware of the bureaucratic nature of his or her university. Certain personnel are designated to handle registration; others health matters; and yet others housing requirements. One learns quickly that if you have a housing problem you do not seek out the registrar. Bureaucracy has come to dominate nearly all the large formal organizations in our society, from the federal government to religious organizations.

The term *bureaucrat* has come to have an extremely negative connotation. We associate bureaucrats with those who are inflexible, give no attention to individual needs and differences, and seek only to see that the rules of the organization are fulfilled. This is the nature of bureaucracy. It is argued that it is the most efficient (cf. Weber, 1968)—and perhaps the only—way to run large scale formal organizations. The frustrations we all encounter in dealing with bureaucracies are, hopefully, offset by the efficient accomplishments of the goals of the organization. In the final analysis universities do educate the young, businesses do turn out the manufactured goods we have come to depend upon, and hospitals do provide a high level of health care for the population. While we may, in a romantic moment, desire to return to a more simple life-style—where the family grew its food, made its clothes, produced its own goods, and interacted primarily with members of small groups—that day is not likely to return.

The readings illustrating the attention which humorists have given to the various forms of human organization begin with Mark Twain's account of "Buck Fanshaw's Funeral." With only slight exaggeration, Twain depicts the use of in-group language when a miner visits a minister and tries to arrange for the burial of one of his companions. The miner opens the meeting with, for him, a perfectly understandable question: "Are you the duck that runs the gospel-mill next door?" It goes downhill from there.

In *Spoiled Children*, Arthur Hoppe describes the behavior of a 32-year-old man, Jerome, who has willfully reverted to behaving as a seven-year-old. The child-rearing patterns of our society, described by some as "permissive," do occasionally permit role behavior on the part of children not unlike that engaged in by Jerome.

Dying for Others is a selection from Joseph Heller's now classic *Catch-22*. Ralph Linton notes that "human beings are so mutable that almost any normal individual can be trained to the adequate performance of almost any role." (1936:115) Heller draws upon this argument to have Yossarian assume the role of a dying boy whose parents have traveled a great distance to see him before he dies. Yossarian is not dying (though see text), but must assume the role of a dying soldier to please his superiors.

In *The Facts of the Great Beef Contract* Mark Twain inherits an obligation of the federal government to pay for thirty barrels of beef delivered (at least in part) to General Sherman's army. His trials and tribulations of dealing with the federal bureaucracy are as relevant today as when Twain wrote—perhaps more so due to the increased size of the government.

 MARK TWAIN

Buck Fanshaw's Funeral

Somebody has said that in order to know a community, one must observe the style of its funerals and know what manner of men they bury with most ceremony. I cannot say which class we buried with most eclat in our "flush times," the distinguished public benefactor or the distinguished rough—possibly the two chief grades or grand divisions of society honored their illustrious dead about equally; and hence, no doubt the philosopher I have quoted from would have needed to see two representative funerals in Virginia [City] before forming his estimate of the people.

There was a grand time over Buck Fanshaw when he died. He was a representative citizen. He had "killed his man"—not in his own quarrel, it is true, but in defence of a stranger unfairly beset by numbers. He had kept a sumptuous saloon. He had been the proprietor of a dashing helpmeet whom he could have discarded without the formality of a divorce. He had held a high position in the fire department and been a very Warwick in politics. When he died there was great lamentation throughout the town, but especially in the vast bottom-stratum of society.

On the inquest it was shown that Buck Fanshaw, in the delirium of a wasting typhoid fever, had taken arsenic, shot himself through the body, cut his throat, and jumped out of a four-story window and broken his neck—and after due deliberation, the jury, sad and tearful, but with intelligence unblinded by its sorrow, brought in a verdict of death "by the visitation of God." What could the world do without juries?

Prodigious preparations were made for the funeral. All the vehicles in town were hired, all the saloons put in mourning, all the municipal and fire-company flags hung at half-mast, and all the firemen ordered to muster in uniform and bring their machines duly draped in black. Now—let us remark in parenthesis—as all the peoples of the earth had representative adventurers in the Silverland, and as each adventurer had brought the slang of his nation or his locality with him, the combination made the slang of Nevada the richest and the most infinitely varied and copious that had ever existed anywhere in the world, perhaps, except in the mines of California in the "early days." Slang was the language of Nevada. It was hard to preach a sermon without it, and be understood. Such phrases as "You bet!" "Oh, no, I reckon not!" "No Irish need apply," and a hundred others, became so common as to fall from the lips of a speaker unconsciously—and very often when they did not touch the subject under discussion and consequently failed to mean anything.

After Buck Fanshaw's inquest, a meeting of the short-haired brotherhood was held, for nothing can be done on the Pacific coast without a public meeting and an expression of sentiment. Regretful resolutions were passed and various committees appointed; among others, a committee of one was deputed to call on the minister, a fragile, gentle, spirituel new fledgling from an Eastern theological seminary, and as yet unacquainted with the ways of the mines. The committeeman, "Scotty" Briggs, made his visit; and in after days it was worth something to hear the minister tell about it. Scotty was a stalwart rough, whose customary suit, when on weighty official business, like committee work, was a fire helmet, flaming red flannel shirt, patent leather belt with spanner and revolver attached, coat hung over arm, and pants stuffed into boot tops. He formed something of a contrast to the pale theological student. It is fair to say of Scotty, however, in passing, that he had a warm heart, and a strong love for his friends, and never entered into a quarrel when he could reasonably keep out of it. Indeed, it was commonly said that whenever one of Scotty's fights was investigated, it always turned out that it had originally been no affair of his, but that out of native goodheartedness he had dropped in of his own accord to help the man who was getting the worst of it. He and Buck Fanshaw were bosom friends, for years, and had often taken adventurous "pot-luck" together. On one occasion, they had thrown off their coats and taken the weaker side in a fight among strangers, and after gaining a hardearned victory, turned and found that the men they were helping had deserted early, and not only that, but had stolen their coats and made off with them! But to return to Scotty's visit to the minister. He was on a sorrowful mission, now, and his face was the picture of woe. Being admitted to the presence he sat down before the clergyman, placed his fire-hat on an unfinished manuscript sermon under the minister's nose, took from it a red silk handkerchief, wiped his brow and heaved a sigh of dismal impressiveness, explanatory of his business. He choked, and even shed tears; but with an effort he mastered his voice and said in lugubrious tones:

"Are you the duck that runs the gospel-mill next door?"

"Am I the—pardon me, I believe I do not understand?"

With another sigh and a half-sob, Scotty rejoined:

"Why you see we are in a bit of trouble, and the boys thought maybe you would give us a lift, if we'd tackle you—that is, if I've got the rights of it and you are the head clerk of the doxology-works next door."

"I am the shepherd in charge of the flock whose fold is next door."

"The which?"

"The spiritual adviser of the little company of believers whose sanctuary adjoins these premises."

Scotty scratched his head, reflected a moment, and then said:

"You ruther hold over me, pard. I reckon I can't call that hand. Ante and pass the buck."

"How? I beg pardon. What did I understand you to say?"

"Well, you've ruther got the bulge on me. Or maybe we've both got the bulge, somehow. You don't smoke me and I don't smoke you. You see, one of the boys has passed in his checks and we want to give him a good send-off, and so the thing I'm on now is to roust out somebody to jerk a little chin-music for us and waltz him through handsome."

"My friend, I seem to grow more and more bewildered. Your observations are wholly incomprehensible to me. Cannot you simplify them in some way? At first I thought perhaps I understood you, but I grope now. Would it not expedite matters if you restricted yourself to categorical statements of fact unencumbered with obstructing accumulations of metaphor and allegory?"

Another pause, and more reflection. Then, said Scotty:

"I'll have to pass, I judge."

"How?"

"You've raised me out, pard."

"I still fail to catch your meaning."

"Why, that last lead of yourn is too many for me—that's the idea. I can't neither trump nor follow suit."

The clergyman sank back in his chair perplexed. Scotty leaned his head on his hand and gave himself up to thought. Presently his face came up, sorrowful but confident.

"I've got it now, so's you can savvy," he said. "What we want is a gospel-sharp. See?"

"A what?"

"Gospel-sharp. Parson."

"Oh! Why did you not say so before? I am a clergyman—a parson."

"Now you talk! You see my blind and straddle it like a man. Put it there!"—extending a brawny paw, which closed over the minister's small hand and gave it a shake indicative of fraternal sympathy and fervent gratification.

"Now we're all right, pard. Let's start fresh. Don't you mind my snuffling a little—becuz we're in a power of trouble. You see, one of the boys has gone up the flume—"

"Gone where?"

"Up the flume—throwed up the sponge, you understand."

"Thrown up the sponge?"

"Yes—kicked the bucket—"

"Ah—has departed to that mysterious country from whose bourne no traveler returns."

"Return! I reckon not. Why pard, he's *dead!*"

"Yes, I understand."

"Oh, you do? Well I thought maybe you might be getting tangled some more. Yes, you see he's dead again—"

"*Again?* Why, has he ever been dead before?"

"Dead before? No! Do you reckon a man has got as many lives as a cat? But you bet you he's awful dead now, poor old boy, and I wish I'd never seen this day. I don't want no better friend than Buck Fanshaw. I knowed him by the back; and when I know a man and like him, I freeze to him—you hear *me*. Take him all round, pard, there never was a bullier man in the mines. No man ever knowed Buck Fanshaw to go back on a friend. But it's all up, you know, it's all up. It ain't no use. They've scooped him."

"Scooped him?"

"Yes—death has. Well, well, well, we've got to give him up. Yes indeed. It's kind of a hard world, after all, *ain't* it? But pard, he was a rustler! You ought to seen him get started once. He was a bully boy with a glass eye! Just spit in his face and give him room according to his strength, and it was just beautiful to see him peel and go in. He was the worst son of a thief that ever drawed breath. Pard, he was *on* it! He was on it bigger than an Injun!"

"On it? On what?"

"On the shoot. On the shoulder. On the fight, you understand. *He* didn't give a continental for *any*body. *Beg* your pardon, friend, for coming so near a cuss-word—but you see I'm on an awful strain, in this palaver, on account of having to cramp down and draw everything so mild. But we've got to give him up. There ain't any getting around that, I don't reckon. Now if we can get you to help plant him—"

"Preach the funeral discourse? Assist at the obsequies?"

"Obs'quies is good. Yes. That's it—that's our little game. We are going to get the thing up regardless, you know. He was always nifty himself, and so you bet you his funeral ain't going to be no slouch—solid silver door-plate on his coffin, six plumes on the hearse, and a nigger on the box in a biled shirt and a plug hat—how's that for high? And we'll take care of *you*, pard. We'll fix you all right. There'll be a kerridge for you; and whatever you want, you just 'scape out and we'll 'tend to it. We've got a shebang fixed up for you to stand behind, in No. 1's house, and don't you be afraid. Just go in and toot your horn, if you don't sell a clam. Put Buck through as bully as you can, pard, for anybody that knowed him will tell you that he was one of the whitest men that was ever in the mines. You can't draw it too strong. He never could stand it to see things going wrong. He's done more to make this town quiet and peaceable than any man in it. I've seen him lick four Greasers in eleven minutes, myself. If a thing wanted regulating, *he* warn't a man to go browsing around after somebody to do it, but he would prance in and regulate it himself. He warn't a Catholic. Scasely. He was down on 'em. His word was, 'No Irish need apply!' But it didn't make no difference about that when it came down to what a man's rights was—and so, when some roughs jumped the Catholic bone-yard and started in to stake out town-lots in it he *went* for 'em! And he *cleaned* 'em, too! I was there, pard, and I seen it myself."

"That was very well indeed—at least the impulse was—whether the act was strictly defensible or not. Had deceased any religious convictions? That is to say, did he feel a dependence upon, or acknowledge allegiance to a higher power?"

More reflection.

"I reckon you've stumped me again, pard. Could you say it over once more, and say it slow?"

"Well, to simplify it somewhat, was he, or rather had he ever been connected with any organization sequestered from secular concerns and devoted to self-sacrifice in the interests of morality?"

"All down but nine—set 'em up on the other alley, pard."

"What did I understand you to say?"

"Why, you're most too many for me, you know. When you get in with your left I hunt grass every time. Every time you draw, you fill; but I don't seem to have any luck. Lets have a new deal."

"How? Begin again?"

"That's it."

"Very well. Was he a good man, and—"

"There—I see that; don't put up another chip till I look at my hand. A good man, says you? Pard, it ain't no name for it. He was the best man that ever—pard, you would have doted on that man. He could lam any galoot of his inches in America. It was him that put down the riot last election before it got a start; and everybody said he was the only man that could have done it. He waltzed in with a spanner in one hand and a trumpet in the other, and sent fourteen men home on a shutter in less than three minutes. He had that riot all broke up and prevented nice before anybody ever got a chance to strike a blow. He was always for peace, and he would *have* peace—he could not stand disturbances. Pard, he was a great loss to this town. It would please the boys if you could chip in something like that and do him justice. Here once when the Micks got to throwing stones through the Methodis' Sunday school windows, Buck Fanshaw, all of his own notion, shut up his saloon and took a couple of six-shooters and mounted guard over the Sunday school. Says he, 'No Irish need apply!' And they didn't. He was the bulliest man in the mountains, pard! He could run faster, jump higher, hit harder, and hold more tangle-foot whisky without spilling it than any man in seventeen counties. Put that in, pard—it'll please the boys more than anything you could say. And you can say, pard, that he never shook his mother."

"Never shook his mother?"

"That's it—any of the boys will tell you so."

"Well, but why *should* he shake her?"

"That's what *I* say—but some people does."

"Not people of any repute?"

"Well, some that averages pretty so-so."

"In my opinion the man that would offer personal violence to his own mother, ought to—"

"Cheese it, pard; you've banked your ball clean outside the string. What I was a drivin' at, was, that he never *throwed off* on his mother—don't you see? No indeedy. He give her a house to live in, and town lots, and plenty of money; and he looked after her and took care of her all the time; and when she was down with the small-pox I'm d—d if he didn't set up nights and nuss her himself! *Beg your pardon for saying it, but it hopped out too quick for yours truly. You've treated me like a gentleman, pard, and I ain't the man to hurt your feelings intentional. I think you're white. I think you're a square man, pard. I like you, and I'll lick any man that don't. I'll lick him till he can't tell himself from a last year's corpse! Put it *there!*" [Another fraternal handshake—and exit.]

The obsequies were all that "the boys" could desire. Such a marvel of funeral pomp had never been seen in Virginia. The plumed hearse, the dirge-breathing brass bands, the closed marts of business, the flags drooping at half mast, the long, plodding procession of uniformed secret societies, military battalions and fire companies, draped engines, carriages of officials, and citizens in vehicles and on foot, attracted multitudes of spectators to the sidewalks, roofs and windows; and for years afterward, the degree of grandeur attained by any civic display in Virginia was determined by comparison with Buck Fanshaw's funeral.

Scotty Briggs, as a pall-bearer and a mourner, occupied a prominent place at the funeral, and when the sermon was finished and the last sentence of the prayer for the dead man's soul ascended, he responded, in a low voice, but with feeling:

"AMEN. No Irish need apply."

As the bulk of the response was without apparent relevancy, it was probably nothing more than a humble tribute to the memory of the friend that was gone; for, as Scotty had once said, it was "his word."

Scotty Briggs, in after days, achieved the distinction of becoming the only convert to religion that was ever gathered from the Virginia roughs; and it transpired that the man who had it in him to espouse the quarrel of the weak out of inborn nobility of spirit was no mean timber whereof to construct a Christian. The making him one did not warp his generosity or diminish his courage; on the contrary it gave intelligent direction to the one and a broader field to the other. If his Sunday-school class progressed faster than the other classes, was it matter for wonder? I think not. He talked to his pioneer small-fry in a language they understood! It was my large privilege, a month before he died, to hear him tell the beautiful story of Joseph and his brethren to his class "without looking at the book." I leave it to the reader to fancy what it was like, as it fell, riddled with slang, from the lips of that grave, earnest teacher, and was listened to by his little learners with a consuming interest that showed that they were as unconscious as he was that any violence was being done to the sacred proprieties!

 **ARTHUR HOPPE**

Spoiled Children

I was talking about spoiled children at lunch the other day with Jerome. A nostalgic look softened his eye. "Yes," he said, "I can remember picking up a plate of creamed succotash at a party, pouring it onto the carpet and shouting, 'I *hate* creamed succotash!' "

"When was that?" I asked.

"Last week," he said.

"But, Jerome," I said, "you're thirty-two years old. Why do you want to behave like a spoiled child?"

"I have made a careful study of children," said Jerome, "and I've found that spoiled children invariably get more than their fair share. So I decided to be spoiled."

"Really, Jerome," I said, "that sounds like the height of self-indulgence."

He looked surprised. "Who else would I prefer to indulge?" he said.

I'll have to admit he had whetted my interest. "What happened after you spilled your succotash?" I asked.

"Oh, the hostess, who was a bit flustered, suggested we all go into the living room. Naturally, I folded my arms and shouted, 'No! Capital N, O. No!' "

"Naturally," I said. "But what did that get you?"

"Another helping of pecan pie with whipped cream. I dearly love pecan pie with whipped cream, and it's loaded with calories. I'm trying to put on another fifteen pounds so I'll get even better at pushing."

"Pushing's helpful?"

"I'd never have gotten in to see Robert Redford at the Palace without shoving my way to the head of the ticket line. Lousy seats, though."

"So you stormed out?"

"No, I lay on my stomach in the middle of the aisle, kicked my feet, and screamed bloody murder so no one could hear what was going on."

"And that got you two in the fifth row center?" I asked, reaching for the basket of bread.

"No, in the loges," he said, snatching the basket out of my hands and clutching it to his chest.

"Come on, Jerome," I said. "Learn to share."

But he just shook his head and said, "Mine!"

I sighed. "Whatever happened to common, ordinary politeness in this country?" I mused.

Jerome shrugged. "Where does it get you?" he said.

I wish I'd seen the waiter coming with the succotash. It would have saved me a shoeshine. "Enough of your spoiled ways, Jerome," I said, rising angrily. "I'm leaving. Fork over your half the check."

He smugly folded his arms, looked up at me with a smirk and said, "I don't have to if I don't want to."

That's when I let him have it with the mashed potatoes. I *hate* mashed potatoes. And talk about the rejuvenating effects of self-indulgence! I walked out of that restaurant feeling like a seven-year-old.

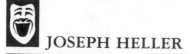

JOSEPH HELLER

Dying For Others

"There are some relatives here to see you. Oh, don't worry," he added with a laugh. "Not your relatives. It's the mother, father and brother of that chap who died. They've traveled all the way from New York to see a dying soldier, and you're the handiest one we've got."

"What are you talking about?" Yossarian asked suspiciously. "I'm not dying."

"Of course you're dying. We're all dying. Where the devil else do you think you're heading?"

"They didn't come to see me," Yossarian objected. "They came to see their son."

"They'll have to take what they can get. As far as we're concerned, one dying boy is just as good as any other, or just as bad. To a scientist, all dying boys are equal. I have a proposition for you. You let them come in and look you over for a few minutes and I won't tell anyone you've been lying about your liver symptoms."

Yossarian drew back from him farther. "You know about that?"

"Of course I do. Give us some credit." The doctor chuckled amiably and lit another cigarette. "How do you expect anyone to believe you have a liver condition if you keep squeezing the nurses' tits every time you get a chance? You're going to have to give up sex if you want to convince people you've got an ailing liver."

"That's a hell of a price to pay just to keep alive. Why didn't you turn me in if you knew I was faking?"

"Why the devil should I?" asked the doctor with a flicker of surprise. "We're all in this business of illusion together. I'm always willing to lend a helping hand to a fellow conspirator along the road to survival if he's willing to do the same for me. These people have come a long way, and I'd rather not disappoint them. I'm sentimental about old people."

"But they came to see their son."

"They came too late. Maybe they won't even notice the difference."

"Suppose they start crying."

"They probably will start crying. That's one of the reasons they came. I'll listen outside the door and break it up if it starts getting tacky."

"It all sounds a bit crazy," Yossarian reflected. "What do they want to watch their son die for, anyway?"

"I've never been able to figure that one out," the doctor admitted, "but they always do. Well, what do you say? All you've got to do is lie there a few minutes and die a little. Is that asking so much?"

"All right," Yossarian gave in. "If it's just for a few minutes and you promise to wait right outside." He warmed to his role. "Say, why don't you wrap a bandage around me for effect?"

"That sounds like a splendid idea," applauded the doctor.

They wrapped a batch of bandages around Yossarian. A team of medical orderlies installed tan shades on each of the two windows and lowered them to douse the room in depressing shadows. Yossarian suggested flowers, and the doctor sent an orderly out to find two small bunches of fading ones with a strong and sickening smell. When everything was in place, they made Yossarian get back into bed and lie down. Then they admitted the visitors.

The visitors entered uncertainly as though they felt they were intruding, tiptoeing in with stares of meek apology, first the grieving mother and father, then the brother, a glowering heavy-set sailor with a deep chest. The man and woman stepped into the room stiffly side by side as though right out of a familiar, though esoteric, anniversary daguerreotype on a wall. They were both short, sere and proud. They seemed made of iron and old, dark clothing. The woman had a long, brooding, oval face of burnt umber, with coarse graying black hair parted severely in the middle and combed back austerely behind her neck without curl, wave or ornamentation. Her mouth was sullen and sad, her lined lips compressed. The father stood very rigid and quaint in a double-breasted suit with padded shoulders that were much too tight for him. He was broad and muscular on a small scale and had a magnificently curled silver mustache on his crinkled face. His eyes were creased and rheumy, and he appeared tragically ill at ease as he stood awkwardly with the brim of his black felt fedora held in his two brawny laborer's hands out in front of his wide lapels. Poverty and hard work had inflicted iniquitous damage on both. The brother was looking for a fight. His round white cap was cocked in an insolent tilt, his hands were clenched, and he glared at everything in the room with a scowl of injured truculence.

The three creaked forward timidly, holding themselves close to each other in a stealthy, funereal group and inching forward almost in step, until they arrived at the side of the bed and stood staring down at Yossarian. There was a gruesome and excruciating silence that threatened to endure forever. Finally Yossarian was unable to bear it any longer and cleared his throat. The old man spoke at last.

"He looks terrible," he said.

"He's sick, Pa."

"Giuseppe," said the mother, who had seated herself in a chair with her veinous fingers clasped in her lap.

"My name is Yossarian," Yossarian said.

"His name is Yossarian, Ma. Yossarian, don't you recognize me? I'm your brother John. Don't you know who I am?"

"Sure I do. You're my brother John."

"He does recognize me! Pa, he knows who I am. Yossarian, here's Papa. Say hello to Papa."

"Hello, Papa," said Yossarian.

"Hello, Giuseppe."

"His name is Yossarian, Pa."

"I can't get over how terrible he looks," the father said.

"He's very sick, Pa. The doctor says he's going to die."

"I didn't know whether to believe the doctor or not," the father said. "You know how crooked those guys are."

"Giuseppe," the mother said again, in a soft, broken chord of muted anguish.

"His name is Yossarian, Ma. She don't remember things too good any more. How're they treating you in here, kid? They treating you pretty good?"

"Pretty good," Yossarian told him.

"That's good. Just don't let anybody in here push you around. You're just as good as anybody else in here even though you are Italian. You've got rights, too."

Yossarian winced and closed his eyes so that he would not have to look at his brother John. He began to feel sick.

"*Now* see how terrible he looks," the father observed.

"Giuseppe," the mother said.

"Ma, his name is Yossarian," the brother interrupted her impatiently. "Can't you remember?"

"It's all right," Yossarian interrupted him. "She can call me Giuseppe if she wants to."

"Giuseppe," she said to him.

"Don't worry, Yossarian," the brother said. "Everything is going to be all right."

"Don't worry, Ma," Yossarian said. "Everything is going to be all right."

"Did you have a priest?" the brother wanted to know.

"Yes," Yossarian lied, wincing again.

"That's good," the brother decided. "Just as long as you're getting everything you've got coming to you. We came all the way from New York. We were afraid we wouldn't get here in time."

"In time for what?"

"In time to see you before you died."

"What difference would it make?"

"We didn't want you to die by yourself."

"What difference would it make?"

"He must be getting delirious," the brother said. "He keeps saying the same thing over and over again."

"That's really very funny," the old man replied. "All the time I thought his name was Giuseppe, and now I find out his name is Yossarian. That's really very funny."

"Ma, make him feel good," the brother urged. "Say something to cheer him up."

"Giuseppe."

"It's not Giuseppe, Ma. It's Yossarian."

"What difference does it make?" the mother answered in the same mourning tone, without looking up. "He's dying."

Her tumid eyes filled with tears and she began to cry, rocking back and forth slowly in her chair with her hands lying in her lap like fallen moths. Yossarian was afraid she would start wailing. The father and brother began crying also. Yossarian remembered suddenly why they were all crying, and he began crying too. A doctor Yossarian had never seen before stepped inside the room and told the visitors courteously that they had to go. The father drew himself up formally to say goodbye.

"Giuseppe," he began.

"Yossarian," corrected the son.

"Yossarian," said the father.

"Giuseppe," corrected Yossarian.

"Soon you're going to die."

Yossarian began to cry again. The doctor threw him a dirty look from the rear of the room, and Yossarian made himself stop.

The father continued solemnly with his head lowered. "When you talk to the man upstairs," he said, "I want you to tell Him something for me. Tell Him it ain't right for people to die when they're young. I mean it. Tell Him if they got to die at all, they got to die when they're old. I want you to tell Him that. I don't think He knows it ain't right, because He's supposed to be good and it's been going on for a long, long time. Okay?"

"And don't let anybody up there push you around," the brother advised. "You'll be just as good as anybody else in heaven, even though you are Italian."

"Dress warm," said the mother, who seemed to know.

 MARK TWAIN

The Facts in the Great Beef Contract

In as few words as possible I wish to lay before the nation what share, howsoever small, I have had in this matter—this matter which has so exercised the public mind, engendered so much ill-feeling, and so filled the newspapers of both continents with distorted statements and extravagant comments.

The origin of this distressful thing was this—and I assert here that every fact in the following résumé can be amply proved by the official records of the General Government:

John Wilson Mackenzie, of Rotterdam, Chemung County, New Jersey, deceased, contracted with the General Government, on or about the 10th day of October, 1861, to furnish to General Sherman the sum total of thirty barrels of beef.

Very well.

He started after Sherman with the beef, but when he got to Washington, Sherman had gone to Manassas; so he took the beef and followed him there, but arrived too late; he followed him to Nashville, and from Nashville to Chattanooga, and from Chattanooga to Atlanta—but he never could overtake him. At Atlanta he took a fresh start and followed him clear through his march to the sea. He arrived too late again by a few days; but hearing that Sherman was going out in the *Quaker City* excursion to the Holy Land, he took shipping for Beirut, calculating to head off the other vessel. When he arrived in Jerusalem with his beef, he learned that Sherman had not sailed in the *Quaker City*, but had gone to the Plains to fight the Indians. He returned to America and started for the Rocky Mountains. After sixty-eight days of arduous travel on the Plains, and when he had got within four miles of Sherman's headquarters, he was tomahawked and scalped, and the Indians got the beef. They got all of it but one barrel. Sherman's army captured that, and so, even in death, the bold navigator partly fulfilled his contract. In his will, which he had kept like a journal, he bequeathed the contract to his son Bartholomew W. Bartholomew W. made out the following bill, and then died:

THE UNITED STATES

   In account with JOHN WILSON MACKENZIE, of New Jersey,
     deceased   Dr.
To thirty barrels of beef for General Sherman, at $100, $ 3,000
To traveling expenses and transportation   14,000

                Total $17,000

        Rec'd Pay't.

He died then; but he left the contract to Wm. J. Martin, who tried to collect it, but died before he got through. *He* left it to Barker J. Allen, and he tried to collect it also. He did not survive. Barker J. Allen left it to Anson G. Rogers, who attempted to collect it, and got along as far as the Ninth Auditor's Office, when Death, the great Leveler, came all unsummoned, and foreclosed on *him* also. He left the bill to a relative of his in Connecticut, Vengeance Hopkins by name, who lasted four weeks and two days, and made the best time on record, coming within one of reaching the Twelfth Auditor. In his will he gave the contract bill to his uncle, by the name of O-be-joyful Johnson. It was too undermining for Joyful. His last words were: "Weep not for me—*I* am willing to go." And so he was, poor soul. Seven people inherited the contract after that; but they all died. So it came into my hands at last. It fell to me through a relative by the name of Hubbard—Bethlehem Hubbard, of Indiana. He had had a grudge against me for a long time; but in his last moments he sent for me, and forgave me everything, and, weeping, gave me the beef contract.

This ends the history of it up to the time that I succeeded to the property. I will now endeavor to set myself straight before the nation in everything that concerns my share in the matter. I took this beef contract, and the bill for mileage and transportation, to the President of the United States.

He said, "Well, sir, what can I do for you?"

I said, "Sire, on or about the 10th day of October, 1861, John Wilson Mackenzie, of Rotterdam, Chemung County, New Jersey, deceased, contracted with the General Government to furnish to General Sherman the sum total of thirty barrels of beef—"

He stopped me there, and dismissed me from his presence—kindly, but firmly. The next day I called on the Secretary of State.

He said, "Well, sir?"

I said, "Your Royal Highness: on or about the 10th day of October, 1861, John Wilson Mackenzie, of Rotterdam, Chemung County, New Jersey, deceased, contracted with the General Government to furnish to General Sherman the sum total of thirty barrels of beef—"

"That will do, sir—that will do; this office has nothing to do with contracts for beef."

I was bowed out. I thought the matter all over, and finally, the following day, I visited the Secretary of the Navy, who said, "Speak quickly, sir; do not keep me waiting."

I said, "Your Royal Highness, on or about the 10th day of October, 1861, John Wilson Mackenzie, of Rotterdam, Chemung County, New Jersey, deceased, contracted with the General Government to General Sherman the sum total of thirty barrels of beef—"

Well, it was as far as I could get. *He* had nothing to do with beef contracts for General Sherman, either. I began to think it was a curious kind of a government. It looked somewhat as if they wanted to get out of paying for that beef. The following day I went to the Secretary of the Interior.

I said, "Your Imperial Highness, on or about the 10th day of October—"

"That is sufficient, sir. I have heard of you before. Go, take your infamous beef contract out of this establishment. The Interior Department has nothing whatever to do with subsistence for the army."

I went away. But I was exasperated now. I said I would haunt them; I would infest every department of this iniquitous government till that contract business was settled. I would collect that bill, or fall, as fell my predecessors, trying. I assailed the Postmaster-General; I besieged the Agricultural Department; I waylaid the Speaker of the House of Representatives. *They* had nothing to do with army contracts for beef. I moved upon the Commissioner of the Patent Office.

I said, "Your August Excellency, on or about—"

"Perdition! have you got *here* with your incendiary beef contract, at last? We have *nothing* to do with beef contracts for the army, my dear sir."

"Oh, that is all very well—but *somebody* has got to pay for that beef. It has got to be paid *now*, too, or I'll confiscate this old Patent Office and everything in it."

"But, my dear sir—"

"It don't make any difference, sir. The Patent Office is liable for that beef, I reckon; and, liable or not liable, the Patent Office has got to pay for it."

Never mind the details. It ended in a fight. The Patent Office won. But I found out something to my advantage. I was told that the Treasury Department was the proper place for me to go to. I went there. I waited two hours and a half, and then I was admitted to the First Lord of the Treasury.

I said, "Most noble, grave, and reverend Signor, on or about the 10th day of October, 1861, John Wilson Macken—"

"That is sufficient, sir. I have heard of you. Go to the First Auditor of the Treasury."

I did so. He sent me to the Second Auditor. The Second Auditor sent me to the Third, and the Third sent me to the First Comptroller of the Corn-Beef Division. This began to look like business. He examined his books and all his loose papers, but found no minute of the beef contract. I went to the Second Comptroller of the Corn-Beef Division. He examined his books and his loose papers, but with no success. I was encouraged. During that week I got as far as the Sixth Comptroller in that division; the next week I got through the Claims Department; the third week I began and completed the Mislaid Contracts Department, and got a foothold in the Dead Reckoning Department. I finished that in three days. There was only one place left for it now. I laid siege to the Commissioner of Odds and Ends. To his clerk, rather—he was not there himself. There were sixteen beautiful young ladies in the room, writing in books, and there were seven well-favored young clerks showing them how. The young women smiled up over their shoulders, and the clerks smiled back at them, and all went merry as a marriage bell. Two or three clerks that were reading the newspapers looked at me rather hard, but went on reading, and nobody said anything. However, I had been used to this kind of alacrity from Fourth Assistant Junior Clerks all through my eventful career, from the very day I entered the first office of the Corn-Beef Bureau clear till I passed out of the last one in the Dead Reckoning Division. I had got so accomplished by this time that I could stand on one foot from the moment I entered an office till a clerk spoke to me, without changing more than two, or maybe three, times.

So I stood there till I had changed four different times. Then I said to one of the clerks who was reading:

"Illustrious Vagrant, where is the Grand Turk?"

"What do you mean, sir? whom do you mean? If you mean the Chief of the Bureau, he is out."

"Will he visit the harem to-day?"

The young man glared upon me awhile, and then went on reading his paper. But I knew the ways of those clerks. I knew I was safe if he got through before another New York mail arrived. He only had two more papers left. After a while he finished them, and then he yawned and asked me what I wanted.

"Renowned and honored Imbecile: on or about—"

"You are the beef-contract man. Give me your papers."

He took them, and for a long time he ransacked his odds and ends. Finally he found the Northwest Passage, as *I* regarded it—he found the long-lost record of that beef contract—he found the rock upon which so many of my ancestors had split before they ever got to it. I was deeply moved. And yet I rejoiced—for I had survived. I said with emotion, "Give it me. The government will settle now." He waved me back, and said there was something yet to be done first.

"Where is this John Wilson Mackenzie?" said he.

"Dead."

"When did he die?"

"He didn't die at all—he was killed."

"How?"

"Tomahawked."

"Who tomahawked him?"

"Why, an Indian, of course. You didn't suppose it was the superintendent of a Sunday-school, did you?"

"No. An Indian, was it?"

"The same."

"Name of the Indian?"

"His name? *I* don't know his name."

"*Must* have his name. Who saw the tomahawking done?"

"I don't know."

"You were not present yourself, then?"

"Which you can see by my hair. I was absent."

"Then how do you know that Mackenzie is dead?"

"Because he certainly died at that time, and I have every reason to believe that he has been dead ever since. I *know* he has, in fact."

"We must have proofs. Have you got the Indian?"

"Of course not."

"Well, you must get him. Have you got the tomahawk?"

"I never thought of such a thing."

"You must get the tomahawk. You must produce the Indian and the tomahawk. If Mackenzie's death can be proven by these, you can then go before the commission appointed to audit claims with some show of getting your bill under such headway that your children may possibly live to receive the money and enjoy it. But that man's death *must* be proven. However, I may as well tell you that the government will never pay that transportation and those traveling expenses of the lamented Mackenzie. It *may* possibly pay for the barrel of beef that Sherman's soldiers captured, if you can get a relief bill through Congress making an appropriation for that purpose; but it will not pay for the twenty-nine barrels the Indians ate."

"Then there is only a hundred dollars due me, and *that* isn't certain! After all Mackenzie's travels in Europe, Asia, and America with that beef; after all his trials and tribulations and transportation; after the slaughter of all those innocents that tried to collect that bill! Young man, why didn't the First Comptroller of the Corn-Beef Division tell me this?"

"He didn't know anything about the genuineness of your claim."

"Why didn't the Second tell me? why didn't the Third? why didn't all those divisions and departments tell me?"

"None of them knew. We do things by routine here. You have followed the routine and found out what you wanted to know. It is the best way. It is the only way. It is very regular, and very slow, but it is very certain."

"Yes, certain death. It has been, to the most of our tribe. I begin to feel that I, too, am called. Young man, you love the bright creature yonder with the gentle blue eyes and the steel pens behind her ears—I see it in your soft glances; you wish to marry her—but you are poor. Here, hold out your hand—here is the beef contract; go, take her and be happy! Heaven bless you, my children!"

This is all I know about the great beef contract that has created so much talk in the community. The clerk to whom I bequeathed it died. I know nothing further about the contract, or any one connected with it. I only know that if a man lives long enough he can tract a thing through the Circumlocution Office of Washington and find out, after much labor and trouble and delay, that which he could have found out on the first day if the business of the Circumlocution

Office were as ingeniously systematized as it would be if it were a great private mercantile institution.

QUESTIONS FOR DISCUSSION

1. While Twain illustrates the in-group language of Buck Fanshaw's friend, Scotty Briggs, he also points to the same trait for the minister. Why do you think groups develop a language peculiar to their members only? What functions does it serve for the group?

2. The parson asks if Buck Fanshaw had ever "been connected with any organization sequestered from secular concerns and devoted to self-sacrifice in the interests of morality." What is this organization? Does Twain's choice of literary dialog mark him as a member of an in-group to which the average college student does not belong? What is it?

3. The various age groups in a society have different norms and values associated with them. Older people (over 65) may behave in a way that young adults may not. How? If a 32-year-old man acted like Jerome in pouring succotash on the carpet, how do you think those around him would react?

4. Jerome refuses to share. He just shakes his head and says "Mine." Do children often act in this fashion? Why shouldn't a 32-year-old man be allowed to refuse to share? Are there societal norms which say adults must share—whether or not they want to—parts of their income with others?

5. Do 22- or 25-year-old rock musicians deviate from behavior associated with people that age? How is this related to status in our society?

6. In the Heller selection, "Dying for Others," the doctor says to Yossarian, "As far as we're concerned, one dying boy is just as good as any other, or just as bad. To a scientist, all dying boys are equal." In the field of medical research the diseases which lead to death obviously vary greatly, but is there a certain painful truth in this statement? Relate this to the concept of *role*. When a student (illegally) takes another student's ex-

am, do you think the professor would say, "One student taking an exam is just as good as any other, or just as bad"?

7. Yossarian asks the doctor: "What do they want to watch their son die for, anyway?" The doctor answers, "I've never been able to figure that one out . . . but they always do." Is the doctor right about parents and dying children? In our day, do children want to see their parents die? Relate this to differing age statuses. Are there cross-cultural differences in how the young attend dying parents? How do you explain our attitudes toward the death of the aged?

8. In "The Facts in the Great Beef Contract," Twain illustrates the frustration which can indeed occur in dealing with a large bureaucracy such as the federal government. Have you experienced similar frustrations in dealing with the university or some other large bureaucracy?

9. Which aspect of bureaucratic organization is implicit in Twain's depiction of being shuffled from one bureau to the next as he is told "this office has nothing to do with contracts for beef"?

10. The clerk says to Twain: "We do things by routine here. . . . It is the best way. It is the only way. It is very regular, and very slow, but it is very certain." Do you think that the bureaucratic organizations of large universities are the best and only way contemporary education can be organized? What would you change to make your education more efficient?

REFERENCES

Linton, Ralph. *The Study of Man.* New York: Appleton-Century-Crofts, 1936.

Rose, Peter I., Glazer, Myron, and Glazer, Penina M. *Sociology.* New York: St. Martin's Press, 1982.

Weber, Max. *Economy and Society.* Ephraim Fischoff, et. al., translators. New York: Bedminster Press, 1968.

Chapter Five

Deviance and Social Control

READINGS

M ost of us conform most of the time to the general norms and values of the society. Nearly all of us deviate at some time from some of these accepted ways of thinking and behaving. When people's behavior deviates too far from accepted norms a problem immediately arises. How serious is the deviation? Must the society react and punish the deviant? Should the punishment be severe or only a polite reminder that "we don't do that"? Deviation from norms is a daily occurrence in any society. It strikes at the very root of a society's ability to function and provide an ongoing and orderly environment in which all members can freely pursue their interests.

Since deviance is such an important matter to any society, it might seem at first that defining deviant behavior would be a simple matter. In one sense, it is: deviance is behavior which violates one or more of the norms which society deems essential. This definition covers many forms of deviant behavior, e.g., theft, physical assault, rape, or murder. Consensus can be reached quickly on the importance of not allowing such behavior in a society and punishing it when it does occur. But consensus on other forms of behavior is not really available. Some groups, the Mormon Church, for example, consider drinking alcohol deviant behavior. Other groups, such as Jews, consume alcohol in their religious ceremonies. Among members of the gay community homosexual intercourse is considered normal behavior. Others consider such behavior abnormal—some going so far as to label homosexuals as "perverts." What is deviant in one society may be normal behavior in another. Newman (1976) found that 90 percent of the population in Iran felt that homosexuality should be prohibited by law. Only 18 percent of the United States population felt this way. On the other hand, in the United States only 6 percent of the population felt that nonviolent public protest should be prohibited by law, but in Iran the corresponding figure was 77 percent.

Current attitudes toward homosexuality and premarital sexual intercourse illustrate another important aspect of deviant behavior. Norms change. Deviant behavior in one generation can become tolerated and, in some cases, accepted behavior in another generation. Certainly our attitudes and behavior with regard to premarital sexuality have undergone what some label a revolution in the past two to three decades. Some argue that this is more of a change in attitudes than behavior, but the increase is such that the traditional norm of premarital chastity clearly no longer has the support it once did.

Journalistic reporting often gives the impression that everyone is participating in a particular activity when data reveal otherwise. For example, journalistic accounts of couples living together without marriage—among college students especially—are widespread. There has been a dramatic increase in the number of such couples: from 523,000 in 1970 to 1,560,000 in 1981. Glick and Spanier have noted that "Rarely does social change occur with such rapidity." (1980:20) Nevertheless, it is well to bear in mind that unmarried couples living together represent only about 3 percent of all households at any given time. This can hardly be described as the *norm* for couples living together. Buchwald (1977:367–68) has delightfully illustrated the problem of a young college student who told his parents that he was living off-campus with a female student. His mother was distressed, but his father was proud of him and doubled his allowance with the comment: "Anyone who is willing to spit in the eye of conformity deserves his father's support." But actually the student was living in a dorm—and for this reason:

> Well, let me tell you, for every girl who's playing house with a male college student, there are a million co-eds who won't even do the dishes.
>
> Then all this talk of students living out of wedlock is exaggerated?
>
> Exaggerated? When I got here, I asked ten girls if they wanted to live with us. The first one said she didn't come to college to iron shirts for the wrong guy, four told me frankly that it would hurt their chances of finding a husband, four told me to drop dead, and one reported me to the campus police. I was lucky to get a room in the dormitory.

Even though norms do change, support for those considered essential to a way of life can be very strong. Ronald Reagan's election, the defeat of the equal rights amendment, and the continuing struggle of the gay community for full acceptance all illustrate how powerful adherence to tradition can be even in the midst of change.

The support for the existing normative structure of a society is attested to by society's ready willingness to apply both *formal* and *informal* sanctions. *Sanctions* refers to both rewards and punishments. Those who conform to the norms are rewarded and those who violate them may be punished. Rewards may come in the form of prestige, high salaries, and what the society generally defines as the "good life." Punishments range all the way from years of imprisonment to eviction from the highest office in the land. Society does not take lightly those who deviate from its norms.

As previously discussed in the Introduction of this book, the control functions of humor are widespread. When normative violation occurs, one way to combat it is through the use of humor. The selections in this chapter address the issue of normative behavior and social control. Art Buchwald, in "What Would You Do?", discusses "one of the major issues of our time, and that is whether Woody Hayes, football coach of the Ohio State football team, should have been fired for slugging a Clemson University player in the Gator Bowl last week." Coach Hayes, in the 1979 Gator Bowl, departed from a common practice of many norm violators: do what you are going to do in secret. Before a national television audience of millions, Coach Hayes struck a football player in the face. Records are not readily available, but it may have been a first for this type of deviant behavior. If the audible gasp of the millions of viewers could have been recorded it might have exceeded a sonic boom. Within 24 hours, Mr. Hayes learned the meaning of sanctions—he was fired.

Mike Royko, in "*Going Bananas*," parodies the gay movement in his account of the Banana Lib Movement. Are sexual life-styles a matter of individual preference? Are monkey–man relationships to be considered normal behavior? This is an ongoing debate which has reached intensity proportions in our society with the onset of acquired immune deficiency syndrome, AIDS, among the homosexual community. Homosexuals themselves are being forced to reconsider what for them has long been considered normal behavior. Moralistic and religious opponents of homosexuality have taken the position that deviance is always, sooner or later, punished. Those who adopt a live and let live attitude have, nevertheless, wanted to isolate homosexuals at times for health reasons. The question of sexual preferences being just preferences is no longer that simple for some.

In "The Hobo and the Hippie," Royko addresses what may seem to be a far less serious issue than homosexuality. But dress styles are not as much a matter of individual preference as one might think. The Wall Street security analyst does *not* wear dirty blue jeans and a red flannel shirt to the office. Dark suits and white shirts for the male are "required," and suitably conservative attire is expected of the female. During the tumultuous years of the 1960s, a sizable number of young people in this society were labeled "hippies." Dress varied, but basically it consisted of blue jeans, often giving no evidence of having ever been washed, lumberjack type shirts and jackets, and many articles of jewelry. Males wore beards and hair ranging from just long to very long. Females disdained giving the usual attention to their hair and clothing which had characterized most females in this society. The hippie image was associated with social protest. While many people other than hippies were arrested for nonviolent protest during this era, the real hippie was practically guaranteed arrest. As Royko points out, however, people with a different dress and life-style have long been a part of this society.

The hippie movement, as such, is no longer a part of the current activities of young people. Indeed, "yuppies" may have replaced hippies as the prevailing image of youth. But protest from segments of the young are as present today as in the 1960s. What is today referred to as "punk rock" has strong parallels to what Royko is describing in "The Hobo and the Hippie." As the bum in Royko's piece notes, hippies could go to parks, play loud rock and roll music, throw flowers at people, and young people loved them. Punk musicians today have a large following among the young. They, too, wear a distinctive dress. Their hair, colored bright orange or otherwise, is, at the least, different from normative hair styles. Their concerts have been seen as deliberate expressions of outrage. Members of some punk rock bands have spit on stage, cursed, thrown things at the audience, and generally engaged in deviant behavior. And among their followers such behavior is literally applauded. As some say, the more things change, the more they remain the same.

The final selection by Russell Baker, "Tougher Sentencing," is a humorous treatment of an important concern in our society: the unequal application of the law to criminal behavior. Are crimes which affect the upper classes treated more severely than lesser crimes? Do courts show favoritism? Is the law not applied equally to all violations? Baker argues, "If we are going to get tough with a few lawbreakers, let's get tough with all."

ART BUCHWALD

What Would You Do?

I believe it's time to do my Woody Hayes' think piece. For a week now, sports pundits, editorial writers and television commentators have been discussing one of the major issues of our time; that is whether Woody Hayes, coach of the Ohio State football team, should have been fired for slugging a Clemson University player in the Gator Bowl last week.

The incident, which is now considered comparable to Gen. Patton hitting a GI in the face during a tour of a hospital in World War II, has ramifications far greater than football. It makes us all ask ourselves, "Whither America's will to win?"

First, the undisputed facts. Ohio State was playing Clemson in the Gator Bowl at Jacksonville, Florida. The Ohio team was losing with 15 points to Clemson's 17. There was one minute and 58 seconds to play. Ohio State had a chance to score. Its quarterback threw a pass, which was intercepted by the Clemson guard, Charley Bauman, who was knocked out of bounds a few feet from coach Hayes on the sidelines. Woody was so furious at the interception that he hit Bauman in the face. Woody wanted to continue the fight but was separated by his own players. The next morning Hayes was fired.

All right, now let's face the tough question. Did Hayes have the right to slug the Clemson guard?

I say the answer to the question is an unequivocal yes.

Let's put ourselves in Woody Hayes' shoes for just a moment. His team is playing in the Gator Bowl, which is in itself a comedown for the Buckeyes, who usually wind up in the Rose, Sugar or Cotton Bowls. The opposition, Clemson, a school with one-tenth the student body of Ohio State, is kicking the hip pads out of the Hayes-coached team. With less than two minutes to go, Hayes' boys have a chance to get in field goal range and win the game.

Then Clemson guard Bauman spoils everything. The Ohio State quarterback throws a pass, Bauman gets in the way and grabs it, thus ending the Buckeyes' chance of winning the game.

If you were the coach of Ohio State, and one of the opposition players snatched victory from your team, would you just stand on the sidelines and do NOTHING? Of course you wouldn't. Your first instinct would be to hit the player who stole your ball. This is what Woody Hayes did.

He didn't do it for himself. He did it for everyone who loves the American game of football. He showed the country on nationwide television that law and order on the gridiron still prevail, and when a kid steals a pass, he's going to pay for it.

It's a coach's job to do everything in his power to win. If this means hitting a player on the other team—so be it. Some say Bauman, the Clemson guard, was the victim of the Hayes attack. I say he invited the slugging match. Bauman knew the pass wasn't for him. He knew it was thrown to an Ohio State receiver. He had no right to get in the way of it, and even less right to catch it and run in the opposite direction.

Unless we are willing to see college football go down the drain, all of us are going to have to speak up and reiterate what American coaches have been telling their players for years, WINNING IS EVERYTHING. If we don't allow coaches to slug players on the other team, then there is no sense suiting our kids up to play the game. Hayes' hit in the mouth might have been the best thing to happen to Bauman, who I am certain will think twice before he ever steals a pass again.

Reprinted with permission of the author.

 MIKE ROYKO

Going Bananas Over Liberation

Is it abnormal for a man to be in love with a monkey? Should a man conceal such a relationship and be tormented by feelings of guilt? Should man-monkey marriages be legal?

These and other such questions are now being confronted as a result of the growing Banana Lib Movement, made up of men who have had such relationships.

They think it is time for them to "come out of the cage." And they want society to accept them as normal citizens.

At one time this would have been unthinkable. Only a few years ago such activity was found only in bars frequented by monkey-man couples.

Now, however, there have been the many defiant Banana Pride parades, with men and their monkey mates marching together; the campus Banana Pride movement has grown, with demands that they be recognized as legitimate student organizations; and the movement is demanding that both political parties adopt planks at their next conventions, declaring their support of Banana Pride.

The movement gained momentum, of course, with the recent declaration by the North American Psychiatric Confederation that it has reversed its previous position and now considers monkey-man relationships to be normal.

"We no longer consider it to be a mental illness when a man falls in love with a monkey, or a monkey falls in love with a man," the confederation said. "We believe it is a matter of individual preference."

One of the leaders of the movement is the Rev. Rodney Treeshaker, the minister who shocked his small-town Montana congregation by revealing that for years he and a monkey had been in love.

He was asked to leave and now heads a congregation of man-monkey couples in Los Angeles.

The Rev. Treeshaker, who has become a frequent guest on the network talk shows, was in town recently to discuss his new book: *Was It Jane That Tarzan Really Loved?* In an interview, he said:

> In this book I describe how I had led a false life, concealing my feelings, burdened with guilt and fear.
> It began when I was 23, and was strolling with my fiancée, a girl, through the zoo. Suddenly, as we walked through the monkey house, I was attracted to a wooly monkey.
> That night I broke my engagement and she returned the ring. The next day I went to the zoo and tried to give the ring to that monkey.
> But the keeper wouldn't let me. He said I could only give it peanuts.
> That was when I realized what it was like to live a lie, throwing peanuts to the monkey I loved when I wanted to give her flowers and perfume. I found myself burdened with the fear of being found out.
> Then I decided, after all these years, that I should not have to furtively cruise around zoos.
> I and the many others like me are normal human beings and we simply want to be accepted as such. We want the same rights other couples have.

The Rev. Treeshaker outlined some of the goals of the Banana Movement.

> First, we want the right to marry. I have been performing such ceremonies, but they are not legally recognized. The California authorities are using a legal loophole because the monkey does not actually say: "I do." It is our contention that if the monkey turns a somersault, this should be considered consent.
>
> Second, we are against job and career discrimination because of our preference. We are filing a federal suit against a company that fired a young executive because he came to his company's awards banquet and danced with his monkey.
>
> Third, we are working to change the discriminatory regulations in the armed forces. An example was the case of that soldier who was discharged when he asked for off-base housing allowance to live with the monkey he loved and that the monkey receive his allotment check.
>
> A man should not to told he can't serve his country merely because he is in love with a monkey, while other men achieve high rank and they are not in love with anybody.

A more militant spokesman is Jack Swing, who has disrupted many TV shows because he believes television distorts the images of monkeys by always showing them swinging from tree branches or doing tricks.

"Why don't they ever show a monkey puttering around the kitchen?" Swing says. "Why don't they show a man and a monkey dancing cheek to cheek, instead of those horrible stereotypes of organ grinders?"

Mr. Swing is in Chicago leading protest marches at zoos.

"Free our sweethearts," he tearfully shouted while unsuccessfully trying to storm the Brookfield Zoo's monkey house.

During an interview, Mr. Swing described his past life.

> The first time I realized how I felt was when I fainted from passion during a campus screening of "King Kong."
>
> But because of society's archaic taboos, I had to hide my emotions.
>
> I finally dropped out of graduate school because there was only one way I could be with my loved one—I opened a pet shop.
>
> This worked out fine, until one day tragedy occurred. While I was at lunch, a new clerk sold my love to a sailor, and I haven't seen her since. That was when I went berserk and burst into that TV variety show, pummeling the man who had the trained monkey act.
>
> Now I live my life in the open. I have found someone else and, when I'm not demonstrating, we reside quietly in a tree.

Reprinted with permission of Mike Royko.

MIKE ROYKO

The Hobo and the Hippie

There is a lot of interest in the hippie movement so I thought I would go out and interview one.

Luck was with me. I spotted a man on a bridge near the Loop who was a perfect specimen of the hippie.

He was wearing a stubble of beard, long sideburns, old tennis shoes, overalls and an Ike jacket.

Excuse me, I said, but how long ago did you drop out of society?

"Oh, a very long time ago."

You choose to wear unusual clothing. Why?

"These are the only clothes I have."

Do you like to get high?

"Yes, sir. I try to get high every day."

And you believe in peace?

"Yep. I don't bother nobody and I don't like nobody to bother me."

Your living conditions—are they drab, barren, simple?

"Just a dumpy, dirty old room is all."

Well, you are a real genuine hippie, aren't you?

"Hippie? No. I'm an old-fashioned Skid Row bum. I'm just standing here on this bridge trying to mooch quarters for wine."

A bum? But you fit the description of a hippie perfectly. You have dropped out, you dress in strange clothing, you get high, you are peace-loving.

"Yes, people are always making that mistake because the two groups are so similar. But there are some very basic differences."

Such as?

"We are a much, much older culture. There have been drunken bums dropping out, getting high, minding their own business for centuries. So it is very unfair."

What is unfair?

"All the publicity and attention they are getting. I go in a bar and look at the TV set and there is a useless, lazy bum, half-high on marijuana, being interviewed about Vietnam, the President and other things.

"I'm just as useless and lazy as any hippie, and I get just as high on wine as he does on marijuana. But am I invited on television talk shows to give my opinions? No. The only time anybody asks me anything is when the judge asks if I want to go to the jail or to the work farm for my thirty days.

"And look how dedicated we are. The average hippie is going to stick with it for a few months, a year or two maybe, then he will shave, get a job, get married, buy a house in the suburbs and tell me to beat it when I ask him for a quarter near the commuter station. But most of us old-fashioned bums are in it for life.

"Do people treat us nicely the way they treat hippies? Of course not. If a hippie goes in a park and plays loud rock 'n' roll music and throws flowers at people and dances, it is called a 'Be-In' or a 'Love-In.'

"But if I go in a park and just sit on a bench it is called loitering.

"If I go up to the University of Chicago and stand around, the intellectuals will say: 'There is a bum. Arrest him.' But if they see a hippie standing around the same way, they will say: 'Oh, you are the hope of the world. Please throw a daisy at me.' "

Why don't you become a hippie?

"I have my pride. And I prefer wine to marijuana or LSD. It tastes better.

"Besides, I don't have a college education and I don't come from a comfortable family background, so I can't qualify socially as a hippie.

"Why, if I went around to where the hippies live they'd just say, 'Scat, you bum.'

"But I've often thought about what it would be like today if my parents had had the money in the old days to put me through college and give me a proper upbringing.

"I sure wouldn't be no dirty, unshaven bum, standing on this bridge mooching quarters for wine so I can get high.

"No sir. I'd be a dirty, unshaven hippie, cashing my allowance check from my dad so I can buy some pot and get high.

"Just shows what a difference the advantages can make."

Reprinted with permission of Mike Royko.

RUSSELL BAKER

Tougher Sentencing

WASHINGTON, Jan. 10—Some people are saying Governor Rockefeller goes too far in wanting to lock up every drug dealer forever. Some say President Nixon's Justice Department shows too much love for the noose in asking Congress to bring back the death penalty, even for hijacking.

The issue is debatable, hotly. What is not debatable, however, is the inequity of getting tough with only a few select crimes such as hijacking and drug dealing.

There is something elitist in these two huge, rich governments selecting drug dealers and hijackers to get tough with. The drug racket and airline hijacking are crimes particularly annoying to big shots who run governments. Here is a classic case of power being used to indulge its own peeves.

What about the dozens of other crimes and misdemeanors which do not affect great men but still make life miserable for those without power to command headlines and Congresses? Why is there no outcry from the top for harder punishments in these cases?

To take a small example, consider double parking. The chief miscreants are trucks, post office vehicles and doctors, three power blocs (Hoffa, postmen, the A.M.A.) which happen to enjoy the patronage of Republican governments.

If hijackers are to hang and drug dealers to be caged eternally because they try the patience of powerful men, then these double parkers who compound the misery of urban life should also suffer punishment more medieval than the occasional ticket left by permissive policemen.

A suitable punishment would be the old torture of "squassation." It would not be used against the vehicle's driver, of course; America is not yet ready to go all the way. It would be applied only to the offending car.

During the witch hunts in Germany, squassation was used to produce confessions. It usually worked. The person under suspicion was bound with arms extended above head. Heavy dangling weights were attached to his feet. Pulleys raised him, arms up, high off the floor. From a high elevation, his body was then allowed to fall free until it stopped with an abrupt jerk just before the attached weights could touch the floor.

After a few post office trucks and doctors' Cadillacs had been subjected to squassation, it is a safe bet that double parking would not be committed quite so cavalierly.

Capital punishment for many minor crimes existed in England well after Elizabeth. For trivial offenses, hands were hacked off, noses slit, ears chopped, cheeks branded.

If we are to get tough, some of this same spirit must be breathed into punishments for offenses which governments now blink at. What about coin machines that grab your silver and give you neither orange soda pop nor change?

Under present namby-pamby sentencing, these thieves have only an occasional kick or punch to fear. No wonder their thefts become increasingly brazen. If governments passed mutilation laws requiring mandatory disfigurement by ax of all machines caught stealing from a human, we would soon have some law and order among these rogues.

Drawing and quartering would not be too hard a punishment for those criminal buses that spew poisonous gases over anyone who dares drive behind them. We can hang muggers and imprison addicts for life, but until the law provides something like drawing and quartering for buses, there will always be crime in the streets.

If we are going to get tough with a few lawbreakers, let's get tough with all. That must be our principle. For false advertisers, the Turkish bastinado. For false advertisers on television, the Chinese bell torture. The electric telephone for household contractors who fail to finish the job; and for businessmen who bribe governments, the Iron Maiden. For bribe-takers, the pillory near a fruit market. If punishment doesn't stop the crime, vengeance at least may satisfy our frustration.

QUESTIONS FOR DISCUSSION

1. Violence is a violation of normative behavior in this society. Woody Hayes was fired from his job for hitting an athlete playing a game. However, hockey players routinely attack one another to the point of causing injuries requiring medical

treatment and, on occasion, hospitalization. Yet, hockey players are not fired—to the contrary, fans applaud their behavior. How do you account for this differential treatment in the world of sports?

2. Many sports are played at night now. In a sports arena one player may physically attack and injure another. Outside, on a dark street, if one person engages in identical behavior toward another, he or she will, if caught, be arrested and accused of assault. Why are there differential norms in lighted sports arenas and dark streets?

3. Buchwald says coaches have been telling their players for years "winning is everything." Is this one of our values in American society?

4. Orlick and Botterill (1975) refer to studies which have shown that many fathers react negatively to their sons when they lose an athletic contest. Does this suggest to children that they have value only if they win? Could we, as a society, develop a sport ethic where playing is motivated by fun as opposed to winning?

5. Should people be allowed to marry monkeys if they want to? How is this related to marriage, not just sexual relationships, between members of the same sex? How do you think members of the gay community responded to Royko's article?

6. At one time our society vigorously condemned homosexual relationships, and homosexuals went to great lengths to hide their sexual orientations. The disease AIDS is present among other groups than homosexuals, but much of the attention has been directed toward the association between homosexuality and the disease. What specific effects do you think this will have with regard to acknowledgment that one is a homosexual? Are employers less likely to employ homosexuals as a result? Are there legal problems here? Are people who might formerly have welcomed homosexuals as friends likely to be more reticent now?

7. The Skid Row bum in Royko's article says that societies have always had "drop outs," and this is indeed true. Why do societies look with disfavor upon those who consciously choose different life-styles from that of the majority? What values, if any, do they call into question?

8. The Skid Row bum also says that "the average hippie is going to stick with it for a few months, a year or two maybe, then he will shave, get a job, get married, buy a house in the suburbs and tell me to beat it when I ask him for a quarter near the commuter station." What became of the hippies of the sixties? Most punk rock musicians are young. What will become of their expressions of outrage as they mature? Are protest and deviant life-styles primarily a function of youth? If so, why?

9. The Environmental Protection Agency (EPA) seeks to monitor and control industrial pollution in our society. Pollution of the air and water can literally threaten the lives of millions. But when industries are found guilty of pollution law violations they are, at most, simply fined a sum of money. Why do you think the fines are minimal compared to the potential disaster of such violations?

10. Baker, in "Tougher Sentencing," expresses a frustration many urban dwellers have over minor civil offenses. In New York City people can amass parking ticket violations in the thousands of dollars. Why are these fines not collected? The city often turns over such violations to a special collection agency. Why can't the city enforce its own laws?

11. On most college campuses, violation of parking rules is widespread. Would stronger sanctions than usually prevail help out in such a situation? For repeating offenders would you support "squassation" of the impounded vehicle? If not, what measures do you think would lead to norm adherence in such situations?

12. Baker says that "if punishment doesn't stop the crime. . . ." Is there any evidence that punishment does deter any crime? Are more murders committed in societies which allow capital punishment than in those which prohibit it?

REFERENCES

Buchwald, Art. "Oh, to be a Swinger," in *Down the Seine and Up the Potomac*. New York: Fawcett Crest, 1977.

Glick, P. D., and Spanier, G. "Married and Unmarried Cohabitation in the United States." *Journal of Marriage and the Family* 42, 1 (1980), 10–30.

Newman, Graham. *Comparative Deviance.* New York: Elsevier, 1976.

Orlick, Terry, and Botterill, Carl. *Every Kid Can Win.* Chicago: Nelson-Hall, 1975.

V

SOCIAL INEQUALITY

Chapter Six

Social Stratification

No formal training in sociology is required to know that there are wide variations in life-styles in the United States. There are millions of people living in poverty; others own both winter and summer homes. In between these extremes is the majority of the population who live quite comfortably. Our overall standard of living is perhaps the highest in the world, and we tend to think of ourselves primarily as a middle class society. Actually, we prefer not to think of ourselves in class terms at all. We pride ourselves on seeing everyone as equal, even in the face of much evidence to the contrary. In 1981, Susan Benjamin of Chicago wrote President Reagan asking him not to cut funds for special education for handicapped children. The wrong form letter was sent to Benjamin. The letter she received in reply to her concern was the Reagans' favorite recipe—crabmeat and artichoke casserole (costing about $20). Benjamin was angry and "appalled by the insensitivity" that money was spent on such expensive recipes at the same time budgets were being cut for the poor. The President's favorite recipe was quickly changed to macaroni and cheese. (*Washington Post*, Dec. 12, 1983)

The understanding of the social stratification of society is an area which has been heavily researched by sociologists and others. We speak of social classes and seek to analytically divide the society into various class levels. Most people speak with ease of the upper, middle, and lower classes. But defining the criteria which enables placement of people into specific classes is quite difficult. Boundaries overlap to some degree, and completely accurate designations are difficult. Nevertheless, the consequences of one's life-style are extremely important, and everything we can understand about social class standings is of great importance for both the society and the individual.

In studying social class, sociologists examine its three major components: wealth, prestige, and power. No society distributes its wealth equally. Prestige is accorded to some and withheld from others. Power, even in a political democracy such as ours, is concentrated in specific groups. The results of the unequal distribution of these three components lead to the formation of social classes. Wealth includes all forms of assets: money, real property, and securities. In terms of money income, the wealthiest

112

one-fifth of families receives about 40 percent of the total income of the society. The lowest fifth receives about 5 percent.

Occupations which pay the highest monetary rewards are usually accorded the greatest prestige. Exceptions do occur. Criminal elements, which may earn millions of dollars in income, are not accorded high prestige rankings. And some occupations, clergy and public school teachers, have low incomes but high prestige.

Power is also closely associated with wealth. Those with great wealth do not pay much more in income taxes than those with far less income. They enjoy tax benefits which are written into the tax laws by those with political power—many of whom themselves possess great wealth. One of the more recent illustrations of this is the tax benefit from leasing property. Some towns have even sold their city halls to groups of wealthy individuals who then lease them back to the town and derive tax benefits from owning and depreciating property. Only the wealthy and those in power to write such laws can participate in these benefits.

Sociologists have employed several methods to delineate carefully the number of social classes in America. The *reputational* method involves asking members of a community how they perceive the class structure of that community. W. L. Warner and Paul Lunt (1941) used this approach in a study of Newburyport, Massachusetts. They found that people identified some members as the "old aristocracy," others as "snobs trying to push up," "poor but decent," "nobodies," or "poor whites." Based upon community responses Warner and Hunt were able to devise a system with six classes: upper upper, lower upper, upper middle, lower middle, upper lower, and lower lower. It is quickly apparent that such a method can be applied only to small communities where people know each other. Such a method also depends heavily upon personal interpretations of the class structure—not a highly reliable method.

The *subjective* approach asks people to identify themselves, not others. It comes as no surprise that most of us tend to identify ourselves as "middle class" or "working class." Reflecting our belief that we are not class-conscious in America, some people (25 percent in a 1978 *New York Times*–CBS survey) say they don't belong to any class at all.

The third approach, the *objective* method, employs "hard" data which are, however, arbitrarily chosen by the sociologist conducting the study. Income, type of residence, level of education, and type of occupation are favorite criteria. These can be readily derived from U.S. Census data and from other agencies which collect these types of information. People can be ranked according to these criteria and class standings can be assigned to the various rankings. While there are some problems with this method, too—e.g., some people in one class may have greater income than those in a higher class, but a different life-style—the consequences of income differences, occupation, and education are so great that such a ranking does enable us to predict with accuracy something about the stratification of the society into various classes.

One of the powerful beliefs in our society is that class barriers, as such, do not really exist. We teach the young that in the United States anyone can become president. Our cultural heroes are often pictured as those who rose from obscurity to positions of power and wealth. And there is some substantiation for this. One can begin in lower class origins and rise to higher class standings. This is referred to as social mobility, which includes, also, movement from *higher* classes to *lower*—but we tend to mask this phenomenon in our society. While we have what is known as an open society—i.e., freedom to move between classes—nevertheless, movement in actual practice is rather limited. Few individuals start out at the bottom of the class structure and end up at the top. Such extreme movements do occur, and when they do their uniqueness is attested to by the amount of attention given to them. But most movement is from one class level to an adjacent one.

Blau and Duncan (1967) analyzed data from over 20,000 men and found that 37 percent of those in white-collar jobs had fathers who were blue-collar workers. Blau and Duncan also offer support for a well-founded belief about social mobility. Education *is* a prime factor in explaining movement from one class level to another. However, probably the most significant finding of the Blau–Duncan study was the fact that *unknown* variables have a tremendous influence upon whether or not an individual experiences upward mobility. It is difficult to measure the intensity of an individual's desire to succeed. Is he or she willing to forgo immediate pleasures for long-term goals? Are there personality traits which drive some individuals to seek advancement? What, if any, role does sheer luck (being in the right place at the right time) have?

All these factors combine to result in movement from one class level to another in America. There is a large amount of upward mobility in America, but increases in one's status are more modest than dramatic. And for some, poverty is a continuing reality passed on from one welfare generation to the next. America, then, is a land of vivid contrasts offering chances of upward mobility for many, continuing poverty for others, and inherited positions of wealth, prestige, and power for yet another segment of the population.

The first humorous selection, "The Money River," is from Kurt Vonnegut's novel, *God Bless You, Mr. Rosewater*. The novel is an attack upon a treasured American value: inherited wealth. The main character in the novel is Eliot Rosewater, president of the Rosewater foundation. The foundation generates income in the amount of "nearly $10,000 a day—Sundays, too." Offspring and siblings of the president become officers of the foundation for life and are allowed the privilege of paying themselves for their services as liberally and lavishly as they like.

Eliot's problem is that, though president and married, he has not provided any offspring to succeed him as head of the foundation. Equally bad, he has ideas which seem to be inappropriate to a Harvard-educated member of the upper class. He wants to care for and love the poor—literally. And he wants to do this with the Rosewater foundation's money. As president he can distribute money to any cause he deems worthy. So he proceeds to return to Rosewater County, Indiana, where he keeps and associates with those whom his father labels as "whores, malingerers, pimps, and thieves."

Apart from his strange associates Eliot has other problems. He drinks heavily, travels around the country to visit fire departments (which he loves), gives his clothes away, and has estranged his wife prior to having any children. His behavior is deviant enough that some question his sanity—especially Norman Mushari, a lawyer. Mushari wants to have Eliot declared insane and control of the family fortune transferred to the Rhode Island branch of the family. Of course, in handling the legal transactions involved in this exchange of control, Mushari expects to profit handsomely.

Eliot and his father disagree on many things—particularly on how hard work makes one wealthy. Eliot argues that the rich are simply born to wealth: they drink early and all their lives from the "Money River." Eliot's father denies the existence of such a river, to which Eliot replies: "When one of us claims that there is no such thing as the Money River I think to myself, 'My gosh, but that's a dishonest and tasteless thing to say.' "

In the selection included in this chapter, Eliot's father, a U.S. Senator, is once again pleading with Eliot to reconcile himself with his wife, "take a good look" at himself, and, in short, behave like a member of one of America's richest families.

Of course, if one is not born on the banks of the Money River, then great attention must be given to moving up the social ladder. J. P. Donleavy offers specific guidance for those not born to wealth. In "Upon Being Not to the Manner Born" and "Useful Rules in Social Climbing," Donleavy suggests how you can overcome the lack of a proper background and still rise in the social order.

Social mobility refers to movement down through the stratification system as well as up. People are sometimes said to marry beneath themselves. We don't discuss this too often in America, but such marriages do occur. When this is the case, Fran Lebowitz thinks you need to know "How Not to Marry a Millionaire: A Guide to the Misfortune Hunter." Some practical hints for the rich include conversation to be avoided with poor people, for example: "I'll call you around noon, will you be up?" Or, "Is that your blue Daimler blocking the driveway?"

The last selection is "*Making It*," by Mike Royko. Royko's account of the old and newly rich competing for space at the opera is more than a parody. It represents attitudes which indeed do exist among members of the aristocracy toward newcomers to wealth. It also represents pretense on the part of a satirist who is talking about one thing when he is actually grappling with a more serious issue.

KURT VONNEGUT, JR.

The Money River

"Eliot—"
   "Sir—?"
   "I want you to take a good look at yourself."

Dutifully, Eliot looked himself over as best he could without a mirror. "I'm looking."

"Now ask yourself, 'Is this a dream? How did I ever get into such a disreputable condition?' "

Again dutifully, and without a trace of whimsicality, Eliot said to himself out loud, "Is this a dream? How did I ever get into such a disreputable condition?"

"Well? What is your answer?"

"Isn't a dream," Eliot reported.

"Don't you wish it *were?*"

"What would I wake up *to?*"

"What you can *be*. What you *used* to be!"

"You want me to start buying paintings for museums again? Would you be prouder of me, if I'd contributed two and a half million dollars to buy Rembrandt's *Aristotle Contemplating a Bust of Homer?*"

"Don't reduce the argument to an absurdity."

"I'm not the one who did *that*. Blame the people who put up that kind of money for that kind of picture. I showed a photograph of it to Diana Moon Glampers, and she said, 'Maybe I'm dumb, Mr. Rosewater, but I wouldn't give that thing house room.' "

"Eliot—"

"Sir—?"

"Ask yourself what Harvard would think of you now."

"I don't have to. I already know."

"Oh?"

"They're crazy about me. You should see the letters I get."

The Senator nodded to himself resignedly, knowing that the Harvard jibe was ill-considered, knowing Eliot told the truth when he spoke of letters from Harvard that were full of respect.

"After all—" said Eliot, "for goodness sakes, I've given those guys three hundred thousand dollars a year, regular as clockwork, ever since the Foundation began. You should *see* the letters."

"Eliot—"

"Sir—?"

"We come to a supremely ironic moment in history, for Senator Rosewater of Indiana now asks his own son, 'Are you or have you ever been a communist?' "

"Oh, I have what a lot of people would probably call communistic thoughts," said Eliot artlessly, "but, for heaven's sakes, Father, nobody can work with the poor and not fall over Karl Marx from time to time—or just fall over the Bible, as far as that goes. I think it's terrible the way people don't share things in this country. I think it's a heartless government that will let one baby be born owning a big piece of the country, the way I was born, and let another baby be born without owning anything. The least a government could do, it seems to me, is to divide things up fairly among the babies. Life is hard enough, without people having to worry themselves sick about *money*, too. There's plenty for everybody in this country, if we'll only *share* more."

"And just what do you think that would do to incentive?"

"You mean fright about not getting enough to eat, about not being able to pay the doctor, about not being able to give your family nice clothes, a safe, cheerful, comfortable place to live, a decent education, and a few good times? You mean shame about not knowing where the Money River is?"

"The *what?*"

"The Money River, where the wealth of the nation flows. We were born on the banks of it—and so were most of the mediocre people we grew up with, went to private schools with, sailed and played tennis with. We can slurp from that mighty river to our hearts' content. And we even take slurping lessons, so we can slurp more efficiently."

"Slurping lessons?"

"From lawyers! From tax consultants! From customers' men! We're born close enough to to the river to drown ourselves and the next ten generations in wealth, simply using dippers and buckets. But we still hire the experts to teach us the use of aqueducts, dams, reservoirs, siphons, bucket brigades, and the Archimedes' screw. And our teachers in turn become rich, and their children become buyers of lessons in slurping."

"I wasn't aware that I slurped."

Eliot was fleetingly heartless, for he was thinking angrily in the abstract. "Born slurpers never are. And they can't imagine what the poor people are talking about when they say they hear somebody slurping. They don't even know what it means when somebody mentions the Money River. When one of us claims that there is no such thing as the Money River I think to myself, 'My gosh, but that's a dishonest and tasteless thing to say.' "

———

"How stimulating to hear you talk of taste," said the Senator clankingly.

"You want me to start going to the opera again? You want me to build a perfect house in a perfect village, and sail and sail and sail?"

"Who cares what I want?"

"I admit this is no Taj Mahal. But should it be, with other Americans having such a rotten time?"

"Perhaps, if they stopped believing in crazy things like the Money River, and got to work, they would stop having such a rotten time."

"If there isn't a Money River, then how did I make ten thousand dollars today, just by snoozing and scratching myself, and occasionally answering the phone?"

"It's still possible for an American to make a fortune on his own."

"Sure—provided somebody tells him when he's young enough that there *is* a Money River, that there's nothing fair about it, that he had damn well better forget about hard work and the merit system and honesty and all that crap, and get to where the river is. 'Go where the rich and the powerful are,' I'd tell him, 'and learn their ways. They can be flattered and they can be scared. Please them enormously or scare them enormously, and one moonless night they will put their fingers to their lips, warning you not to make a sound. And they will lead you through the dark to the widest, deepest river of wealth ever known to man. You'll be shown your place on the riverbank, and handed a bucket all your own. Slurp as much as you want, but try to keep the racket of your slurping down. A poor man might hear.' "

The Senator cursed.

"Why did you say that, Father?" It was a tender question.

The Senator cursed again.

"I just wish there didn't have to be this *arcrimony*, this tension, every time we talk. I love you so."

There was more cursing, made harsher by the fact that the Senator was close to tears.

"Why would you swear when I say I love you, Father?"

"You're the man who stands on a street corner with a roll of toilet paper, and written on each square are the words, 'I love you.' And each passer-by, no matter who, gets a square all his or her own. I don't want *my* square of toilet paper."

"I didn't realize it *was* toilet paper."

"Until you stop drinking, you're not going to realize anything!" the Senator cried brokenly. "I'm going to put your wife on the phone. Do you realize you've lost her? Do you realize what a good wife she was?"

———

"Eliot—?" Sylvia's was such a breathy and frightened greeting. The girl weighed no more than a wedding veil.

"Sylvia—" This was formal, manly, but even. Eliot had written to her a thousand times, had called and called. Until now, there had been no reply.

"I—I am aware that—that I have behaved badly."

"As long as the behavior was human—"

"Can I help being human?"

"No."

"Can anybody?"

"Not that I know of."

———

"Eliot—?"

"Yes?"

"How is everybody?"

"Here?"

"Anywhere."

"Fine."

"I'm glad."

———

"If—if I ask about certain people, I'll cry," said Sylvia.

"Don't ask."

"I still care about them, even if the doctors tell me I mustn't ever go there again."

"Don't ask."

"Somebody had a baby?"

"Don't ask."

"Didn't you tell your father somebody had a baby?"

"Don't ask."

"Who had a baby, Eliot?—I care, I care."

"Oh Christ, don't ask."

"I care, I care!"

"Mary Moody."

"Twins?"

"Of course." Eliot revealed here that he had no illusions about the people to whom he was devoting his life. "And firebugs, too, no doubt, no doubt." The Moody family had a long history of not only twinning but arson.

"Are they cute?"

"I haven't seen them." Eliot added with an irritability that had always been a private thing between himself and Sylvia. "They always are."

"Have you sent their presents yet?"

"What makes you think I still send presents?" This had reference to Eliot's old custom of sending a share of International Business Machines stock to each child born in the county.

"You don't do it any more?"

"I still do it." Eliot sounded sick of doing it.

"You seem tired."

"It must be a bad connection."

"Tell me some more news."

"My wife is divorcing me for medical reasons."

"Can't we skip that news?" This was not a flippant suggestion. It was a tragic one. The tragedy was beyond discussion.

"Hippity hop," said Eliot emptily.

————

Eliot took a drink of Southern Comfort, was uncomforted. He coughed, and his father coughed, too. This coincidence, where father and son matched each other unknowingly, inconsolable hack for hack, was heard not only by Sylvia, but by Norman Mushari, too. Mushari had slipped out of the living room, had found a telephone extension in the Senator's study. He was listening in with ears ablaze.

"I—I suppose I should say goodbye," said Sylvia guiltily. Tears were streaming down her checks.

"That would be up to your doctor to say."

"Give—give my love to everyone."

"I will, I will."

"Tell them I dream about them all the time."

"That will make them proud."

"Congratulate Mary Moody on her twins."

"I will. I'll be baptizing them tomorrow."

"Baptizing?" This was something new.

Mushari rolled his eyes.

"I—I didn't know you—you did things like that," said Sylvia carefully.

Mushari was gratified to hear the anxiety in her voice. It meant to him that Eliot's lunacy was not stabilized, but was about to make the great leap forward into religion.

"I couldn't get out of it," said Eliot. "She insisted on it, and nobody else would do it."

"Oh." Sylvia relaxed.

Mushari did not register disappointment. The baptism would hold up very well in court as evidence that Eliot thought of himself as a Messiah.

"I told her," said Eliot, and Mushari's mind, which was equipped with ratchets, declined to accept this evidence, "that I wasn't a religious person by any stretch of the imagination. I told her nothing I did would count in Heaven, but she insisted just the same."

"What will you say? What will you do?"

"Oh—I don't know." Eliot's sorrow and exhaustion dropped away for a moment as he became enchanted by the problem. A birdy little smile played over his lips. "Go over to her shack, I guess. Sprinkle some water on the babies, say, 'Hello, babies. Welcome to Earth. It's hot in the summer and cold in the winter. It's round and wet and crowded. At the outside, babies, you've got about a hundred years here. There's only one rule that I know of, babies—:

" 'God damn it, you've got to be kind.' "

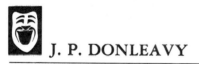 J. P. DONLEAVY

Upon Being Not to the Manner Born

When this unpleasant remark is made about you, stand up, making sure your flies are closed and announce in a firm voice.

"To hell with that shit."

You may add, with a hint of hurt modesty flavouring the voice.

"I was born, wasn't I, and that's enough for me."

Of course your opponent's high pitched riposte will be.

"But sir, that is not enough for us."

Sit down and think. A valuable antique chair helps. Cross your legs and pull up your socks. Right away if your socks are white or otherwise bright you are in trouble unless you happen to be in yachting or tennis gear. In these latter equipages you can assume you are not entirely without hope.

Examine your background. If you really stare it straight in the status it's surprising the amount of dignity which can be salvaged from the unvarnished truth. Even from the unmitigated wrong side of the tracks or floor of the apartment building, there's bound to be something that will entitle you to make an effective reply to the lousy remark above. This is why everybody should research around a little in his lineage. Back far enough or out to the side, someone must have been something once.

For orphans who do not know who their parents were, this is sad but by no means socially fatal, and affords you a fresh start. If you have received a Red Cross Life Saving Certificate, riposte pronto with this information. After their first few ha ha ha's, your temporarily superior opponents will cringe at your hopeless effort to give an accounting of yourself. And you will really feel rotten. Your crestfallen demeanour, however, will make them clear off. They will not be inviting you to their parties. But you are left with a marvellous incitement to social climb.

Useful Rules in Social Climbing

Sketch out and firmly keep in mind your own personal dreams of grandeur in which circumstances you figure you will be when you finally get there. Forthrightly behave as if you had already made it. This will require you to strike various seemingly affected poses and possibly expose you to ridicule, especially in the matter of pretending to descend a grand staircase. It is entirely essential to be indifferent to those who laugh, point and smirk.

Impose a limit upon the speed at which you socially rise. This makes your ascent more graceful. Plus you do not always find yourself surrounded by a bunch of total strangers which can happen when you've sped right by everybody. Also any calm casualness by which you can proceed will recommend you to the discerning eye of other dedicated climbers.

Until you are firmly socially established, under no circumstances give large parties with fountains of good champagne and chilled marble bowls of caviar nestled on orchid covered tables. Instead indulge yourself semi privately with these extravagant deliciousnesses. When you get a lot of your folk crammed in your house slamming back the goodies, a socially demeaning conspiracy could get going against you as well as firm friendships which depressingly exclude you.

The smile ranks only after money and ass kissing as the major tool in climbing. It is recommended to smile as often as you can without appearing like a nut. Should someone accost you to say they do not like your smile. Wait. Until you are both on safari. When a lot of suitable ripostes connected with camels will rapidly come to mind and the setting will lend a helpful hand to the thrust.

Be easily amused. This is a socially superior characteristic, only improved upon by being highly amused. But for your own safety it is as well to temper this latter quality by never explosively convulsing with laughter except in the presence of established intimates. If however you are temporarily not easily amused and someone who may be of social advantage has put much effort into the telling of a joke, make every effort possible to remark.

"Hey that's really rich."

The greatest social strides forward are always made by unhesitatingly letting people know straight to their faces how wonderful they are, especially in the matter of their apparel.

"Gee I like the roll on your lapels, I really do."

The phrase "I really do" offers reassurance to a guy who is not entirely certain his lapels are not for the birds and thinks you're spoofing him. Also it provides an air of surprise that you couldn't help blurting out your feelings. This is helpful when a member of the socially elite is suspicious of you. Small expletives such as "gee," "hey" and "boy o boy" can always help make your remarks endearingly credible. When they might otherwise come dangerously close to gross insult. As happens when these small expletives are repeated more than once.

Don't look back. The faces are not nice to see. Your ascent will cause those whom you have left behind, below and under, to suffer a personality corrosion which will etch upon them looks of deeply grieved resentment.

Permission by J. P. Donleavy.

FRAN LEBOWITZ

How Not to Marry a Millionaire: A Guide for the Misfortune Hunter

The recent marriage of a well-known Greek shipping heiress and an unemployed Russian Communist has given rise to the speculation that we may, in fact, be witnessing an incipient trend. It is not unlikely that working your way down may shortly become the romantic vogue among the truly rich—with interest ranging from the merely less fortunate to the genuinely poor. Should this become the case, our more affluent brethren will undoubtedly be in need of some practical advice and careful guidance. Thus I offer the following course of instruction:

I. Where Poorer People Congregate

Meeting the poorer person is a problem in itself, for the more conventional avenues of acquaintance are closed to you. The poorer person did not prep with your brother, form a racehorse syndicate with your broker or lose to you gracefully in Deauville. He does not share your aesthetic interest in pre-Columbian jewelry, your childhood passion for teasing the cook or your knowledge of land values in Gstaad. Therefore, it is not probable that the poorer person is someone whom you are just going to run into by chance. He must be actively sought. In seeking the poorer person, one must be ever mindful of both his habits and his daily routine:

a. The very backbone of the mass-transit system *is* the poorer person, who when he must go somewhere will usually avail himself of the vivid camaraderie to be found on buses and subways. Should you choose this method, take special care that you do not give yourself away by an awkward and superfluous attempt to hail the E train or by referring to the bus driver as "the captain."

b. The poorer person performs most personal services for himself. Thus he can commonly be found in the acts of purchasing food, laundering clothing, shopping for hardware, picking up prescriptions and returning empty bottles. These tasks can be accomplished at locations throughout the city and are all open to the public, which can, if you like, include yourself.

c.   Generally speaking, the poorer person summers where he winters.

d.   Unless he's an extremely poorer person (i.e., a welfare recipient) he will spend a substantial portion of each day or night at work. Work may occur in any number of places: stores, offices, restaurants, houses, airports or the front seats of taxicabs. With the possible exception of the last, you yourself have easy and frequent access to all such locales—a circumstance that can often be used to advantage, as it affords you the opportunity of making that crucial first gesture.

II.   Breaking the Ice With Poorer People

In approaching the poorer person, one can employ, of course, the same tactics that one might use in approaching someone on more equal footing with oneself. Charm, wit, tact, direct eye contact, simple human warmth, the feigning of interest in his deeper feelings— all of these may be beneficial in establishing rapport. Such strategies are, however, not without risk, for they are every one open to misinterpretation and most certainly cannot be counted upon for immediate results. Poorer people, being, alas, not only poorer but also people, are quirky; they too have their little moods, their sore spots, their prickly defenses. Therefore their responses to any of the above might well be erratic and not quite all that one has hoped. Do not lose heart, though, for it is here that your own position as a richer person can best be exploited and can, in fact, assure you of almost instantaneous success in getting to know the poorer person more intimately.

Buy the poorer person an expensive present: a car; a house; a color television set; a dining-room table. Something nice. The poorer person, without exception, loves all these things. Buy him one of them and he will definitely like you enough to at least chat.

III.   What Not to Say to Poorer People

It is at this juncture that the utmost care be exercised lest you lose your hard-won toehold. For it is in actual conversation with the poorer person that even the most attentive and conscientious student tends to falter.

Having been softened up with a lavish gift, the poorer person will indeed be in an expansive, even friendly, frame of mind. He is not, however, completely and irrevocably yours yet; it is still possible to raise his hackles and make as naught all of your previous efforts. A thoughtless remark, an inopportune question, an unsuitable reference—any of these may offend the poorer person to the point where you may totally alienate him. Below are some examples of the sort of thing one really must strive to avoid:

a. Is that your blue Daimler blocking the driveway?

b. ... and in the end, of course, it's always the larger stockholder who is blamed.

c. I'll call you around noon. Will you be up?

d. Who do you think you are, anyway—Lucius Beebe?

e. Don't you believe it for a minute—these waiters make an absolute fortune.

f. Oh, a uniform. What a great idea.

IV.   A Short Glossary of Words Used by Poorer People

sale—An event common to the retail business, during the course of which merchandise is reduced in price. Not to be confused with *sail*, which is, at any rate, a good word not to say to poorer people.

meatloaf—A marvelously rough kind of pâté. Sometimes served hot.

overworked—An overwhelming feeling of fatigue; exhaustion; weariness. Similar to jet lag.

rent—A waste of money. It's so much cheaper to buy.

MIKE ROYKO

Making It

The Metropolitan Opera peacefully integrated its top-society box seats for last week's opening night.

The evening was the talk of international society because the old, established rich had to give up some of their exclusive box seats to some of the newly rich.

The newly rich got the seats for the first time because they contributed new money to build the new opera house.

Although many of the old rich appeared tense or a bit stiff, there were no reports of violence.

The inside story of the peaceful move-in is told here for the first time.

Much of the credit belongs to the secretly created Metropolitan Opera Human Relations Commission.

It was formed months ago and did hush-hush work behind the scenes, breaking the news to the old, established rich that the newly rich would be sitting with them.

In an exclusive interview, I. Dugood Deeds, the commission's director, explained the agency's role.

"Our job was mainly educational. We had to break down the fears and prejudices of the old rich and keep them from panicking and running to the movies instead of the opera."

Was it a difficult thing to do?

"Not really. Most of the old rich are decent, law-abiding, peace-loving people. But like everyone else, they were afraid. You must remember that many of the old rich have never seen a new rich. They had many false notions."

Such as?

"Well, Mrs. Barry Doe Deeply III was typical. She thought they were all former used-car dealers and would try to sell her something on an easy-payment plan during intermission."

How did you educate them?

"We formed human relations 'teams,' as many suburbs have done, to go have quiet talks with the old rich; to explain that the opera integration is inevitable."

The teams were made up of clergymen, I suppose?

"A clergyman, yes. Also a banker, a polo player, a stockholder, a hairdresser, a tennis instructor and a Hungarian nobleman."

They went door-to-door in the neighborhood?

"No. The old rich don't all live in the same block. Or country. We had to dash around the world a bit."

Where?

"We found Finlay Mustymoney on his yacht in the Mediterranean. When we told him about the planned movein he was so upset that he threw a cabin boy over the side."

He refused to co-operate?

"At first. But after we assured him that none of the newly rich had a bigger yacht or wanted him to marry their daughters, he was quite reasonable. He even sent a small boat to look for the cabin boy."

Then yacht size was a big objection?

"Not in every case. Some of the old rich feared the presence of the new rich would depreciate their property—such as money."

How?

"Mrs. Vanderocker was particularly upset. She said she didn't trust new money. She thought she would lose the little nest egg her great-great-grandfather, Avaricious P. Vanderocker, worked so hard to set aside when he cornered the world market in food, clothing and medicine."

What did you tell her?

"We showed her some new money. At first she covered her eyes and refused to look at it. She said we were worse than pornography peddlers and threatened to call the DAR. But finally she peeked and was quite surprised to find that it looked just like her money."

That eased her fears?

"Not really. It upset her to know that other money looks like her money. She asked us if FDR caused that, too. But she agreed to the new opera seating when we promised her the newly rich would not wear their money or toss it to people on the main floor."

So most of the fears were economic?

"No. Some were simply afraid the newly rich wouldn't know how to act at an opera. Mrs. Mary Wizely, Jr., thought they would clap too much or act like they were enjoying themselves and embarrass their neighbors. I remember her saying: 'Those people have too much rhythm.' "

She refused to attend?

"No. She was quite agreeable when we told her that the newly rich don't like opera any more than she does."

Your work seems to have paid off. There were no incidents?

"Just one. After the first act, everyone was shouting 'Bravo, Bravo'—except Mr. I. M. Solvent. We had to talk to him."

He was booing?

"No. He was shouting, 'Old power! Old power!' "

Reprinted with permission of Mike Royko.

QUESTIONS FOR DISCUSSION

1. Do you agree with Eliot Rosewater that there is a Money River for some but not all? Eliot's father says, "Perhaps, if [Americans] stopped believing in crazy things like the Money River, and got to work, they would stop having such a rotten time." Do some opponents of the welfare system seem to agree with this philosophy?

2. Eliot wants to share the money of this country—"there's plenty for everybody...." In 1982 the richest fifth of the population received almost half (43 percent) of the total income in the United States. The poorest fifth received 5 percent of the total income. This disparity in the distribution of income has remained about the same for the past 30 years in spite of federal programs for job training, welfare, and the like. Would you support some method of more equally distributing the income in the United States?

3. Each year *Forbes* magazine publishes a list of America's 400 wealthiest individuals. A significant proportion of these individuals inherited their wealth. Eliot's father says that to redistribute income in the United States would destroy any incentive the poor have to work harder to have more money. Yet, Eliot's position is that the rich simply "slurp" from the Money River. Which of these two arguments has the most evidence to support it?

4. Steven Jobs, cofounder, major stockholder, and for several years chairperson of Apple Computer (he was forced to resign in 1985), is one of America's wealthiest individuals. He represents Eliot's father's argument that "it's still possible for an American to make a fortune on his own." Do success stories

of individuals like Jobs negate the force of Eliot's argument that wealth is simply inherited?

5. Donleavy and Eliot Rosewater are discussing very similar concerns about being born into the "right" families. Donleavy suggests that when someone says you are "not to the manner born," you may reply, "I was born, wasn't I?" But your opponent will reply, "But, sir, that is not enough for me." Why does Donleavy refer to such people as *opponents*? What are they opposing?

6. "Examine your background," says Donleavy, to see if there is not something that will raise your dignity. Do those who are born wealthy have to do this? If not, does this, again, support Eliot Rosewater's argument about the Money River?

7. Donleavy suggests that one rule for social climbing is to be easily amused. Can you think of a social situation where you laughed at jokes which you did not think were funny? Why did you laugh? Donleavy also suggests that we not look back. Are there friends from your high school days which, for some reason, you no longer associate with on a social level? Why is this?

8. You probably do not think of yourself as a poor person, but are the habits of the poorer members of society described by Lebowitz similar to some of your habits? Lebowitz refers to "poorer" people as contrasted with the rich. From her description, though, to what social class does she actually seem to be referring in her essay?

9. Lebowitz, too, seems to argue for sharing the wealth: "Buy the poorer person an expensive present . . . he will definitely like you enough to at least chat." Does the repeated occurrence of this theme in literature, the social sciences, and Congress suggest that there is a problem associated with the distribution of wealth in our society?

10. More than sharing the wealth, though, what does Lebowitz seem to think would break down class barriers in our society?

11. In a news article in *Fortune* magazine (August 18, 1983), Steven Jobs, then chairperson of Apple Computer, was pictured seated at a table with a cheap coffee cup, a V-neck sweater with no shirt, and barefoot. Other executives featured

in the same article had on business suits and ties and were standing outside corporate headquarters or seated in formal offices. Obviously, the founder of Apple Computer has newly earned wealth. From his casual dress style would you think Jobs would scare the old rich discussed in Royko's "Making It"? Why?

12. Royko's "Making It" originally appeared in the 1960s, a time of great civil and racial unrest in this country. His reference to "opera integration" obviously has other meanings, too. He says that Finlay Mustymoney had to be assured that "none of the newly rich ... wanted him to marry their daughters...." Are there similar restrictions on relationships between members of different social classes and different racial groups in our society?

13. Mrs. Mary Wisely, Jr., was afraid that the newly rich "would clap too much" at the opera and "embarrass their neighbors." Mrs. Wisely says that "those people have too much rhythm." Who?

14. Twenty years later, has the "opera" been successfully integrated?

15. Do socialist countries, with official policies of a classless society and equal distribution of wealth, seem to have done as well as or more poorly than the United States in redistributing income?

REFERENCES

Blau, Peter M., and Duncan, Otis D. *The American Occupational Structure.* New York: John Wiley, 1967.

Warner, W. Lloyd, and Hunt, Paul S. *The Social Life of a Modern Community.* New Haven: Yale Univ. Press, 1941.

Chapter Seven

Race and Ethnic Relations

*O*urs is a pluralistic society. It always has been. The only true Americans are those descendants of the Indians who met the *Mayflower*. There are jokes about this, of course, but the truth is that the Indians were quickly displaced (using any means necessary) by the newcomers, who in time came to see themselves as the "true" Americans. From the beginning of the country we have had severe problems trying to establish harmony among the various racial and ethnic groups which make up the population of the United States. The enslavement of millions of blacks and the murder of unknown numbers of them, the massacres of the Indians, the imprisonment of Japanese-Americans during World War II, the race riots of 1967 and other years, and the My Lai episode in Vietnam demonstrate the unpleasant truth that prejudice and discrimination toward racial and ethnic groups in our society have long been a part of our history. On the other hand, we did fight a bloody civil war to free the slaves, many ethnic groups have risen to positions of prestige and political power in the United States, and we have enacted civil rights legislation to guarantee that all minority groups have equal social and political rights. We now have black mayors of some of our largest cities, black and Hispanic-American members of Congress, and in 1984 Jesse Jackson was the first black to be a serious contender for the presidential nomination in a major political party. Miss America of 1983, and the first runner-up, were for the first time in the history of the pageant, black contestants. Ours is a paradoxical case of proclaiming that "we hold these truths to be self-evident, that all men are created equal," but we still have not reached in practice that ideal.

Race is a term which has come under increasing scholarly criticism. Biologists and anthropologists have virtually abandoned the concept as having any more than partial descriptive value. Sociologists know, however, that if people are defined as belonging to a given race—especially one that has a skin color other than white—then treatment of such individuals can take on negative overtones. Thus, it does little good to point out that some "blacks" have lighter skin than some "whites." If a person is defined as black that is sufficient in the minds of many. In Louisiana in 1982 a descendant of an eighteenth-century black slave, Susie G. Phipps, asked the courts of Louisiana to declare

134

her to be a white person. Her birth certificate identifies her as a "colored" person since she is the great-great-great-great granddaughter of a black slave and a white plantation owner. Her birth certificate had been filed by her parents who listed her as "colored". Slave owners often classified the child of a slave as the same race of the mother irrespective of the male parent's racial category. When Susie Phipps recently went to obtain a copy of her birth certificate for passport purposes, she found that she was listed as "colored."

Complicating the matter is the fact that other relatives of Susie Phipps, two aunts, state that they see themselves as colored. One stated, simply: "I was raised colored." Yet, one of the aunts who considers herself colored has two children, one son and one daughter. The son considers himself black but the daughter identifies herself as white. The issue is pending in court.

Defining who belongs to a particular *ethnic group* is a somewhat simpler matter than racial designation. An ethnic group may be thought of as "a community group based upon the ascribed status of a diffuse ancestry that is maintained by similarities of culture, language, and/or phenotype." (Burkey, 1978:12) Ethnic groups often have different life-styles, dress, and food habits, and may live in relatively well-defined community neighborhoods. Within our society we have Polish, Italian, Jewish, Hmong, and other ethnic communities.

Minority groups make up a third category which it is necessary to understand in order to discuss patterns of prejudice and discrimination in a society. Louis Wirth (1945) may have been the first sociologist to use the term *minority groups*. For Wirth minority groups were a "people who, because of their physical or cultural characteristics, are singled out from others in the society in which they live for differential and unequal treatment and who therefore regard themselves as objects of collective discrimination." It is important to note that the term *minority* does not necessarily carry with it the implication of size. Minority group members may greatly outnumber the dominant group—as in the case of blacks in the Union of South Africa. What minority groups experience is the differential and unequal treatment which Wirth referred to in his definition. Blacks, Jews, and many of the ethnic groups in our society are also minority groups.

Racial groups, ethnic groups, and minorities experience both discrimination and prejudice from members of the dominant groups in society. Simply by belonging to a particular group individuals may be discriminated against. They are often considered to be inferior to other peoples. In the above case of Susie G. Phipps, her attorney stated quite simply that "in her part of the country, colored is considered inferior." In the mid-nineteenth century, Irish immigrants were considered dirty drunkards best avoided as social companions. Later on the Irish held these same attitudes toward immigrants from Europe who had come to America after them. Such attitudes collectively become known as *stereotypes*. Thus, one drunken Irishman (in this case, usually an Irish*man*) quickly leads to the stereotype of all Irish as drunkards. One black arrested for drug dealing gives rise to the idea of "black pushers" and so on. Such stereotypes persist even in the face of data which indicates that not all members, or even a majority, of a given racial or minority group behave in a stated fashion. Fortunately, stereotypes can and do change. Today pressures brought to bear by groups who have suffered from stereotypes have not completely eliminated them, but movies and the television industry, for example, are extremely careful about picturing racial or ethnic groups with widely held stereotypes of the past.

Stereotypes result from *prejudices* which we hold. Prejudice is a prejudgment of individuals which we have prior to an encounter with the individual. If we meet a Jew and we are holding prejudicial attitudes toward Jews, we have already formed an evaluative judgment of him or her. It does not matter if the particular Jew in question is an astronaut and not in the business world at all, he or she may still be viewed as "dishonest."

Prejudice is an attitude which may lead to *discrimination*, a form of behavior. For years blacks, simply because they were black, were denied the right to vote or hold political office—irrespective of their individual qualifications. Discrimination denies any member of a group opportunities not denied to others. In this sense women constitute, numerically, the largest minority group in the country. While great strides have been made in the equalization of opportunities for women in the United States, they still suffer numerous difficulties not experienced by males.

If prejudice and discrimination are powerful enough, efforts may be made to segregate all racial, ethnic, and minority groups from more than minimal contact with the dominant group. Even following their release from slavery, blacks were still segregated from the white population by the Jim Crow laws in the South and by de facto segregation in the rest of the country. Official segregation is outlawed in the United States now, but full integration is far from complete. American Indians are no longer officially segregated, but their integration into the society lags behind that of other minority groups. Hispanic-Americans, recent arrivals from Asia such as the South Vietnamese, and the refugees from Haiti all illustrate the continuing problem of integrating minority groups into the life of the total society.

Survey data for several years now indicate that deeply ingrained prejudicial attitudes are not easy to change, but at least the public expression of prejudice is no longer socially acceptable. Few are willing to state categorically that any group should be denied the opportunity to make it in America. Those who are willing to support this position sometimes make the evening news, since it is a denial of one of our basic values. The fact that humorists can now address this issue openly represents a small but important step forward toward a fully integrated society.

The first selection, Harry Golden's "Vertical Negro Plan," was written in the late 1950s and uses a form of verbal irony. Since the Southerner does not mind *standing* by the Negro in bank lines, at the grocery store, and elsewhere, the school system could be peacefully integrated by removing the desks and requiring students to stand. The Southerner does not oppose vertical integration.

Arthur Hoppe discusses both social mobility and racial integration in "Horatio Finds Friendship." The problems of upwardly mobile successful blacks integrating white neighborhoods is often perilously close to the humorous account offered here.

In "The Pocketbook Game," Alice Childress portrays the stereotype that many whites have concerning blacks, that they steal, or "borrow," or just "take" things even when you "trust" them as your employee. If one black employee has been found guilty of theft, then of course all of them are potential thieves.

Stereotypes are difficult enough to contend with, but Childress raises an even more profound issue of *caste* in "The Health Card." In a caste system the members of the outcaste are considered to be unclean, and physical contact with such caste members is strictly forbidden. During slavery and for many years following, blacks in this country were basically considered unclean. Thus, segregated toilets and other public facilities were established. If they were employed as domestic help they would,

as Childress indicates, be required to present a health card
showing that, in essence, they were "clean."

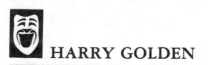

HARRY GOLDEN

The Vertical Negro Plan

Those who love North Carolina will jump at the chance to share in
the great responsibility confronting our Governor and the State
Legislature. A special session of the Legislature (July 25–28, 1956)
passed a series of amendments to the State Constitution. These
proposals submitted by the Governor and his Advisory Education
Committee included the following:

> (A) The elimination of the compulsory attendance law, "to prevent any
> child from being forced to attend a school with a child of another race."
> (B) The establishment of "Education Expense Grants" for education in
> a private school, "in the case of a child assigned to a public school
> attended by a child of another race."
> (C) A "uniform system of local option" whereby a majority of the folks
> in a school district may suspend or close a school if the situation
> becomes "intolerable."

But suppose a Negro child applies for this "Education Expense
Grant" and says he wants to go to the private school too? There are
fourteen Supreme Court decisions involving the use of public funds;
there are only two "decisions" involving the elimination of racial
discrimination in the public schools.

The Governor has said that critics of these proposals have not
offered any constructive advice or alternatives. Permit me, therefore, to offer an idea for the consideration of the members of the
regular sessions. A careful study of my plan, I believe, will show that
it will save millions of dollars in tax funds and eliminate forever the
danger to our public education system. Before I outline my plan, I
would like to give you a little background.

One of the factors involved in our tremendous industrial growth
and economic prosperity is the fact that the South, voluntarily, has

all but eliminated VERTICAL SEGREGATION. The tremendous buying power of the twelve million Negroes in the South has been based wholly on the absence of racial segregation. The white and Negro stand at the same grocery and supermarket counters; deposit money at the same bank teller's window; pay phone and light bills to the same clerk; walk through the same dime and department stores, and stand at the same drugstore counters.

It is only when the Negro "sets" that the fur begins to fly.

Now, since we are not even thinking about restoring VERTICAL SEGREGATION, I think my plan would not only comply with the Supreme Court decisions, but would maintain "sitting-down" segregation. Now here is the GOLDEN VERTICAL NEGRO PLAN. Instead of all those complicated proposals, all the next session needs to do is pass one small amendment which would provide *only* desks in all the public schools of our state—*no seats.*

The desks should be those standing-up jobs, like the old-fashioned bookkeeping desk. Since no one in the South pays the slightest attention to a VERTICAL NEGRO, this will completely solve our problem. And it is not such a terrible inconvenience for young people to stand up during their classroom studies. In fact, this may be a blessing in disguise. They are not learning to read sitting down, anyway; maybe standing up will help. This will save more millions of dollars in the cost of our remedial English course when the kids enter college. In whatever direction you look with the GOLDEN VERTICAL NEGRO PLAN, you save millions of dollars, to say nothing of eliminating forever any danger to our public education system upon which rests the destiny, hopes, and happiness of this society.

My WHITE BABY PLAN offers another possible solution to the segregation problem—this time in a field other than education.

Here is an actual case history of the "White Baby Plan To End Racial Segregation":

Some months ago there was a revival of the Laurence Olivier movie, *Hamlet*, and several Negro schoolteachers were eager to see it. One Saturday afternoon they asked some white friends to lend them two of their little children, a three-year-old girl and a six-year-old boy, and, holding these white children by the hands, they obtained tickets from the movie-house cashier without a moment's hesitation. They were in like Flynn.

This would also solve the baby-sitting problem for thousands and thousands of white working mothers. There can be a mutual exchange of references, then the people can sort of pool their children at a central point in each neighborhood, and every time a

Negro wants to go to the movies all she need do is pick up a white child—and go.

Eventually the Negro community can set up a factory and manufacture white babies made of plastic, and when they want to go to the opera or to a concert, all they need do is carry that plastic doll in their arms. The dolls, of course, should all have blond curls and blue eyes, which would go even further; it would give the Negro woman and her husband priority over the whites for the very best seats in the house.

While I still have faith in the WHITE BABY PLAN, my final proposal may prove to be the most practical of all.

Only after a successful test was I ready to announce formally the GOLDEN "OUT-OF-ORDER" PLAN.

I tried my plan in a city of North Carolina, where the Negroes represent 39 per cent of the population.

I prevailed upon the manager of a department store to shut the water off in his "white" water fountain and put up a sign, "Out-of-Order." For the first day or two the whites were hesitant, but little by little they began to drink out of the water fountain belonging to the "coloreds"—and by the end of the third week everybody was drinking the "segregated" water; with not a single solitary complaint to date.

I believe the test is of such sociological significance that the Governor should appoint a special committee of two members of the House and two Senators to investigate the GOLDEN "OUT-OF-ORDER" PLAN. We kept daily reports on the use of the unsegregated water fountain which should be of great value to this committee. This may be the answer to the necessary uplifting of the white morale. It is possible that the whites may accept desegregation if they are assured that the facilities are still "separate," albeit "Out-of-Order."

As I see it now, the key to my Plan is to keep the "Out-of-Order" sign up for at least two years. We must do this thing gradually.

ARTHUR HOPPE

Horatio Finds Friendship

Once upon a time there was a young Negro lad named Horatio Alger who, despite his humble origins, was determined to persevere.

"In this great land of ours," he would earnestly tell his school chums in the ghetto, "any poor boy can grow up to be rich, successful and respected."

"Man, you're out of your skull," his little friends would reply. "Let's go steal hubcaps."

But young Horatio persevered. He eschewed bad companions. He devoted every waking moment to reading worth-while books, doing isometric exercises and slaving diligently at honest employment. By the time he had put himself through college he was superbly conditioned, brilliantly educated and possessed of the highest moral character, marked by an indomitable will to persevere. He got a job in a bank which desperately needed to hire one Negro in order to escape prosecution under the fair employment laws. Horatio persevered. He married a lovely girl, had a lovely son, rose through incredible efforts to a vice-presidency and at last achieved his lifelong dream: a $75,000 house in the suburbs with radio-controlled garage doors and an automatic sprinkler system.

The riots lasted five days.

After the welcome died down, Horatio wiped the rotten eggs off his suit, replaced the broken windows of his new home and told his little family: "Don't worry, we have some bad neighbors and some good neighbors. But if we persevere, all the neighbors will come to treat us equally."

And this came true. The bad neighbors (53.2 percent) never smiled at the Algers. The good neighbors (46.8 percent) smiled overly profusely. But all the neighbors (100 percent) wouldn't let their daughters go dancing with Horatio's son. So while Horatio was rich and successful, he didn't feel respected somehow in White middle-class society. In fact, he felt downright lonely.

"At least," he said to himself, "I have won the respect of my own people by the splendid example I have set in becoming rich and successful." And he went back to the ghetto to enjoy it.

"Persevere, friends," Horatio told his old down-and-out school chums, "and you can all become rich and successful like me."

After he had wiped the rotten eggs off his suit (and had his head bandaged for a nasty wound caused by a flying brick), Horatio decided on the only possible course: He sold his home with the automatic sprinkler system and his two cars and his gray flannel suit, gave the money to S.N.C.C., moved back to the ghetto, went on relief and became a leading advocate of Black Power.

"You're a born troublemaker, Alger," a social worker told him after his third arrest for inciting to riot. "If you had only persevered, just think where you'd be today."

Horatio sighed. "Without a friend in the world," he said.

Moral: In this great land of ours any young Negro lad can grow up to be rich and successful. If he isn't lucky.

 ALICE CHILDRESS

"The Pocketbook Game"

Marge ... day's work is an education! Well, I mean workin' in different homes you learn much more than if you was steady in one place.... I tell you, it really keeps your mind sharp tryin' to watch for what folks will put over on you.

What? ... No, Marge, I do not want to help shell no beans, but I'd be more than glad to stay and have supper with you, and I'll wash the dishes after. Is that all right? ...

Who put anything over on who? ... Oh yes! It's like this.... I been working for Mrs. E ... one day a week for several months and I notice that she has some peculiar ways. Well, there was only one thing that really bothered me and that was her pocketbook habit.... No, not those little novels.... I mean her purse—her handbag.

Marge, she's got a big old pocketbook with two long straps on it ... and whenever I'd go there, she'd be propped up in a chair with her handbag double wrapped tight around her wrist, and from room to room she'd roam with that purse hugged to her bosom.... Yes, girl! This happens every time! No, there's *nobody* there but me and her.... Marge, I couldn't say nothin' to her! It's her purse, ain't it? She can hold onto it if she wants to!

I held my peace for months, tryin' to figure out how I'd make my point.... Well, bless Bess! *Today was the day!* ... Please, Marge, keep shellin' the beans so we can eat! I know you're listenin', but you listen with your ears, not your hands.... Well, anyway, I was almost ready to go home when she steps in the room hangin' onto her bag as usual and says, "Mildred will you ask the super to come up and fix the kitchen faucet?" "Yes, Mrs. E ...," I says, "as soon as I leave." "Oh, no," she says, "he may be gone by then. Please go now." "All right," I says, and out the door I went, still wearin' my Hoover apron.

I just went down the hall and stood there a few minutes ... and then I rushed back to the door and knocked on it as hard and frantic as I could. She flung open the door sayin', "What's the matter? Did you see the super?" ... "No," I says, gaspin' hard for breath, "I was almost downstairs when I remembered ... *I left my pocketbook!*"

With that I dashed in, grabbed my purse and then went down to get the super! Later, when I was leavin' she says real timid-like, "Mildred, I hope that you don't think I distrust you because ..." I cut her off real quick.... "That's all right, Mrs. E ..., I understand. 'Cause if I paid anybody as little as you pay me, I'd hold my pocketbook too!"

Marge, you fool ... lookout! ... You gonna drop the beans on the floor!

ALICE CHILDRESS

The Health Card

Well, Marge, I started an extra job today.... Just wait, girl. Don't laugh yet. Just wait till I tell you.... The woman seems real nice.... Well, you know what I mean.... She was pretty nice, anyway. Shows me this and shows me that, but she was real cautious about loadin' on too much work the first morning. And she stopped short when she caught the light in my eye.

Comes the afternoon, I was busy waxin' woodwork when I notice her hoverin' over me kind of timid-like. She passed me once and smiled and then she turned and blushed a little. I put down the wax can and gave her an inquirin' look. The lady takes a deep breath and comes up with, "Do you live in Harlem, Mildred?"

Now you know I expected somethin' more than that after all the hesitatin'. I had already given her my address so I didn't quite get the idea behind the question. "Yes, Mrs. Jones," I answered, "that is where I live."

Well, she backed away and retired to the living room and I could hear her and the husband just a-buzzin'. A little later on I was in the kitchen washin' glasses. I looks up and there she was in the doorway, lookin' kind of strained around the gills. First she stuttered and then she stammered and after beatin' all around the bush she comes out with, "Do you have a health card, Mildred?"

That let the cat out of the bag. I thought real fast. Honey, my brain was runnin' on wheels. "Yes, Mrs. Jones," I says, "I have a health card." Now Marge, this is a lie. I do not have a health card. "I'll bring it tomorrow," I add real sweet-like.

She beams like a chromium platter and all you could see above her taffeta house coat is smile. "Mildred," she said, "I don't mean any offense, but one must be careful, mustn't one?"

Well, all she got from me was solid agreement. "Sure, I said, "indeed *one* must, and I am glad you are so understandin', 'cause I was just worryin' and studyin' on how I was goin' to ask you for yours, and of course you'll let me see one from your husband and one for each of the three children."

By that time she was the same color as the housecoat, which is green, but I continue on: "Since I have to handle laundry and make beds, you know ..." She stops me right there and after excusin' herself she scurries from the room and has another conference with hubby.

Inside fifteen minutes she was back. "Mildred, you don't have to bring a health card. I am sure it will be all right."

I looked up real casual kind-of and said, "On second thought, you folks look real clean, too, so ..." And then she smiled and I smiled and then she smiled again.... Oh, stop laughin' so loud, Marge, everybody on this bus is starin'.

QUESTIONS FOR DISCUSSION

1. Golden's "Vertical Negro Plan" presents an accurate picture of the South in the late 1950s and early 1960s. Whites and blacks did indeed stand by each other but would not sit next to each other. Why do you think this was the case?

2. Sometimes it is difficult for the individual who has not actually experienced what a humorist is discussing to know when he or she is being factual or being facetious. Golden is correctly reporting the fact that black females could accompany white children to a theater or other public event to which they (being black) would have been denied entrance had they appeared alone. How do you explain such seemingly irrational behavior? Are all norms by which people live rational?

3. Is the "Out-of-Order" plan for drinking fountains a reference to the caste idea of unclean?

4. Some blacks, especially in the entertainment and sports world, have had successful careers and bought homes in largely white neighborhoods. Legally, a black can buy a home anywhere he or she can afford to pay the price. Is Hoppe's account of Horatio's troubles an exaggeration, or can you offer evidence of parallel happenings in the United States?

5. Is the proportion of blacks who have grown up to be rich and successful as great as, or less than, the proportion of whites? Do blacks have the same chance to "slurp" from the Money River (see Chapter 6) as whites do?

6. Horatio was "rich and successful, [but] he didn't feel respected somehow in White middle-class society." Do you think this is the case today with successful black men and women in the business profession? Would it be more true of businesspersons and professionals than of blue-collar workers? Why? Would this apply equally well to other racial and ethnic groups such as Jews, Polish-Americans, or Hispanic-Americans?

7. What does Marge's friend, Mildred, mean when she says to her employer: "... if I paid anybody as little as you pay me, I'd hold my pocketbook too!"

8. Mildred does live in Harlem. Much of Harlem is what could be defined as a slum. Is there any evidence that slum dwellers

suffer more from disease than those who live, for example, in the suburbs? Is this the basis of Mildred's employer's concern about the health card?

9. Even though blacks have been considered "unclean" by some whites, they have nevertheless long served as preparers of food in homes and commercial establishments. How do you explain this apparent anomaly?

REFERENCES

Burkey, Richard. *Ethnic and Racial Groups.* Menlo Park, Calif.: Cummings Publishing Co., 1978.

Wirth, Louis. "The Problem of Minority Groups," in *The Science of Man in the World Crisis.* Ralph Linton, ed. New York: Columbia Univ. Press, 1945.

VI

THE INSTITUTIONAL SPHERE

Chapter Eight

The Family

*T*ired clichés abound when any discussion of the family in contemporary America takes place. The family is in a "crisis"; it is undergoing dramatic change; it is no longer useful; it must be replaced by some other viable alternative. Interestingly enough, those sociologists who study the family are seldom responsible for these popular views. Most sociologists would readily agree that the family is undergoing changes—some of which are dramatic, others of which are fairly predictable and hardly worthy of the melodramatic imagery used by those who must come up with copy for widely circulated magazines. Sociological analysis suggests that the family is an enduring institution whose history is as old as any of our other stable ways of coping with the environment. The so-called "traditional" family is still with us. Taubin and Mudd succinctly summarize data to support this view:

> Census data (Glick, 1979; U.S. Bureau of the Census, 1981) document continuing conventional choices and a surprising stability in family patterns. Permanent marriage is still, for most, both the ideal and the reality. Although persons may be marrying somewhat later than in the recent past, over 95 percent of the adult population still marry at some point in their life, and more than 60 percent of all married couples remain married. Although the divorce rate has been rising steadily, the great majority of divorced men and women remarry, with the rate depending somewhat on their age at divorce.
>
> Lifelong mutual sexual fidelity has been and is still preferred (Glenn and Weaver, 1979; Yankelovich, 1981), although evidence suggests that clandestine affairs and occasional indulgence in sexual opportunities are common and apparently non-disruptive of many marriages (e.g., Bell, et. al. 1975) ... Over 90 percent of all married couples have children, although the number of children per couple has declined. Moreover, more than three-quarters of all children under 18 (excluding those who are maintaining their own households) are living at any given time in a household with two parents, at least one of whom is their natural or adoptive parent. (1983:259)

It is highly probable that some form of the family (similar to what we now have) is likely to continue into the foreseeable future.

The importance of the family for the society cannot be overly stressed and thus has generated much important sociological research. The child spends his or her early formative years in the context of the family. Many personality traits which he or she will carry into adult life are formed in the family (these may be, of course, negative as well as positive). The child's life chances are heavily influenced by the type of family in which he or she is raised. We do not know, at this time, how these life chances may be affected for those children currently being raised in families which do depart from the conventional nuclear family of husband–wife and biological offspring. The adaptability of *Homo sapiens* suggests, however, that whatever form of family a child is reared in, the influence of family life will continue to be great in the child's life.

The primacy of and interest in the family is of such magnitude that it might be supposed that sociologists could, at the least, satisfactorily define who or what constitutes a "family." Such is not the case, however. In America the "typical" family is a statistical abstraction (1.8 children?!). There are suburban middle-class families, ghetto families, ethnic families, and so on. Television portrayals of the "typical" family may be more of a caricature than a depiction of reality. "The Waltons" can still be found in America, but they hardly represent a dominant family type. Since it is necessary to have some framework within which to operate, sociologists have offered working definitions of the family. Many of these stress: (1) the importance of kinship and (2) the functions which are performed by the family. Hammond, et. al. suggest that "the family can be defined simply as the institution in which roles are related by kinship. People most often become kinsman either by blood or by marriage." (1972:213) Thus, a man and woman who marry and produce offspring provide the basis for a family. What this unit of husband–wife and children do is important, also. Zelditch proposes four functions of the family:

> (1) A family is a social group in which sexual access is permitted between adult members, (2) reproduction legitimately occurs, (3) the group is responsible to society for the care and upbringing of children, and (4) the group is an economic unit at least in consumption. (1964:681)

Zelditch's use of the term *group* is important since it is obvious that there are groups other than a husband–wife and offspring (which we commonly think of as the American family) which can perform some of the functions commonly attributed to the family. Nevertheless, people related by blood and marriage and perform-

ing the functions suggested by Zelditch are generally considered
to be a family.

The family has long been a stable diet for humorous writings.
In the selection "The First Children," Mark Twain depicts the reaction of a father to the coming of the first child. Children are
seen as strangers whose ways and habits fathers must adjust to
and try to understand.

In "Researching the Myth of Mom," Bill Vaughan has a reporter seek out a "typical" mom. The contrast between this mother and what is often portrayed on television and in magazines as
the average American mother provides a study in contrast.

The final selection by Jean Shepherd, "Wanda Hickey's Night
of Golden Memories," is a vivid portrayal of one of the few rites
of passage for American young people: the senior prom. This is
the time when the child moves, hesitantly, toward assumption of
adult status and roles. This process is quite ambiguous in our society. *When* does a boy become a man and a girl a woman? Certainly the senior prom helps to define this transition. It may be
the first time the child is away from direct parental or adult control. It may be the first time the female, especially, is away from
home all evening and through the night with parental approval.

The selection by Shepherd characterizes proms in the late
1950s (note the reference to the waiter's hair "glistening with
Vaseline Hair Oil"). But Judith Martin, a contemporary observer
of American manners and mores, reveals that anxieties about the
senior prom are still present today among young people:

> Dear Miss Manners:
>
> I am a senior in high school, and I have a few questions about
> proper etiquette.... Do you have any suggestions that would make
> either graduation or senior prom night more enjoyable?
>
> Gentle Reader:
>
> No.... just run along and have a wonderful time. (1982)

Shepherd presents a lifelike account of this wonderful night of
"golden memories."

MARK TWAIN

The First Children

Next Year

We have named it Cain. She caught it while I was up country trapping on the North Shore of the Erie; caught it in the timber a couple of miles from our dug-out—or it might have been four, she isn't certain which. It resembles us in some ways, and may be a relation. That is what she thinks, but this is an error, in my judgment. The difference in size warrants the conclusion that it is a different and new kind of animal—a fish, perhaps, though when I put it in the water to see, it sank, and she plunged in and snatched it out before there was opportunity for the experiment to determine the matter. I still think it is a fish, but she is indifferent about what it is, and will not let me have it to try. I do not understand this. The coming of the creature seems to have changed her whole nature and made her unreasonable about experiments. She thinks more of it than she does of any of the other animals, but is not able to explain why. Her mind is disordered—everything shows it. Sometimes she carries the fish in her arms half the night when it complains and wants to get to the water. At such times the water comes out of the places in her face that she looks out of, and she pats the fish on the back and makes soft sounds with her mouth to soothe it, and betrays sorrow and solicitude in a hundred ways. I have never seen her do like this with any other fish, and it troubles me greatly. She used to carry the young tigers around so, and play with them, before we lost our property; but it was only play; she never took on about them like this when their dinner disagreed with them.

Sunday

She doesn't work Sundays, but lies around all tired out, and likes to have the fish wallow over her; and she makes fool noises to amuse it, and pretends to chew its paws, and that makes it laugh. I have not seen a fish before that could laugh. This makes me doubt.... I have come to like Sunday myself. Superintending all the week tires a body so. There ought to be more Sundays. In the old days they were tough, but now they come handy.

Wednesday

It isn't a fish. I cannot quite make out what it is. It makes curious, devilish noises when not satisfied, and says "goo-goo" when it is. It is not one of us, for it doesn't walk; it is not a bird, for it doesn't fly; it is not a frog, for it doesn't hop; it is not a snake, for it doesn't crawl; I feel sure it is not a fish, though I cannot get a chance to find out whether it can swim or not. It merely lies around, and mostly on its back, with its feet up. I have not seen any other animal do that before. I said I believed it was an enigma, but she only admired the word without understanding it. In my judgment it is either an enigma or some kind of a bug. If it dies, I will take it apart and see what its arrangements are. I never had a thing perplex me so.

Three Months Later

The perplexity augments instead of diminishing. I sleep but little. It has ceased from lying around, and goes about on its four legs now. Yet it differs from the other four-legged animals in that its front legs are unusually short, consequently this causes the main part of its person to stick up uncomfortably high in the air, and this is not attractive. It is built much as we are, but its method of travelling shows that it is not of our breed. The short front legs and long hind ones indicate that it is of the kangaroo family, but it is a marked variation of the species, since the true kangaroo hops, whereas this one never does. Still, it is a curious and interesting variety, and has not been catalogued before. As I discovered it, I have felt justified in securing the credit of the discovery by attaching my name to it, and hence have called it *Kangaroorum Adamiensis* . . . . It must have been a young one when it came, for it has grown exceedingly since. It must be five times as big, now, as it was then, and when discontented is able to make from twenty-two to thirty-eight times the noise it made at first. Coercion does not modify this, but has the contrary effect. For this reason I discontinued the system. She reconciles it by persuasion, and by giving it things which she had previously told it she wouldn't give it. As already observed, I was not at home when it first came, and she told me she found it in the woods. It seems odd that it should be the only one, yet it must be so, for I have worn myself out these many weeks trying to find another one to add to my collection, and for this one to play with; for surely then it would be quieter, and we could tame it more easily. But I find none, nor any vestige of any; and strangest of all, no tracks. It has to live on the ground, it cannot help itself; therefore, how does it get about without leaving a track? I have set a dozen traps, but they do no good. I catch all small animals except that one; animals that merely go into the trap out of curiosity, I think, to see what the milk is there for. They never drink it.

Three Months Later

The kangaroo still continues to grow, which is very strange and perplexing. I never knew one to be so long getting its growth. It has fur on its head now; not like kangaroo fur, but exactly like our hair, except that it is much finer and softer, and instead of being black is red. I am like to lose my mind over the capricious and harassing developments of this unclassifiable zoological freak. If I could catch another one—but that is hopeless; it is a new variety, and the only sample; this is plain. But I caught a true kangaroo and brought it in, thinking that this one, being lonesome, would rather have that for company than have no kin at all, or any animal it could feel a nearness to or get sympathy from in its forlorn condition here among strangers who do not know its ways or habits, or what to do to make it feel that it is among friends; but it was a mistake—it went into such fits at the sight of the kangaroo that I was convinced it had never seen one before. I pity the poor noisy little animal, but there is nothing I can do to make it happy. If I could tame it—but that is out of the question; the more I try, the worse I seem to make it. It grieves me to the heart to see it in its little storms of sorrow and passion. I wanted to let it go, but she wouldn't hear of it. That seemed cruel and not like her; and yet she may be right. It might be lonelier than ever; for since I cannot find another one, how could *it*?

Five Months Later

It is not a kangaroo. No, for it supports itself by holding to her finger, and thus goes a few steps on its hind legs, and then falls down. It is probably some kind of a bear; and yet it has no tail—as yet—and no fur, except on its head. It still keeps on growing—that is a curious circumstance, for bears get their growth earlier than this. Bears are dangerous—since our catastrophe—and I shall not be satisfied to have this one prowling about the place much longer without a muzzle on. I have offered to get her a kangaroo if she would let this one go, but it did no good—she is determined to run us into all sorts of foolish risks, I think. She was not like this before she lost her mind.

A Fortnight Later

I examined its mouth. There is no danger yet; it has only one tooth. It has no tail yet. It makes more noise now than it ever did before—and mainly at night. I have moved out. But I shall go over, mornings, to breakfast, and to see if it has more teeth. If it gets a mouthful of teeth, it will be time for it to go, tail or no tail, for a bear does not need a tail in order to be dangerous.

Four Months Later

I have been off hunting and fishing a month, up in the region that she calls Buffalo; I don't know why, unless it is because there are not any buffaloes there. Meantime the bear has learned to paddle around all by itself on its hind legs, and says "poppa" and "momma." It is certainly a new species. This resemblance to words may be purely accidental, of course, and may have no purpose or meaning; but even in that case it is still extraordinary, and is a thing which no other bear can do. This imitation of speech, taken together with general absence of fur and entire absence of tail, sufficiently indicates that this is a new kind of bear. The further study of it will be exceedingly interesting. Meantime I will go off on a far expedition among the forests of the North and make an exhaustive search. There must certainly be another one somewhere, and this one will be less dangerous when it has company of its own species. I will go straightway; but I will muzzle this one first.

Three Months Later

It has been a weary, weary hunt, yet I have had no success. In the mean time, without stirring from the home estate, she has caught another one! I never saw such luck. I might have hunted these woods a hundred years, I never should have run across that thing.

Next Day

I have been comparing the new one with the old one, and it is perfectly plain that they are the same breed. I was going to stuff one of them for my collection, but she is prejudiced against it for some reason or other; so I have relinquished the idea, though I think it is a mistake. It would be an irreparable loss to science if they should get away. The old one is tamer than it was, and can laugh and talk like the parrot, having learned this, no doubt, from being with the parrot so much, and having the imitative faculty in a highly developed degree. I shall be astonished if it turns out to be a new kind of parrot; and yet I ought not to be astonished, for it has already been everything else it could think of, since those first days when it was a fish. The new one is as ugly now as the old one was at first; has the same sulphur-and-raw-meat complexion and the same singular head without any fur on it. She calls it Abel.

Ten Years Later

They are boys; we found it out long ago. It was their coming in that small, immature shape that puzzled us; we were not used to it. There are some girls now. Abel is a good boy, but if Cain had stayed a bear it would have improved him. After all these years, I see that I was mistaken about Eve in the beginning; it is better to live outside the Garden with her than inside it without her. At first I thought she talked too much; but now I should be sorry to have that voice fall silent and pass out of my life. Blessed be the chestnut that brought us near together and taught me to know the goodness of her heart and the sweetness of her spirit!

 BILL VAUGHAN

Researching the Myth of Mom . . .

Q—You are a mother?

A—Boy, you polltakers are getting smarter all the time. You wade up to the door through twenty feet of tricycles, scooters, buggies, and roller skates; there's a clothesline full of tiny garments right in plain view; I'm holding what any fairly perceptive human being could identify as a baby; and you ask me if I'm a mother.

Q—Are you a typical mother?

A—You want a fat lip, mister? You want to talk to a typical mother, go see the duchess next door. She's the typical mother. One kid and a full-time maid.

Q—This makes her typical?

A—Well, it makes her look like the typical mother that I see in the ads, who's always showing her husband how clean she got the kid's clothes with some soap chip or other. Those things kill me. Here you see this gal who's obviously spent the day in the beauty parlor. Which is O.K. I'm not knocking it. I wish I had the time. Anyway, she gets all fixed up for her old man and he comes home, maybe after a hard day at the wherever, and would like to have a cold beer and listen to the ball game. She drags out little Leroy's shirt.

"See, Harold," she says, "how fresh, clean, and sweet-smelling little Leroy's shirt is."

In the ads the husband says, "My, what a clever little manager lucky me married."

In real life what would he say—or, anyway, what would my old man say? "I didn't come home to smell no laundry. How come there's only one cold beer?"

These typical mothers really do me in.

"Dr. Tuckerman," they say to the dentist, "I am concerned about Lily Belle. She will not brush her teeth up and down."

She goes to the dentist to tell him this. It's a wonder she didn't call him at two a.m. and get sore because he doesn't make night calls.

Another thing they do is when the dog comes in with its muddy paws and jumps in the clean laundry. They smile and shake their heads and say, "Bad Doggy."

If that flea-bearing free loader of ours ever pulled that trick it would be the sorriest day of his mangy life.

Q—Could you make your answers a little briefer? The blanks on this form are really quite small.

A—So shove off—who asked you in anyway?

Q—No, no. It's quite all right. I just have a few more questions. What do you think of Mother's Day?

A—I think it's great. I sent my mother a wire.

Q—Splendid; what was the sentiment?

A—*"Come quick; I'm going nuts."*

Q—Will she come?

A—Sure. She's my mom.

Q—You do approve of motherhood, then?

A—I gave up Hollywood for it, didn't I?

Q—Hollywood?

A—Hollywood, North Dakota. It's one of my husband's little jokes.

Q—In the papers the other day there was a story about a mother who saved her child from injury by singlehandedly lifting a station wagon under which the little rascal was pinned. Do you think you could do the same for one of yours?

A—I'd have to. The mister has a slipped disk.

Q—Yes. Now as a mother do you love your children? Do you tenderly nurture them, look out for their wants, guide them on the right path, warm them with your maternal affection?

A—Yeah. Sure. What else can you do with kids?

Q—You feel, don't you, that Mother's Day should be observed the year around?

A—You mean that I should get five handkerchiefs and a hand-woven pot holder every day all year?

Q—Not necessarily. I mean that mothers should be appreciated the year around. Don't you think so?

A—Mister, I'm appreciated about all I can stand as it is. From five a.m. until nearly midnight, it's "Maw, I'd appreciate it if you'd iron my dress" or "Maw, I'd appreciate it if you'd hit us a few fungoes." Just one day without any appreciation, that's what I need.

Q—You know what I think?

A—No, and I don't much care.

Q—I think you're a typical mother.

A—Get out of here before I find something heavier than this baby to hit you with.

 JEAN SHEPHERD

Wanda Hickey's Night of Golden Memories

An aura of undefined sin was always connected with the name Red Rooster. Sly winks, nudgings, and adolescent cacklings about what purportedly went on at the Rooster made it the "in" spot for such a momentous revel. Its waiters were rumored really to be secret henchmen of the Mafia. But the only thing we knew for sure about the Rooster was that anybody on the far side of seven years old could procure any known drink without question.

The decor ran heavily to red-checkered-oilcloth table covers and plastic violets, and the musical background was provided by a legendary jukebox that stood a full seven feet high, featuring red and blue cascading waterfalls that gushed endlessly through its voluptuous façade. In full 200-watt operation, it could be *felt*, if not clearly heard, as far north as Gary and as far south as Kankakee. A triumph of American aesthetics.

Surging with anticipation, I guided Wanda through the uproarious throng of my peers. Schwartz and Clara Mae trailed behind, exchanging ribald remarks with the gang.

We occupied the only remaining table. Immediately, a beady-eyed waiter, hair glistening with Vaseline Hair Oil, sidled over and hovered like a vulture. Quickly distributing the famous Red Rooster Ala Carte Deluxe Menu, he stood back, smirking, and waited for us to impress our dates.

"Can I bring you anything to drink, gentlemen?" he said, heavily accenting the "gentlemen."

My first impulse was to order my favorite drink of the period, a bottled chocolate concoction called Kayo, the Wonder Drink; but remembering that better things were expected of me on prom night, I said, in my deepest voice, "Uh ... make mine ... bourbon."

Schwartz grunted in admiration. Wanda ogled me with great, swimming, lovesick eyes. Bourbon was the only drink that I had actually heard of. My old man ordered it often down at the Bluebird Tavern. I had always wondered what it tasted like. I was soon to find out.

"How will you have it, sir?"

"Well, in a glass, I guess." I had failed to grasp the subtlety of his question, but the waiter snorted in appreciation of my humorous sally.

"Rocks?" he continued.

Rocks? I had heard about getting your rocks, but never in a restaurant. Oh, well, what the hell.

"Sure," I said. "Why not?"

All around me, the merrymaking throng was swinging into high gear. Carried away by it all, I added a phrase I had heard my old man use often: "And make it a triple." I had some vague idea that this was a brand or something.

"A *triple?* Yes, sir." His eyes snapped wide—in respect, I gathered. He knew he was in the presence of a serious drinker.

The waiter turned his gaze in Schwartz' direction. "And you, sir?"

"Make it the same." Schwartz had never been a leader.

The die was cast. Pink ladies, at the waiter's suggestion, were ordered for the girls, and we then proceeded to scan the immense menu with feigned disinterest. When the waiter returned with our drinks, I ordered—for reasons that even today I am unable to explain—lamb chops, yellow turnips, mashed potatoes and gravy, a side dish of the famous Red Rooster Roquefort Italian Cole Slaw—and a strawberry shortcake. The others wisely decided to stick with their drinks.

Munching bread sticks, Wanda, Schwartz, Clara, and I engaged in sophisticated postprom repartee. Moment by moment, I felt my strength and maturity, my dashing bonhomie, my clean-cut handsomeness enveloping my friends in its benevolent warmth. Schwartz, too, seemed to scintillate as never before. Clara giggled and Wanda sighed, overcome by the romance of it all. Even when Flick, sitting three tables away, clipped Schwartz behind the left ear with a poppyseed roll, our urbanity remained unruffled.

Before me reposed a sparkling tumbler of beautiful amber liquid, ice cubes bobbing merrily on its surface, a plastic swizzle stick sporting an enormous red rooster sticking out at a jaunty angle. Schwartz was similarly equipped. And the fluffy pink ladies looked lovely in the reflected light of the pulsating jukebox.

I had seen my old man deal with just this sort of situation. Raising my beaded glass, I looked around at my companions and said suavely, "Well, here's mud in yer eye." Clara giggled; Wanda sighed dreamily, now totally in love with this man of the world who sat across from her on this, our finest night.

"Yep," Schwartz parried wittily, hoisting his glass high and slopping a little bourbon on his pants as he did so.

Swiftly, I brought the bourbon to my lips, intending to down it in a single devil-may-care draught, the way Gary Cooper used to do in the Silver Dollar Saloon. I did, and Schwartz followed suit. Down it went—a screaming 90-proof rocket searing savagely down my gullet. For an instant, I sat stunned, unable to comprehend what had happened. Eyes watering copiously, I had a brief urge to sneeze, but my throat seemed to be paralyzed. Wanda and Clara Mae swam before my misted vision; and Schwartz seemed to have disappeared under the table. He popped up again—face beet-red, eyes bugging, jaw slack, tongue lolling.

"Isn't this romantic? Isn't this the most wonderful night in all our lives? I will forever treasure the memories of this wonderful night." From far off, echoing as from some subterranean tunnel, I heard Wanda speaking.

Deep down in the pit of my stomach, I felt crackling flames licking at my innards. I struggled to reply, to maintain my élan, my fabled *savoir-faire*. "Urk ... urk ... yeah," I finally managed with superhuman effort.

Wanda swam hazily into focus. She was gazing across the table at me with adoring eyes.

"Another, gents?" The waiter was back, still smirking.

Schwartz nodded dumbly. I just sat there, afraid to move. An instant later, two more triple bourbons materialized in front of us.

Clara raised her pink lady high and said reverently, "Let's drink to the happiest night of our lives."

There was no turning back. Another screamer rocketed down the hatch. For an instant, it seemed as though this one wasn't going to be as lethal as the first, but the room suddenly tilted sideways. I felt torrents of cold sweat pouring from my forehead. Clinging to the edge of the table, I watched as Schwartz gagged across from me. Flick, I noticed, had just chugalugged his third rum-and-Coke and was eating a cheeseburger with the works.

The conflagration deep inside me was now clearly out of control. My feet were smoking; my diaphragm heaved convulsively, jiggling my cummerbund; and Schwartz began to shrink, his face alternating between purple-red and chalk-white, his eyes black holes staring fixedly at the ketchup bottle. He sat stock-still. Wanda, meanwhile, cooed on ecstatically—but I was beyond understanding what she was saying. Faster and faster, in ever-widening circles, the room, the jukebox, the crowd swirled dizzily about me. In all the excitement of preparations for the prom, I realized that I hadn't eaten a single thing all day.

Out of the maelstrom, a plate mysteriously appeared before me; paper-pantied lamb chops hissing in bubbling grease, piled yellow turnips, gray mashed potatoes awash in rich brown gravy. Maybe this would help, I thought incoherently. Grasping my knife and fork as firmly as I could, I poised to whack off a piece of meat. Suddenly, the landscape listed forty-five degrees to starboard and the chop I was about to attack skidded off my plate—plowing a swath through the mashed potatoes—and right into the aisle.

Pretending not to notice, I addressed myself to the remaining chop, which slid around, eluding my grasp, until I managed to skewer it with my fork. Hacking off a chunk, I jammed it fiercely mouthward, missing my target completely. Still impaled on my fork, the chop slithered over my cheekbone, spraying gravy as it went, all over my white lapels. On the next try, I had better luck, and finally I managed to get the whole chop down.

To my surprise, I didn't feel any better. Maybe the turnips will help, I thought. Lowering my head to within an inch of the plate to prevent embarrassing mishaps, I shoveled them in—but the flames within only fanned higher and higher. I tried the potatoes and gravy. My legs began to turn cold. I wolfed down the Red Rooster Roquefort Italian Cole Slaw. My stomach began to rise like a helium balloon, bobbing slowly up the alimentary canal.

My nose low over the heaping dish of strawberry shortcake, piled high with whipped cream and running with juice, I knew at last for a dead certainty what I had to do before it happened right here in front of everybody. I struggled to my feet. A strange rubbery numbness had struck my extremities. I tottered from chair to chair, grasping for the wall. There was a buzzing in my ears.

Twenty seconds later, I was on my knees, gripping the bowl of the john like a life preserver in pitching seas. Schwartz, imitating me as usual, lay almost prostrate on the tiles beside me, his body racked with heaving sobs. Lamb chops, bourbon, turnips, mashed potatoes, cole slaw—all of it came rushing out of me in a great roaring torrent—out of my mouth, my nose, my ears, my very soul. Then Schwartz opened up, and we took turns retching and shuddering. A head thrust itself between us directly into the pot. It was Flick moaning wretchedly. Up came the cheeseburger, the rum-and-Cokes, pretzels, potato chips, punch, gumdrops, a corned-beef sandwich, a fingernail or two—everything he'd eaten for the last week. For long minutes, the three of us lay there limp and quivering, smelling to high heaven, too weak to get up. It was the absolute high point of the junior prom; the rest was anticlimax.

Finally, we returned to the table, ashen-faced and shaking. Schwartz, his coat stained and rumpled, sat Zombie-like across from me. The girls didn't say much. Pink ladies just aren't straight bourbon.

But our little group played the scene out bravely to the end. My dinner jacket was now even more redolent and disreputable than when I'd first seen it on the hanger at Al's. And my bow tie, which had hung for a while by one clip, had somehow disappeared completely, perhaps flushed into eternity with all the rest. But as time wore on, my hearing and eyesight began slowly to return; my legs began to lose their rubberiness and the room slowly resumed its even keel—at least even enough to consider getting up and leaving. The waiter seemed to know. He returned as if on cue, bearing a slip of paper.

"The damages, gentlemen."

Taking the old man's twenty dollars out of my wallet, I handed it to him with as much of a flourish as I could muster. There wouldn't have been any point in looking over the check; I wouldn't have been able to read it, anyway. In one last attempt to recoup my cosmopolitan image, I said offhandedly, "Keep the change." Wanda beamed in unconcealed ecstasy.

The drive home in the damp car was not quite the same as the one that had begun the evening so many weeks earlier. Our rapidly fermenting coats made the enclosed air rich and gamy, and Schwartz, who had stopped belching, sat with head pulled low between his shoulder blades, staring straight ahead. Only the girls preserved the joyousness of the occasion. Women always survive.

In a daze, I dropped off Schwartz and Clara Mae and drove in silence toward Wanda's home, the faint light of dawn beginning to show in the east.

We stood on her porch for the last ritual encounter. A chill dawn wind rustled the lilac bushes.

"This was the most wonderful, wonderful night of my whole life. I always dreamed the prom would be like this," breathed Wanda, gazing passionately up into my watering eyes.

"Me, too," was all I could manage.

I knew what was expected of me now. Her eyes closed dreamily. Swaying slightly, I leaned forward—and the faint odor of sauerkraut from her parted lips coiled slowly up to my nostrils. This was not in the script. I knew I had better get off that porch fast, or else. Backpedaling desperately and down the stairs, I blurted, "Bye!" and—fighting down my rising gorge—clamped my mouth tight, leaped into the Ford, burned rubber, and tore off into the dawn. Two blocks away, I squealed to a stop alongside a vacant lot containing only a huge Sherwin-Williams paint sign. WE COVER THE WORLD, it aptly read. In the blessed darkness behind the sign, concealed from prying eyes, I completed the final rite of the ceremony.

The sun was just rising as I swung the car up the driveway and eased myself quietly into the kitchen. The old man, who was going fishing that morning, sat at the enamel table sipping black coffee. He looked up as I came in. I was in no mood for idle chatter.

"You look like you had a hell of a prom," was all he said.

"I sure did."

The yellow kitchen light glared harshly on my muddy pants, my maroon-streaked, vomit-stained white coat, my cracked fingernail, my greasy shirt.

"You want anything to eat?" he asked sardonically.

At the word "eat," my stomach heaved convulsively. I shook my head numbly.

"That's what I thought," he said. "Get some sleep. You'll feel better in a couple of days, when your head stops banging."

He went back to reading his paper. I staggered into my bedroom, dropping bits of clothing as I went. My soggy Hollywood paisley cummerbund, the veteran of another gala night, was flung beneath my dresser as I toppled into bed. My brother muttered in his sleep across the room. He was still a kid. But his time would come.

Excerpts from WANDA HICKEY'S NIGHT OF GOLDEN MEMORIES & OTHER DISASTERS by Jean Shepherd. Copyright (c) 1969 by HMH Publishing, Inc. Reprinted by permission of Doubleday & Co., Inc.

QUESTIONS FOR DISCUSSION

1. Sociologists have long recognized that dyadic relationships (between two persons) can be dramatically altered by the addition of a third party. It becomes possible, for example, for two members of the triad to form a coalition against the third member. Does the arrival of a first child offer such possibilities in a family? In a subtle fashion, is this being hinted at in "The First Child"?

2. Adam sees the first child as a stranger—"it is not one of us, for it doesn't walk." Are children strangers to their parents? Adam says, "I never had a thing perplex me so...." Is this a likely statement by most young parents regarding their first child?

3. The "thing" says Adam, has "the imitative faculty in a highly developed degree." What theory of socialization is being referred to here?

4. What is the difference between the disciplinary efforts by Adam and Eve—"she reconciles it by persuasion...." Do such differences exist among contemporary fathers and mothers regarding disciplining of children?

5. The response to the first child by Adam and Eve is quite different. Adam is perplexed; Eve seems to understand from the outset. Does this suggest that motherhood is "natural" and fathers are more often than not "strangers" who must get to know their children?

6. Is the mother being interviewed in "The Myth of Mom" offering a correct assessment of most husbands when she says that he would bellow, "I didn't come home to smell no laundry. How come there's only one cold beer?" If so, why do TV ads picture husbands (and wives) so differently from reality?

7. Are the mothers portrayed on TV and in magazines more or less "typical" than the mother *you* were reared by? Is there any such thing as a "typical" mother? (Before you quickly say "no," how many suburban mothers do you think would recognize themselves in Vaughan's piece?)

8. The interviewer asks: "Now as a mother do you love your children? Do you tenderly nurture them, look out for their wants, guide them on the right path, warm them with your maternal affection?" Is there an assumption here that mothers—more than anyone else (including fathers)—do provide such care for their offspring? Is this related to Twain's description of the father as largely perplexed by children?

9. Senior proms are still a part of family and school concerns. Is this a rite of passage for American young people? Note the reference to adult behavior: "I had seen my old man deal with just this sort of situation"; "Bourbon was the only drink that I had actually heard of. My old man ordered it often ..."; "I added a phrase I had heard my old man use often...." Is this one manner in which the young assume adult status?

10. Why do societies prohibit behavior for the young which is approved for adults? Is the senior prom an effective means of

introducing the young to adult behavior patterns? How else could this be done?

REFERENCES

Bell, R. R., Turner, S., and Rosen, L. "A multi-variate analysis of female extra-marital coitus." *Journal of Marriage and the Family* 37 (1975), 375–84.

Glenn, N. D., and Weaver, C. N. "Attitude toward premarital, extra-marital, and homosexual relations in the U.S. in the 1970's." *Journal of Sex Research* 15 (1979), 108–18.

Glick, P. C. "Future American Families." *The Washington COFO Memo* 2, Summer/Fall (1979), 2–5.

Hammond, Philip, et. al. *The Structure of Human Society.* Lexington, Mass.: D. C. Heath, 1975.

Martin, Judith. *Miss Manners' Guide to Excruciatingly Correct Behavior.* New York: Warner Books, 1982.

Taubin, S. B., and Mudd, E. H. "Contemporary Traditional Families: The Undefined Majority," in *Contemporary Families and Alternative Life Styles.* E. D. Macklin and R. H. Rubin, eds. Beverly Hills, Calif.: Sage Publications, 1983.

U.S. Bureau of the Census. "Marital Status and Living Arrangement: March, 1980." *Current Population Reports*, Series P–20, No. 365. Washington, D.C.: Government Printing Office, 1981.

Yankelovich, D. "New Rules in American Life: Searching for Self-Fulfillment in a World Turned Upside Down." *Psychology Today* 15.4 (1981), 35–91.

Zelditch, Morris. "Family, Marriage, and Kinship," in *Handbook of Modern Sociology.* Robert E. L. Faris, ed. Skokie, Ill.: Rand McNally, 1964.

Chapter Nine

Courtship and Marriage

.

READINGS

M arriage is still an important life goal for most young people in our society. Even though both males and females are marrying at a later age and the number never married has increased over the past two decades, young people still plan to and eventually do marry.

Marriage in our society (but not in all) is preceded by a period of courtship which may be a few days, weeks, months, or in some cases, years. Courtship behaviors have always been a matter of serious importance to a society. How young people meet, date, and engage in premarital (not necessarily sexual) activities has always been, to some degree, controlled by the norms of society. Up until the Second World War, dating in our society was a carefully regulated activity. Parents of teenage females, especially, wanted to know who the young man was, where the couple was going, what time they intended to be home (often telling them what time they *had* to be home), and so on.

Today there are fewer restrictions on dating relationships between young men and women. Dating begins at a very early age (around 14 years). In the beginning parents have some control over dating activities simply because the couple must be taken where they are going and later picked up and returned to their respective homes. As soon as the teenagers are able to drive, however, new norms come into play. How and by whom these new norms are determined is a point of genuine concern for most parents. Bowman and Spanier state that "survivors of a previous era cannot be expected to set the standard for our current one." (1978:73) They point out that new standards have evolved around three major areas: (1) more freedom, especially for the female; (2) less formal activities; and (3) more group activities.

Few young people of this generation need to have pointed out to them that today's female can do things her mother never would have entertained in her wildest dreams. Young couples, unchaperoned, spend weekends at the beach, go backpacking, or engage in virtually any activities they so desire. Formality is often eschewed by young couples. Jogging may be an occasion for a date—and decided upon 30 minutes ahead of time rather than a week or two in advance. Dating is no longer primarily a young man and young woman going to a movie or some other solo activity. Many dates involve group activities; many such informal

170

gatherings on college campuses form the basis of meeting and dating. All these are new norms which guide, and put an enormous responsibility on, young people who participate in courtship today.

Even though there is more freedom of choice by young people regarding dating activities, it should not be assumed that parental influence is totally lacking. Leslie, et. al. (1986), building on the work of Bates (1942) and others, sought to determine what influence, if any, parental reaction to dating relationships had on the dating partners' relationships. Using 159 college sophomores and juniors (who might be assumed to be free from parental influence in such matters), the authors also investigated whether or not young adult children tried to influence parents about their dating relationships. They did. While parental influence is primarily indirect, the authors argue that parents are still trying to provide a "proper" environment for their offspring to develop dating/mating relationships—this is "still quite in vogue in the 1980's." The study suggests that while freedom is indeed more available to today's young adults, parental approval and concern is, to some degree, present.

If sufficient interest develops between a couple they may eventually form a cohabiting relationship. While this is not a new norm—it has always existed—certainly the prevalence of it and the openness with which it is done represents a dramatic change from earlier eras. Its practice on college campuses would lead to the conclusion that "everyone" does this. Such is not the case, of course, but nearly two million couples (1984) living together in a nonmarital union represents a significant change in behavior in our society's norms. Macklin summarizes this change succinctly:

> The years 1966–1975 appear to have been watershed years in U.S. culture with regard to sexual values and associated life styles. Prior to this time, only the most avant-garde or the most impoverished, or those otherwise considered to be on the social periphery of society, were to be found openly cohabiting outside of marriage, and unmarried persons known to be living together could expect to be referred to derogatorily as "shacking up." (1983:52)

Of course, not all behavior is approved even when practiced. Yet, approval of cohabitation is found not only among college students but among the general population as well. Yankelovich (1981) and associates conducted a survey for *Time* magazine and reported that 52% of the respondents did not believe cohabitation to be morally wrong for unmarried couples.

Most courtship among couples does not lead to cohabitation outside marriage but rather to cohabitation within marriage. Marriage is still the norm. The wedding ceremony, even the traditional June wedding, is still a part of the normative structure of today. Magazines devoted to weddings, such as *Bride's* and *Modern Bride*, and advertisements in other magazines are sufficient evidence that the traditional wedding is far from vanquished. Some young people wish to write their own marriage vows now, and great latitude is permitted in most Protestant churches in the United States. Nevertheless, a majority of all marriage ceremonies are still performed by a member of the clergy of some faith, and most of these ceremonies remain fairly traditional.

The various departures from traditional marriages—open marriages, group marriages, trial marriages, "swinging" singles, homosexual unions (still to be recognized as legal marriages), or group sex and other "orgies"—are a part of contemporary society and provide very real choices for some people. However, at least one sociologist has tried to put all this in perspective:

> As some sober fact finders have asserted, there may be much more talk than action. . . . People have been heard to complain that though wild orgies seem to be occurring on every block, they never seem to be invited to them, so that once again there may be more rhetoric than consummation. Nevertheless, most readers of this book can observe that action moves steadily in conformity with rhetoric. . . .
>
> On the other hand, at the risk of seeming to be both conservative and pessimistic, it must be said that for most people these options are more illusionary than real. . . . Few of us are so secure inwardly that we can live comfortably from day to day in relationships where the other person feels no obligation to continue giving us support or affection beyond the whim of the moment. For that matter, few of us are so attractive, or attractive over many years, that we can be sure there *will* be another partner who will become available when we need him or her. (Goode, 1977:393–94)

The first humorous selection in this chapter examines the propriety of dating behavior. In "Propriety," Miss Manners seeks to instruct a "sexually free" young woman who started dating at 14. The young woman acknowledges that she doesn't know the "proper" way to act on a date. Like most young people, she fears rejection if she does not know the proper dating behavior. Miss Manners seeks to educate her.

The second selection, "Living Together," struggles with what is both a humorous and serious matter: what do young couples who live with each other, but are not married, call each other? The U.S. Census has had to come up with a term. In good bureaucratic style it has, for the moment, hit on POSSLQ—Persons of Opposite Sex Sharing Living Quarters. Miss Manners thinks a possible winner is: "Uhmmer." As in, "This is my daughter's uhm ... uhm ... uhm."

Stephanie Brush asks the question, "So Why Invest in a Man at All?" In this day in which there are increasing numbers of females classified as never married (17% of all females 18 and over in 1980), it is a question which is, for some, being answered with "no reason." Brush disagrees, and she offers what she feels are still abiding reasons for having a man around—all the time.

The final selection is by Garrison Keillor. "Your Wedding and You" examines the nontraditional weddings which occur among young people. The June bride may still be with us, but Keillor presents "case studies" of those who reject the stereotypes and want their weddings "to express that unique personalness, the *beingness*, that each of us, and only us, can bring to our marriage."

JUDITH MARTIN

Propriety

DEAR MISS MANNERS:

I'm sure you're aware of the confusion of "male-female" roles in courtship these days. I, for one, am particularly confused. You see, I was rather a, uh, sexually free young lady, starting at fourteen.

The problem is that I don't know the "proper" way to act on a date because I have never before attempted to be "proper." What does one say? Can one get personal? Do you kiss and hug on the first date? How soon is it OK to ask a man over for dinner? Obviously, I don't know the etiquette and I am so tired of those shallow, quickly ended relationships. Actually, I'm a bit frightened of men—will this one and the next reject me, too? I have been told that I "try too hard" and "fall too fast," so I'm trying to restrain myself.

GENTLE READER:

Welcome to the world of propriety. We have more fun here than you may have been led to believe, just as the world of promiscuity, as you have discovered, offers less fun than you may have been led to believe. Like fast food, it tends to be of poor quality and may leave you with worse problems than the hunger it was intended to quell. So stop gobbling and learn to prepare something decent. It takes time and effort, but the preparation can be fun in itself and the results will be better.

No getting personal. No hugging and kissing. No come-over-to-my-place. Your feelings of fright are the correct ones, not your ones of c'mere, honey. In the proper world, romance is supposed to develop out of friendship. A gentleman and a lady both pretend that they are cultivating each other for common interests, shared humor, or whatever—and then they both act surprised when passion strikes them like lightning. This shock is considered exciting by proper ladies and gentlemen, who regard instant matings, based on the idea that we all have standard parts that may be fitted together interchangeably, to be dull as well as distasteful. You will find that rejection by a friend who does not become a lover is less painful than rejection by a lover who does not want to go on to become a friend.

Now, are you willing to try? Can you act friendly to a man while being reserved enough to discourage either emotional or physical intimacies? Can you treat him as a pleasant enhancement to your life, and not the answer to your prayers? Miss Manners doesn't want to upset you by too quick a transition. But can you hold out until the second date?

 JUDITH MARTIN

Living Together

It has come to Miss Manners' attention that not all ladies and gentlemen who live together in pairs are husband and wife, or even brother and sister. While Miss Manners would never dream of inquiring into anyone's living arrangements, she is always pleased to hear of increased sociability in the world.

However, it seems that these people have a problem. They don't know what to call each other. The terms "husband" and "wife" are not accurate; nor are "fiancé" and "fiancée," which lead to questions these people do not wish to entertain. "The person I live with" is not only unwieldy, but it ends in a proposition, where these arrangements tend to start.

Miss Manners has long endeavored to avoid this problem by inquiring querulously why people need to declare their sexual affiliations at all. Why can't they simply introduce one another by their names?

However, she has finally conceded that a term is needed for couples who reject legal sanction for their union but demand social sanction.

She must set down certain rules for this search. The word must be simple, sensible and dignified, appropriate for public, daytime usage. It must not describe graphically the private purpose of the liaison, which is none of society's business. But it should not be so conventional as to be easily confused with other existing relationships, thus casting an implication of sexuality onto them.

Allow Miss Manners to illustrate these principles by explaining her objections to the terms that she has heard proposed.

"Paramour," "lover," "the person I share my life with," "significant other," "meaningful associate": These are too vivid. If you imagine a long-married person introducing his or her spouse to you as "my lover," you will understand, as your gorge rises, Miss Manners' distaste. Such terms are also bound to be at least occasionally inaccurate during the normal ups and downs of life. Miss Manners once heard the term "my fondest friend" proposed to a lady in need of a term for the gentleman with whom she lived, and the lady replied, "But actually, I can think of people I'm fonder of."

"Mistress": This suggests some financial arrangement favoring the lady, and what, pray, is the corresponding term for the gentleman involved?

"Roommate," "housemate," "live-in friend": These are infringements on the meaning of a different relationship. A roommate is a person who tells one's parents that one is asleep when one is actually keeping scandalous hours, and who leaves hairs in the sink.

"Companion," "partner": Similarly, these carry confusing connotations. A companion is an impoverished but genteel person who has taken a situation traveling with someone elderly, rich, and cranky in the hope of increasing that person's friction with his or her legitimate heirs and thus figuring prominently in the will. Miss Manners used to favor the term partner, on the grounds that it represented "marriage partner" without the marriage, but has become convinced that it is the proper property of cigar-smoking gentlemen who suspect each other of cheating on the books, and of those who come from a part of the country where they pronounce "How do you do?" as "Howdy."

"Consort," "co-vivant," "comrade": Each of these conjures an irrelevant image in Miss Manners' mind. Consort suggests Prince Philip permanently assigned to walking three paces behind his wife. Co-vivant sounds like someone who will cook only with expensive copper pots. Comrade, etymologically impeccable, as one Gentle Reader pointed out, because it derives from the Latin *camera* for "chamber," has come to be associated with people who think it their patriotic duty to report you to the authorities.

"Comate": This is etymologically disastrous. One meaning is that of companion, but another, if you will take the trouble to look it up, as Miss Manners did, is hairy.

"POSSLQ": This term, the acronym for Persons of Opposite Sex Sharing Living Quarters, invented by the Census Bureau, is a possible winner. People do have an antipathy to newly invented words, however—there are still many who object to the practical "Ms."—and this is not an easy one to spell. Miss Manners is therefore reserving judgment.

"Uhmmer": Another possible winner, this has a natural origin, from popular usage, as in "This is my daughter's uhm . . . uhm . . . uhm."

In her heart, Miss Manners believes that a more nearly perfect term exists, and she is waiting for a kind and Gentle Reader to send it to her.

STEPHANIE BRUSH

So Why Invest in a Man at All?

There are still a number of very sound reasons, and don't listen to anybody who tells you there aren't.

Now that the eighties are upon us (and so far they've been a terrible idea—there's no denying that), we all have hard practical considerations to take into account. Among them, safety: Living completely alone can be terribly unwise. Self-defense manuals will tell you, "When living alone and answering the door, always yell, 'I'll get it, Bruce!' for the benefit of whatever pervert is lurking on the other side."

Well. I, for one, come from a long line of unconvincing liars. Lying in a low voice is one thing, but lying at extremely high decibel levels is outside the range of many women's capabilities. Life in the eighties is war. If a real Bruce will help you sleep nights, and he's making himself available, are you sure you want to fight him off?

Some women insist that pets, and even fine furniture, can fill the same function as men in one's life. Many women swear by cats. Actually, cats are much more difficult than men. Men do not give you small rodents as kiss-and-make-up gifts, men do not try to eat everything smaller than they are, and men do not require tiny little doors just to be let out of the house.

Many women insist that living with a man is a hindrance to getting to know one's "selfhood." But living with one's "selfhood" has become inconvenient for a number of reasons. It is difficult to share the rent with one's selfhood. It is difficult to fold sheets with one's selfhood. It is very silly to bring one's selfhood home to meet one's parents since, presumably, you've all already met.

But I won't kid you with a lot of cogent reasoning and fancy talk and intricately crafted arguments—

The Main Reason to Live with a Man:

You will never have to go on dates again. The principal difference between dates and Nazi torture is that Nazi torture took place in the 1940s and was seriously criticized at the Nuremburg trials. Dating, however, is STILL LEGAL and remains one of the least-understood atrocities that humans can commit. (Why, one wonders, is "to date" a transitive verb—something you do to another person? You could replace the verb "to date" with "to offend," "to assault," or "to dive-bomb.")

ANY NORMAL WOMAN OUT OF HIGH SCHOOL WHO DOES NOT WANT TO THROW UP BEFORE A DATE IS PROBABLY ON DRUGS, OR MENTALLY DEFICIENT. (For what it's worth, this is probably true of men, too.)

Casual dating (which is already a contradiction in terms) brings up so many irksome, niggling questions:

- Will you enjoy each other's company?

- Will you laugh at the same places in the movie?

- Will you agree, afterward, that you've *seen* the same movie?

- Will he want to pay for the meal?

- Will you need to pay him for paying for the meal?

If you are living with a man you do not have to worry about whether you should sleep with him after dinner. Which is to say, you'd bleeding well *better* sleep with him; but at least it's a black-and-white issue—there are no fine points of law involved. And if you are living with a man, he won't respect you any less in the morning than he does now.

A lot of women say, "I'm afraid to live with a man. He'll know *everything* about me."

Every women has an "It" about herself that she doesn't want known. Something private and dark and terrible. Lizzie Borden, for example, had a tough time on evenings out after she was acquitted, whenever her date said, "So, do your folks live in the area?" Once you begin living with a man, though, he forgives many of your trespasses, and you even forget rapidly what dates used to be like: God is merciful. (All you have to do is spend an evening with a single friend and *her* date to remember the horror of it all over again. Watch the anguish on your friend's face as her date mispronounces "Fassbinder" or makes Chinaman jokes or eats his salad with his oyster fork.)

Another Good Reason

Living with a man means, at least theoretically, not having to sit home and wait for him to call. You will look back with amazement on the days when you were expecting a call from some Special Guy. You canceled all your appointments for two days, filled a Hefty bag with Doritos, and camped out by the phone table. Sometimes you turned the phone upside down to see if all the wires were connected. When the phone rang, it was your mother, and you screamed into the receiver. Then you waited some more.

When darkness fell, you did not turn on the lights. You did not turn on the television or read a book, because your heart was pounding so fast that the excitement of reading *Martin Chuzzlewit* yet again would give you a coronary. You rehearsed the nonchalant tone you would affect when the call finally came.

Only it didn't.

Further Good Reasons

People often decide to live together simply because they need more personal contact in an impersonal world. Some claim this "contact" can be provided just as easily by one's immediate family, or even by another *woman*, but they are mistaken. Living with your family after the age of twenty-one is admitting that they have a Monopoly on your life. It is returning to "GO" without collecting two hundred dollars.

As for female roommates: They are indeed kind, loyal, thrifty, brave, and obedient; as well as modern and politically acceptable to other women. But all too often living with another woman is like waking up in the middle of a Rona Jaffe novel. Do you really want to spend the rest of your adult life arguing about who ate the last Figurine? Can another woman give you grandchildren?

And there can be no better reason for favoring men than this: esthetics. All male roommates at 7 A.M. look appreciably rumpled, yet adorable. They exude innocence, huggableness—a sort of helpless, charming *je ne sais quoi*.

All female roommates at 7 A.M. look like Lon Chaney.

No one knows why this is true, but it is.

GARRISON KEILLOR

YOUR WEDDING AND YOU

A Few Thoughts on Making It More Personally Rewarding, Shared by Reverend Bob Osman

Courtesy of
THE HUNDRED FLOWERS BRIDAL SHOP
Designers—Consultants—Caterers
"We Care"

In the past decade, a very rapidly increased change in our views of marriage as an institution and the wedding ceremony as an expression of two persons' feelings about marriage and about themselves and each other, their place in the community and society, and their relationship to the planet itself (and, of course, God) has undoubtedly taken place. Perhaps this change is summed up fairly well by two young people whom I'll call *Pat* and *Mike*.

"People like us reject the stereotypes, the role-playing, that seem to be so much a part of other people's relationships," they confided to me one day during premarital counseling. "We are individuals with an infinite capacity for loving, sharing, knowing, caring, growing, and expanding. We want our wedding to express that unique personalness, that *beingness*, that each of us, and only us, can bring to marriage. Do you know what we mean?"

More and more, most of us do—especially those in the eighteen-to-thirty-five age group in which most first marriages take place. Oftentimes writing their own ceremonies and creating their own symbols, language, music, feelings, this generation of young couples is seeking new modes, new marriage styles, to express what one minister called "the naturally religious, the realistically mystical, the practically impossible."

Heavy, right?

Not necessarily. In fact, the emphasis is definitely *away* from heaviness and *toward* lightness and informality. Comfortable. Feeling good. Being yourself. Being okay.

That is what the "New Wedding" is all about.

What is the "New Wedding"?

O.K., let's get down to specifics.

First of all, the New Wedding is less likely to occur in a formal place of worship or government but, rather, in an environment where the couple feels comfortable—a natural hillside or valley, a favorite restaurant, a nearby park or playground, or the home of a close friend.

Second, it is less likely to involve formal Judeo-Christian-establishment language but, rather, words that the couple would want to say to each other even if they weren't getting married.

Third, it is more likely to make each person attending the ceremony feel like a participant in something that is very interesting indeed.

Of course, many couples still elect a more traditional ceremony: the white tunics and daisy crowns, the lighting of matches by the congregation, the beautiful Peter, Paul, and Mary songs, and such a ceremony can be deeply meaningful in its own way. Certainly no couple should reject it just to be "different." An Alternative Wedding should be chosen only after careful and sincere discussion of the couple's own values, dreams, and attitudes at this most important moment in their life.

What is an "Alternative Wedding"?

That's a good question. I'd say, "It depends pretty much on the individual," so let's look at some individual cases.

Sam and *Judy*, for example. They chose to emphasize their mutual commitment to air and water quality, exchanging vows while chained to each other and to the plant gate of a major industrial polluter.

Lyle and *Marcia*, recognizing their dependence on each other, were joined in matrimony in a crowd of total strangers and had but $3.85 and a couple of tokens between them.

Al and *Tammy*, on the other hand, sharing a commitment to challenge and excitement, were married in 6.12 seconds in *Al's* Supercharged Funny Car, with a minister on her lap and four bridesmaids on the floor (a new track record).

Bud and *Karen* chose a simple ceremony in their own apartment, with *Karen* fixing pizza in the kitchen, *Bud* asleep on the sofa, and their *two children* watching television in the bedroom.

Charles and *Frank*, however, selected the Early Traditional style, complete with morning coats, Wagner and Mendelssohn, and crustless sandwiches.

Others have been married in canoes or small powerboats, under bridges, in tunnels, beside creeks, on towers, over the telephone (with the groom calling from a distant tavern), and on ski tows, islands, mountain peaks, peninsulas, rooftops, and rocks. A New, or Alternative, Wedding means freedom to be married in exactly the way you always wanted to be.

What is an "Alternative, or New, Wedding"?

Very well, let's look at three basic elements of the marriage ceremony in terms of personal experience today: readings, or literature; ceremony itself, or drama; and singing, or music. All are forms of *celebration*, from the Latin word *celebratio*, meaning "to get along famously, or quickly."

MUSIC: The music of Scott Joplin, Bob Dylan, Barbra Streisand, the Carpenters, the Grateful Dead, "Sesame Street," Pepsi-Cola, and the Fifties is often chosen, though many couples are now creating their own music. *Henry* and *Phyllis* were members of the Beloveds, a bliss-rock band, and decided to hold their wedding in a large auditorium, with a sellout crowd sharing the joy and excitement of a Beloveds concert. Although the band had never played outside of small coffeehouses and was little known on the music scene, with the help and concern of a supportive promoter the concert was arranged, with ticket prices scaled upward accordingly. "It was a wonderful wedding, and we all got off on it, especially the aspect of total sharing," remarked *Phyllis* afterward. "And there would've been even more to share, except the promoter took 60 percent off the top, and expenses wiped out the rest. Which goes to show the importance of having a good wedding contract." Alternatively, you may want to invite guests to bring their own instruments or a favorite record.

CEREMONY: It is customary for the bride and groom to write their own ceremony, reflecting their own tastes suitable to the occasion. *Vern* and *LaVerne* wanted their wedding to be a "rite of passage" from the empty, structured urban life they had known to a new rural life based on community and trusting and showing concern for tradition and love of the land, and they set out to do exactly that. Leaving the midwestern city in which they had long lived, the couple drove south looking for a community that was just right. A few hours later, they came across a small white frame church in the country. Its oak-shaded yard was crowded with aged parishioners eating fried-chicken lunches and displaying native crafts and abilities. The minister, a kindly old man in a black frock coat and starched shirt, greeted them warmly, and when *Vern* and *LaVerne* indicated their intentions he let out a joyous yell and slapped his thigh. "Bust my buttons! Caroline, fetch my collar!" he whooped and shouted. In no time, the entire congregation was seated in the church and singing old-time shape-note hymns, fanning vigorously, and crying "Amen!" at every opportunity.

Minister: "Well, Lord, You sure gave us one heck of a hard winter and I reckon some of us wondered if there'd be no end to it, but, dang it, this troubled ol' earth just keeps a-rotatin' and here we are at plantin' time agin and the trees are puttin' out their blossoms and the ol' bull is lookin' across the fence at the heifers and it sorta speaks to us of what they call *renewal* and *rededication*, don't it?

"And that's why we're here today, ain't it, Lord, 'cause these-here kids want ter sorta carry on them *natural processes* and kinder do their part to *create life* and be what Y' might call *at one* with You and each other and the trees and the birds and this great big ball of humanity we got down here and what we might call the *life force*—anyhow, that's the way I see it.

"Well, Lord, they're a-waitin' for me, and Caroline here is clearin' her throat somethin' fierce, so I guess I said enough, but—well, You take real good care of 'em now, Y'hear? Good-bye, God. Be talkin' to Y'later."

Vern and *LaVerne* also wrote their own vows. *Rod* and *Mary Elizabeth*, on the other hand, employed the regular vows of their church but added two pages of dialogue from *Love Knows No Night*—a scene in which *Curly* and *Jo-Jo*, pinned by the mud slide, promise to love each other forever if they are rescued soon. Or a couple might wish to speak extemporaneously.

LITERATURE: Readings from Walt Whitman, Thoreau, Dylan Thomas, E. E. Cummings, Frost, the Song of Solomon, and Carl Rogers are popular at weddings today, and, properly chosen, can be every bit as personal and creative as your own poems, essays, songs, or articles. The key, of course, is to make them your own, expressing your own feelings and desires.

Sometimes, selections may be incorporated into the ceremony itself. (Some states have recognized Marlowe's "Come live with me and be my love" as a legally binding contract, but be sure to check with local authorities about this, to avoid misunderstandings later.) Or you might want to write your own dialogue and incorporate *that* into the ceremony, as a young couple did not long ago who asked that their names not be used:

Man: And shall we then be husband and wife, and love and trust each other in the spirit of mutual adventure and joy, giving nurture and sustenance the one to the other and yet also preserving the independence and solitude of each, W——?

Woman: I—I—don't know what to say ... just that I'm ...

Man: I'm here. Cleave to me.

Woman: ... so happy. Happy and mixed up and—I don't know. It's like—

Man: Like we were two but now we are two in one?

Woman: Like what Carl Rogers once wrote. "When I love you, I am loving myself, for you are me."

Man: "When you love me, you are loving yourself, for I am you."

Both: "When we love ourselves, we are loving the world, for we are it."

Woman: P——, read that short poem you wrote for us recently.

Man: Oh, I don't know—it's sort of personal.

Woman: Please.

Man: Well, all right:

> maybe it will always be that sunday
> > when
> we sang to the little bouncing ball
> > dribbled
> down the dewy grass-green fairways
> > of our
> consciousness landing in hard woods
> > of where
> and when   so let us always
> and not just the day before tomorrow
> > slice
> together the loaf of our caring and
> > hook
> the fish of our first flowing self no
> kidding swinging love's clubs between
> the hazards of water the traps of
> > sand
> in the baggy morning crazy happy
> > yelling "For! For!"

Woman: P——!

Man: W——!

Or you might enclose your poem in the wedding invitation or have it printed on napkins. *Stan* and *Debbie*, although they were not poets, nonetheless wanted their wedding to be a "marriage of minds" and a time of sharing with family and friends, and sent out the invitations three months before, including a short reading list:

Bhagavad Gita
Couples, Updike
Crime and Punishment, Dostoevski
The Golden Bough, Frazer
The Great Gatsby, Fitzgerald
How to Be Your Own Best Friend, Newman and Berkowitz
On Aggression, Lorenz
The Portable Nietzsche, Nietzsche
The Republic, Plato
Them, Oates
We, Lindbergh

In the church, the couple entered together from the rear and sat in front facing the guests. The attendants passed up and down the aisles distributing notebooks and pencils. The minister introduced *Stan* and *Debbie*, who took turns addressing the audience from a small lectern. *Debbie* spoke on "Views of Home in Post-Marriage Culture." *Stan* spoke on "The Goddess and the Mom: Woman as Totemic Figure and Family Technician in Contemporary Mythology." After a brief discussion and a multiple-choice quiz, the service was over. (To conserve time, *Stan* and *Debbie* had been married three weeks before at their apartment.)

Or you can simply speak to each guest briefly during the reception, to make sure the main points of your wedding are clearly understood. And if you have already selected your married life-style you may wish to discuss that, too. (See my "Choosing a Life-style" or call me and make an appointment.)

Garrison Keillor, "Your Wedding And You," from HAPPY TO BE HERE. Copyright (c) 1982 Garrison Keillor. Reprinted with permission of Atheneum Publishers Inc.

QUESTIONS FOR DISCUSSION

1. Do you agree with Miss Manners that in the world of propriety (norms) "we have more fun than you may have been led to believe"? If so, why are so many of the traditional norms which Miss Manners refers to—"no hugging and kissing"—being rejected today?

2. Miss Manners says "learn to prepare something decent." How do you decide which dating norms are decent and which are indecent?

3. Miss Manners would appear to be supporting rather traditional normative behavior—"No come-over-to-my-place." But, at the end she asks, "Can you hold out until the second date?" Is this the type of ending to the piece you would have anticipated?

4. What do you call someone with whom you are living but to whom you are not married?

5. Some people do ask, "What difference does a piece of paper make?" (meaning, of course, a marriage license). Miss Manners has a sharp retort: she has a safe box full of papers that do make a difference. What important social and legal differences does a marriage license make for a couple? Is a license a form of protection for both male and female? Have legal problems already arisen in this society over couples living together without the "piece of paper"?

6. Miss Manners is not pleased with the idea that a long-married person would introduce his or her spouse with the term "my lover." What is being implied here about the differences in sexual relationships between those just living together and those who are long-married? Is there data to support this assumption?

7. Macklin (1983) reports that she was one of the first to try and define nonmarital cohabitation. She wanted to use the following operational definition: "sharing a bedroom and/or bed for four or more nights a week for three or more consecutive months with someone of the opposite sex to whom one is not married." She reports that "many have considered this too similar to contemporary dating...." Do you think this proposed definition is virtually the same as dating today?

8. Brush notes that some women feel they cannot know their "selfhood" if they live with a man. Is there some truth to this argument? Does this mean, then, that a lot of women (millions of them) do not know who they are since they are married?

9. The main reason to live with a man, according to Brush, is that "you will never have to go on dates again." She then

compares dates with Nazi torture. Relate this to Macklin's contention that her definition of sharing a bed for several nights is the same as contemporary dating. What aspects of dating do you think Brush is referring to?

10. Brush says that another woman cannot provide the same emotional and physical companionship that a man can. Do you agree with her evaluation?

11. The "new weddings" are said to occur in places where the couple feels comfortable. What does this say about the relationship of some young people to the institutional church?

12. A new wedding "means freedom to be married in exactly the way you always wanted to be." Are there any societal restrictions upon how a couple may be married? What are they?

13. A lot of emphasis is given today to the words of the marriage ceremony. Why do you think the traditional vows exchanged in religious rituals have lasted as long as they have? How powerful a factor is ritual in all our behavior—not just marriage?

REFERENCES

Bates, Alan. "Parental Roles in Courtship." *Social Forces* 20 (1942), 482–86.

Bowman, Henry Al, and Spanier, Graham B. *Modern Marriage.* New York: McGraw-Hill, 1978.

Goode, William J. *Principles of Sociology.* New York: McGraw-Hill, 1977.

Leslie, L. A., Huston, T. L., and Johnson, M. P. "Parental Reactions to Dating Relationships: Do They Make a Difference?" *Journal of Marriage and the Family* 48, (February 1986), 57–66.

Macklin, Eleanor D. "Nonmarital Heterosexual Cohabitation: An Overview," in *Contemporary Families and Alternative Life Styles.* Macklin, Eleanor D., and Rubin, Roger H., eds. Beverly Hills: Sage Publications, 1983, 49–74.

Yankelovich, D. "New Rules in American Life: Searching for Self-Fulfillment in a World Turned Upside Down." *Psychology Today* 15, 4 (1981), 35–91.

Chapter Ten

The Political Order

READINGS

E very school child learns that our form of political organization is a representative democracy. The founders of our country went to great lengths to establish a government "of the people, by the people, and for the people." It was not, however, until the election of Andrew Jackson as the eighth president that we elected "one of the people" to the highest office in the land. Over the years the concept of a government of the people has experienced strain and pressures. The "people" seem to have a basic distrust of those whom they elect to office, and those who govern barely conceal a distrust of the "people." H. L. Mencken was one who hotly disputed the theory that a popular democracy was based on the wisdom of the people. It was his judgment that "if x is the population of the United States and y is the degree of imbecility of the average American, then democracy is the theory that $x \times y$ is less than y." Will Rogers was not too sure of either those who lead or those who are led. Al Smith, the first Roman Catholic to run for president, was the subject of much anti-Catholicism in his campaign. Said Rogers:

> Al Smith explains that if elected President all Protestants would not be exterminated; ... that the Knights of Columbus would not replace the Boy Scouts and Kiwanis; that mass would not replace golf on Sunday morning; and, that those fortunate enough to have meat could eat it on Friday.
>
> It's no compliment to a nation's intelligence when these things have to be explained.

For a representative democracy to work, great emphasis must be put upon the participation of the populace in elections. But our history is a checkered one in this respect. In early colonial New England only church members could vote. Blacks, as slaves, obviously were denied the right to vote, but even after emancipation more than 100 years passed before they were able to participate fully in the electoral process. The same restrictions were put on Native Americans. The idea of women voting was not seriously entertained for years. When the issue was brought to the forefront, women underwent struggles similar to those of blacks for voting rights. Today, of course, no citizen may be denied the franchise.

While full participation in voting for candidates is the ideal, this very ideal leads to problems in practice. The competing interests of the various groups in a pluralistic society mean that any candidate for office must be able to convince everyone that he or she is the one who can best meet their needs if elected. Minority groups such as blacks, Hispanic-Americans, and women exercise great influence—or, at the least, are perceived to exercise influence—in elections. To secure their votes, party platforms must include positions which minorities feel are essential if they are to move ahead. Thus, "to the extent that a minority group has some resource that the leadership wishes (in this case, votes), the desires of that group will be allowed to affect policy somewhat, even in a modified form." (Goode, 1977:411) Women constitute one of the most vocal political minority groups in our society today. This was not lost on the Democratic presidential candidates in the 1984 election. Reporting on this the *New York Times* editorialized:

> Politicians are often said to woo voters, but seldom if ever has there been such a wooing as occurred in Washington last Saturday night. Six suitors stood before 2,000 delegates to the annual convention of the National Organization for Women and declared themselves ready, willing, even eager for a truly meaningful relationship.
>
> All would be delighted, should the chips fall that way, to enter the White House with a woman by their sides. All favored—nay, embraced—the Equal Rights Amendment. All gave the lie to that old tale about the women's movement being dead; else why would these gentlemen be telling NOW all this?
>
> "Anyone who takes you for granted will regret it," said Walter Mondale. "As for Vice President, I see some contenders in this room."
>
> "I will not only consider" a female veep, said Ernest Hollings, "I recommended it a year and a half ago."
>
> "A very likely prospect," said George McGovern.
>
> "I will not let sex, race or creed or color or size determine or prevent anyone from being considered," promised Alan Cranston.
>
> "To men, their rights and nothing more," intoned John Glenn, quoting Elizabeth Cady Stanton. "To women, their rights and nothing less."
>
> "I would be proud," said Gary Hart, topping everyone, "to run with a woman on either end of the ticket."
>
> Although the gentlemen's attentions appear honorable, the objects of their affection are being cautious. Once we vote for Fritz

or George or Alan or John or Gary, they seem to be asking themselves, will he still respect us? (October 4, 1983).

Minority groups' interests may, and often do, conflict with those of other powerful groups such as labor or business. The resolution of these competing interests is why some refer to politics as the "art of compromise."

Once in office the party's candidate and his or her administration must satisfy the various groups which put the party into power. Powerful groups have their own lobbies in Washington who work daily to see that their politics are enacted into laws which continue their privileged positions. With ample resources at their command businesses are able to exercise a great deal of influence in the halls of Congress. As the Nixon campaign of 1972 made clear, campaign contributors are expected to be rewarded later. Buchwald (1973) parodies this political fact of life in commenting on the Nixon election of 1972:

I was sitting with Helmut Strudel, president of Strudel Industries, at President Nixon's inauguration. Strudel had donated a million dollars to the Committee for the Reelection of the President and had flown all the way into Washington in his private plane to see what he had gotten for his money.

... when Mr. Nixon started to talk about domestic matters, my friend became quite upset. The President said:

"Let each of us remember that America was built not by government, but by people—not by welfare, but by work—not by shirking responsibility, but by seeking responsibility."

Strudel began to perspire. "It sounds like he's not going to bail my company out of bankruptcy," he said worriedly.

"Don't be silly," I told Strudel. "When he speaks of people on welfare, the President's talking about the little guy who's freeloading on the government. He is not talking about companies that get large government subsidies."

The President said, "In the challenges we face together let each of us ask not just how government can help but how can I help?"

"You know, of course," Strudel whispered to me, "that my company has a contract to build four thousand gazebos for the U.S. Air Force at eight million dollars each. Well, since we got the order, gazebos have gone up to $10 million, and unless the government helps us, we won't be able to deliver them."

"Of course the government will help you," I assured Strudel. "When the President said, 'Ask not what the government will do for me but what can I do for myself,' he was talking about teachers and farmers and old people on Social Security, who are always at the government trough. Contractors are not in that category.

Buchwald's parody is an updated version of Ambrose Bierce's epigrammatic definition of politics in *The Devil's Dictionary*: "Politics, n.: A strife of interests masquerading as a contest of principles. The conduct of public affairs for private advantage." (1911)

Since governmental decisions affect nearly all areas of life from birth (the abortion issue) to the grave (legal efforts to define when death has occurred), it is not surprising that political humor is pervasive in our society. The humorous selections in this chapter probe areas of our political life beginning with our initial effort to declare ourselves free from the political control of Great Britain. In "Let's See Who Salutes," Buchwald imagines the difficulties Thomas Jefferson would have had with the Declaration of Independence if it had been prepared for television presentation. Political parties must make sure they are speaking to "the people," and Jefferson had used words like "despotism, annihilation, migration, and tenure. Those are all egghead words and don't mean a damn thing to the public." In addition, the sponsor for the program, the Boston Tea Company, "is interested in selling tea, not independence." Serving the interests of everyone is not an easy undertaking.

In "The Favorite Son," Arthur Hoppe discusses the difficulties in choosing a candidate who appeals to all people. One might think that in our society Jesus Christ would have some desirable qualities as a political candidate. Hoppe points out the problems associated with such a candidate.

In "At Last, a Candordate," Russell Baker offers a vivid contrast between the usual television announcement of a *candidate* for president and that of a *candordate*. The "candordate" tries to be entirely honest in stating why he wants to be president. The outcome will be predictable—according to his advisers.

Mark Twain, in "Female Suffrage," takes us back to the era when women did not have the right to vote. He, like many others in his day, argues against the right of women to vote on many grounds, e.g., "they would swamp the country with debt"; "they shall neglect the duties of the household to go out and take a drink with candidates; and men shall nurse the baby while their wives travel to the polls to vote." The replies to Twain's arguments from would-be female voters are indicative of why women eventually won their battle.

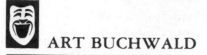

ART BUCHWALD

Let's See Who Salutes

Have you ever wondered what would have happened if the people who are in charge of television today were passing on the draft of the Declaration of Independence?

The scene is Philadelphia at WJULY TV. Several men are sitting around holding copies of the Declaration.

Thomas Jefferson comes in nervously.

"Tommy," says the producer, "it's just great. I would say it was a masterpiece."

"We love it, Tommy boy," the advertising agency man says. "It sings. Lots of drama, and it holds your interest. There are a few things that have to be changed, but otherwise it stays intact."

"What's wrong with it?" Mr. Jefferson asks.

There's a pause. Everyone looks at the man from the network.

"Well, frankly, Tommy, it smacks of being a little anti-British. I mean, we've got quite a few British listeners and something like this might bring in a lot of mail."

"Now don't get sore, Tommy boy," the agency man says. "You're the best declaration of independence writer in the business. That's why we hired you. But our sponsor the Boston Tea Company is interested in selling tea, not independence. Mr. Cornwallis, the sponsor's representative, is here, and I think he has a few thoughts on the matter. Go ahead, Corney. Let's hear what you think."

Mr. Cornwallis stands up. "Mr. Jefferson, all of us in this room want this to be a whale of a document. I think we'll agree on that."

Everyone in the room nods his head.

"At the same time we feel—I think I can speak for everybody— that we don't want to go over the heads of the mass of people who we hope will buy our product. You use words like despotism, annihilation, migration, and tenure. Those are all egghead words and don't mean a damn thing to the public. Now I like your stuff about 'Life, Liberty, and the pursuit of Happiness.' They all tie in great with tea, particularly pursuit of happiness, but it's the feeling of all of us that you're really getting into controversial water when you start attacking the King of Britain."

Mr. Jefferson says, "But every word of it is true. I've got documentary proof."

"Let me take a crack at it, Corney," the agency man says. "Look, Tommy boy, it isn't a question of whether it's true or not. All of us here know what a louse George can be. But I don't think the people want to be reminded of it all the time. They have enough worries. They want escape. This thing has to be upbeat. If you remind people of all those taxes George has laid on us, they're not going to go out and buy tea. They're not going to go out and buy anything."

"Frankly," says the network man, "I have some strong objections on different grounds. I know you didn't mean it this way, but the script strikes me as pretty left-wing. I may have read the last paragraph wrong, but it seems to me that you're calling for the overthrow of the present government by force. The network could never allow anything like that."

"I'm sure Tommy didn't mean anything like that," the producer says. "Tommy's just a strong writer. Maybe he got a little carried away with himself. Suppose Tommy took out all references to the British and the King. Suppose we said in a special preamble this Declaration of Independence had nothing to do with persons living or dead, and the whole thing is fictitious. Wouldn't that solve it?"

Mr. Jefferson says, "Gentlemen, I was told to write a Declaration of Independence. I discussed it with many people before I did the actual writing. I've worked hard on this declaration—harder than I've worked on anything in my life. You either take it or leave it as it is."

"We're sorry you feel that way about it, Tommy," the agency man says. "We owe a responsibility to the country, but we owe a bigger responsibility to the sponsor. He's paying for it. We're not in the business of offending people, British people or any other kind of people. The truth is, the British are the biggest tea drinkers of anyone in the colonies. We're not going to antagonize them with a document like this. Isn't that so, Mr. Cornwallis?"

"Check—unless Mr. Jefferson changes it the way we want him to."

Mr. Jefferson grabs the Declaration and says, "Not for all the tea in China," and exits.

The producer shakes his head. "I don't know, fellows. Maybe we've made a mistake. We could at least have run it up a flagpole to see who saluted."

"As far as I'm concerned," Mr. Cornwallis says, "the subject is closed. Let's talk about an hour Western on the French and Indian War."

Reprinted with permission of the author.

 ARTHUR HOPPE

The Favorite Son

With President Johnson and Richard Nixon both slipping in the polls, the emergence of a fresh, new candidate was not unexpected. The revelation came in a nationwide poll asking voters the routine question: "If Lyndon Johnson and Richard Nixon are the nominees of their parties, which candidate would get your vote?"

In reply, 7.2 percent said Johnson, 6.8 percent said Nixon and 61.4 percent said Jesus Christ. The remainder was split among lesser-known candidates. The surprising showing of a candidate whose influence had so far been felt in American politics created a sensation. Support was strong in the Bible Belt. Doves were enthusiastic over what they believed would be The Candidate's position on Vietnam. And indeed, no political figure voiced anything but unqualified approval in public. Both major parties vied with each other in saying how much they had long admired The Candidate and espoused The Candidate's principles. Spokesmen for each expressed confidence The Candidate would accept a draft to head their ticket. Initially, then, the Nation looked forward to a landslide. But a few cracks began to appear in this consensus.

The Candidate's known view on money-lending caused shudders on Wall Street and the Dow-Jones average plummeted 30 points. In general, the Eastern Establishment was cool, murmuring discreet remarks about "working-class background" and "radical social view." Hate literature, such as *The Cross and the Flag*, published exposes of The Candidate's ethnic background, causing more than one expert to worry in print, "Is the Country Ready for a Jewish President?" Negro militants denounced the doctrine of "turn the other cheek" as "just another Honky trap." And Conservatives, while praising The Candidate's record of feeding the multitudes, noted that this tended to sap individual initiative and the multitudes ought to feed themselves. Liberals talked uneasily about "separation of church and state" and the churches, as usual, couldn't agree on anything:

As quickly as the boom had soared, just as quickly did it fizzle out. Overnight the issue was dead. Everyone agreed that The Candidate, while praiseworthy and all that, simply wasn't electable. Many expert reasons were given, but a hard-headed politician, who had carefully studied The Candidate's record and voter appeal, went to the heart of the matter.

"Basically, it was the image," he said. "Beard, robes, a lot of talk about love—how would it come across on TV? People aren't ready for stuff like that.

"These days," he said, shaking his head, "a candidate like that would get crucified."

 **RUSSELL BAKER**

At Last, a Candordate

WASHINGTON, Jan. 10—My fellow Americans:

Painful as it is for me to speak to you on television, because of my distaste for talking to machinery, I have chosen this way to announce to you today that I shall be a candidate for President of the United States.

My reason for using television is not flattering to you. To be honest about it, I have been advised that a great many of you whose votes I shall need rarely read anything more adult than the television schedules, and that it would be impossible to communicate with you except through this piece of furniture you are now watching. I believe this to be true.

I tell you this, though some of you will doubtless be offended by it, because I believe it is time to re-establish trust between the American people and their Government. This can only be done if the man at the very apex of Government, the President, will follow a policy of pure candor in dealing with you, the people.

In line with this policy, I must tell you that I am wearing a heavy application of cosmetics around my eyes and mouth, and on my cheeks. The purpose of this make-up is to deceive you with the impression that I am younger, less worn and less fatigued than, in fact, I am.

The gray spots in my hair have been dyed for the same reason. My hair style, this suit I am wearing, this shirt and this necktie were all selected by a committee of men and women who are professional experts in manipulating public opinion and enticing you to buy things you don't need.

I was strongly advised by these professionals not to appear on television at all, but to hire a performer who looked more like a potentially great leader than I do, and to have him appear pretending to be me.

I rejected this proposal because I deplore the recent trend which has turned so many of our great actors into performers for television commercials, and it would break my heart to see members of this great profession reduced to playing politicians in political campaigns.

I must also inform you that I am not now sitting in a studio speaking to you. My advisers told me that to make this announcement "live" would be dangerous. I might make some natural gesture, such as rubbing my nose or scratching my chin, which would betray my natural nervousness under stress.

For this reason, this speech was recorded two weeks ago. Seventeen versions were taped. Snippets of nine of them were spliced together to create this announcement of my Presidential candidacy, which you are now hearing. I do not know where I am at this moment, but if it is being shown in prime evening time, as I hope, the chances are excellent that I am sitting at home with a large snifter of brandy, thoroughly enjoying myself on television.

I tell you this because I think it important for you to know that I am just as vain as the next man. I do most certainly enjoy seeing myself on television, even when I do not look much like me, as in this particular appearance.

I also enjoy seeing my picture in newspapers and magazines, and I am certain that I would enjoy the sensation of knowing that my words and acts were being discussed around the earth every day. I like the idea of everybody having to stand up when I walk into the room.

Frankly, ladies and gentlemen, I like to feel important, and one of the reasons I want to be President is to satisfy my vanity. It will almost certainly be an important factor in my decision—if I am elected—to run for a second term.

In my effort to be entirely honest with you, I am not going to overemphasize my interest in the vacation possibilities of the Presidency. Frankly, the knowledge that, as President, I would have my own jetliner and helicopters, chauffeured limousines and yacht, as well as sundry vacation White Houses in climates of my choosing— all these make the Presidency far more attractive to me than it would be if it required one to ride to work on the bus and offered only a two-week vacation in the family station wagon.

I would never, however, accept any job simply because the fringe benefits were excellent. For me, a job must also be absorbing, interesting and rich in ego gratification and pay a good salary.

The Presidency appeals to me on all these grounds. It would be immensely absorbing to me to fly to all the vacation spas for conferences with Prime Ministers, other Presidents, Chancellors and the more debonair dictators.

It would be both interesting and gratifying to see the most brilliant minds of the Ivy League sparkle and glisten at my command. The salary is excellent. Even if I served only one term, it would solve the serious financial problem of my children's educations. The expense account, needless to say, is superb, and free housing will be a godsend, since mortgage payments, utilities and upkeep on my present house are now so high that I have not been able to afford a suit in the past three years.

In all honesty, I have no program as yet. Any program I may announce before the election will almost surely be abandoned if I am elected. All I promise is complete honesty and absolute refusal to try to deceive you. My advisers tell me that not one in twenty among you will vote for such a candidate, and, in all honesty, I must tell you that I believe them.

MARK TWAIN

Female Suffrage

Editors Missouri Democrat:

I have read the long list of lady petitioners in favor of female suffrage, and as a husband and a father I want to protest against the whole business. It will never do to allow women to vote. It will never do to allow them to hold office. You know, and I know, that if they were granted these privileges there would be no more peace on earth. They would swamp the country with debt. They like to hold office too well. They like to be Mrs. President Smith of the Dorcas society, or Mrs. Secretary Jones of the Hindoo aid association, or Mrs. Treasurer of something or other. They are fond of the distinction of the thing, you know; they revel in the sweet jingle of the title. They are always setting up sanctified confederations of all kinds, and then running for president of them. They are even so fond of office that they are willing to serve without pay. But you allow them to vote and to go to the Legislature once, and then see how it will be. They will go to work and start a thousand more societies, and cram them full of salaried offices. You will see a state of things then that will stir your feelings to the bottom of your pockets. The first fee bill would exasperate you some. Instead of the usual schedule for judges, State printer, Supreme court clerks, &c., the list would read something like this:

OFFICES AND SALARIES.

President Dorcas society	$ 4,000
Subordinate officers of same, each	2,000
President Ladies' Union prayer meeting	3,000
President Pawnee Educational society	4,000
President of Ladies' society for Dissemination of Belles Lettres among the Shoshones	5,000
State Crinoline Directress	10,000
State Superintendent of waterfalls	10,000
State Hair Oil inspectress	10,000
State milliner	50,000

You know what a state of anarchy and social chaos that fee bill would create. Every woman in the commonwealth of Missouri would let go everything and run for State Milliner. And instead of ventilating each other's political antecedents, as men do, they would go straight after each other's private moral character. (I know them—they are all like my wife.) Before the canvass was three days old it would be an established proposition that every woman in the State was "no better than she ought to be." Only think how it would lacerate me to have an opposition candidate say that about my wife. That is the idea, you know—having other people say these hard things. Now, I know that my wife isn't any better than she ought to be, poor devil—in fact, in matters of orthodox doctrine, she is particularly shaky—but still I would not like these things aired in a political contest. I don't really suppose that that woman will stand any more show hereafter than—however, she may improve—she may even become a beacon light for the saving of others—but if she does, she will burn rather dim, and she will flicker a good deal, too. But, as I was saying, a female political canvass would be an outrageous thing.

Think of the torch-light processions that would distress our eyes. Think of the curious legends on the transparencies:

"Robbins forever! Vote for Sallie Robbins, the only virtuous candidate in the field!"

And this:

"Chastity, modesty, patriotism! Let the great people stand by Maria Sanders, the champion of morality and progress, and the only candidate with a stainless reputation!"

And this: "Vote for Judy McGinniss, the incorruptible! Nine children—one at the breast!"

In that day a man shall say to his servant, "What is the matter with the baby?" And the servant shall reply, "It has been sick for hours." "And where is its mother?" "She is out electioneering for Sallie Robbins." And such conversations as these shall transpire between ladies and servants applying for situations: "Can you cook?" "Yes." "Wash?" "Yes." "Do general housework?" "Yes." "All right; who is your choice for State milliner?" "Judy McGinniss." "Well, you can tramp." And women shall talk politics instead of discussing the fashions; and they shall neglect the duties of the household to go out and take a drink with candidates; and men shall nurse the baby while their wives travel to the polls to vote. And also in that day the man who hath beautiful whiskers shall beat the homely man of wisdom for Governor, and the youth who waltzes with exquisite grace shall be Chief of Police, in preference to the man of practiced sagacity and determined energy.

Every man, I take it, has a selfish end in view when he pours out eloquence in behalf of the public good in the newspapers, and such is the case with me. I do not want the privileges of women extended, because my wife already holds office in nineteen different infernal female associations and I have to do all her clerking. If you give the women full sweep with the men in political affairs, she will proceed to run for every confounded office under the new dispensation. That will finish me. It is bound to finish me. She would not have time to do anything at all then, and the one solitary thing I have shirked up to the present time would fall on me and my family would go to destruction; for I am *not* qualified for a wet nurse.

MARK TWAIN

A Volley From the Down-Trodden

DEFENSE

Editors Missouri Democrat:

I should think you would be ashamed of yourselves. I would, anyway—to publish the vile, witless drivelings of that poor creature who degrades me with his name. I say you ought to be ashamed of yourselves. Two hundred noble, Spartan women cast themselves into the breach to free their sex from bondage, and instead of standing with bowed heads before the majesty of such a spectacle, you permit this flippant ass, my husband, to print a weak satire upon it. The wretch! I combed him with a piano stool for it. And I mean to comb every newspaper villain I can lay my hands on. They are nothing but villains anyhow. They published our names when nobody asked them to, and therefore they are low, mean and depraved, and fit for any crime however black and infamous.

Mr. Editor, I have not been appointed the champion of my sex in this matter; still, if I could know that any argument of mine in favor of female suffrage which has been presented in the above communication will win over any enemy to our cause, it would soften and soothe my dying hour; ah, yes, it would soothe it as never another soother could soothe it.

MRS. MARK TWAIN
President Afghanistan Aid Association,
Secretary of the Society
for introducing the Gospel into New Jersey, etc., etc., etc.

[The old woman states a case well, don't she? She states a case mighty well, for a woman of her years? She even soars into moving eloquence in that place where she says: "two hundred noble Spartan women cast themselves into the breaches," etc. And those "arguments" of hers afford her a prodigious satisfaction, don't they? She may possibly die easy on account of them, but she won't if I am around to stir her up in her last moments. That woman has made my life a burthen to me, and I mean to have a hand in soothing her myself when her time is up.—MARK TWAIN]

MORE DEFENSE

Editors Missouri Democrat:

I have read the article in your paper on female suffrage, by the atrocious scoundrel Mark Twain. But do not imagine that such a thing as that will deter us from demanding and enforcing our rights. Sir, we will have our rights, though the heavens fall. And as for this wretch, he had better find something else to do than meddling with matters he is incapable of understanding. I suppose he votes—such is law!—such is justice!—he is allowed to vote, but women a thousand times his superiors in intelligence are ruled out!—he!—a creature who don't know enough to follow the wires and find the telegraph office. Comment is unnecessary. If I get my hands on that whelp I will snatch hair out of his head till he is as bald as a phrenological bust.

Mr. Editor, I may not have done as much good for my species as I ought, in my time, but if any of the arguments I have presented in this article in favor of female suffrage shall aid in extending the privileges of woman, I shall die happy and content.

MRS. ZEB. LEAVENWORTH
*Originator and President of the Association for the
Establishment of a Female College in Kamschatka.*

[I perceive that I have drawn the fire of another heavy gun. I feel as anxious as any man could to answer this old Kamschatkan, but I do not know where to take hold. Her "arguments" are too subtle for me. If she can die happy and content on that mild sort of gruel, though, let her slide.—MARK TWAIN]

MORE YET

Editors Missouri Democrat:

The depths of my heart of hearts are stirred. Gentle chiding from those that love me has ever fallen upon my wounded spirit like soothing moonlight upon a troubled sea, but harsh words from wretches is more than I can bear. I am not formed like others of my sex. All with me is ideal—is romance. I live in a world of my own that is peopled with the fairy creatures of fancy. When that is rudely invaded, my ethereal soul recoils in horror. For long years I have collected buttons, and door-plates and dictionaries, and all such things as I thought would make the poor savages of the South seas contented with their lot and lift them out of their ignorance and degradation—and no longer than a month ago I sent them Horace Greeley's speeches and some other cheerful literature, and the pure delight I felt was only marred by the reflection that the poor creatures could not read them—and yet I may not vote! Our petition for our rights is humanly attacked by one who has no heart, no soul, no gentle emotions, no poesy! In tuneful numbers I will bid this cold world adieu, and perchance when I am gone, Legislatures will drop a tear over one whose budding life they blighted, and be torn with vain regrets when it is all too late:

> In sorrow I sorrow, O sorrowful day!
> In grief-stricken tears O joy speed away!
> I weep and I wail, and I waft broken sighs,
> And I cry in my anguish, O Woman arise!
>
> But I shout it in vain! for Demons have come,
> Who drown my appeal with foul blasphemous tongue;
> Yes, in sorrow I fade, and flicker and die!
> Lo! a martyr to Suffrage in the tomb let me lie!

If I dared to hope that any argument I have here presented may be the means of securing justice to my down-trodden sex, I could lay me down and pass away as peacefully as the sighing of a breeze in summer forests.

MISS AUGUSTA JOSEPHINE MAITLAND,
*Secretary of the Society for the Dissemination
of Poetry among the Pawnees.*

[Now, this old maid is a little spooney, of course, but she does not abuse me as much as the others, and it really touches me to know that she is going to fade, and flicker out. Her "arguments" are a little vague, but that is of no consequence. I haven't anything in the world against her, except that inspired atrocity of inflicting Horace Greeley's speeches on the poor heathen of the South Seas. What harm have they ever done her, that she should want to . . . ?

You must excuse me. I see a procession of ladies filing in at my street door with tar-buckets and feather-beds, and other arrangements. I do not wish to crowd them. I will go out the back way. But I will singe that pestilent old wild-cat, my wife, for leading them.—MARK TWAIN]

QUESTIONS FOR DISCUSSION

1. The television network advisers argue, among other things, that Jefferson's Declaration of Independence seems to be "pretty left-wing" and appears to be "calling for the overthrow of the present government by force. The network could never allow anything like that." There are those who argue that the media does indeed control the presentation of news and allow only what the establishment wants to appear. Is there evidence to support this argument?

2. The agency man says to Jefferson: "Look, Tommy boy, it isn't a question of whether it's true or not. All of us here know what a louse George can be. But I don't think the people want to be reminded of it all the time. They have enough worries. They want escape." TV has been accused of being a "vast wasteland" with its game shows, soaps, sitcoms, and other less than intellectually challenging fare. Is there evidence that this is what the public wants or is this, again, what the sponsors think will sell "tea"?

3. Mr. Cornwallis, the sponsor's representative, says: "... we don't want to go over the heads of the mass of people who we hope will buy our product. You use words like despotism, annihilation, migration, and tenure. Those are all egghead words and don't mean a damn thing to the public." One of the most consistently high-rated programs on TV is "60 Minutes." It regularly uses "egghead words" but has a large following. How do you account for this?

4. The Moral Majority backs political candidates who, assumedly, espouse the views of Jesus Christ, the candidate in Arthur Hoppe's "Favorite Son." Which of Jesus' "radical social views" are offered by candidates supported by the Moral Majority? Do candidates backed by the Moral Majority seem to embrace views just the opposite of those ascribed to the candidate in Hoppe's "Favorite Son"?

5. Are some of Jesus' views (such as feeding the multitudes) a part of official government policy in this society? There are those who think this tends to "sap individual initiative and the multitudes ought to feed themselves." Where does the Moral Majority stand on such social programs as these?

6. The office of the president does carry with it what are known as "perks"—i.e., financial and other benefits in addition to just straight salary. It is often humorously pointed out that the president has free housing, for example. Senators and members of Congress have free mailing privileges. All such perks are expenses borne by the taxpayer. What do you think the reaction of the public would be if a presidential candidate did forthrightly express his or her interest in such perks?

7. Baker's "Candordate" says that he is wearing cosmetics "to deceive you with the impression that I am younger, less worn, and less fatigued than, in fact, I am." Some political analysts think that John Kennedy defeated Richard Nixon for the presidency because Nixon did appear to be fatigued, older, and less enthused than Kennedy in their television debates. Does the public vote for presidential candidates primarily on the basis of their "sex appeal": their looks, youthfulness, etc.? Is the public really aware of the political issues and the differing stands which candidates have on such issues? Is this a cynical approach to American politics?

8. (Baker's article originally appeared in 1972, nearly a decade before Ronald Reagan was elected president.) The "Candordate" says that "I was strongly advised by ... professionals not to appear on television but to hire a performer who looked more like a potentially great leader than I do, and have him appear pretending to be me.... I rejected this proposal ... it would break my heart to see members of this great profession reduced to playing politicians in political campaigns." Do you think, as has been suggested, that Reagan's experience as an actor has assisted him in his ability to portray leadership? If so, what does this say for future presidential contests?

9. "Any program I may announce before the election will almost surely be abandoned if I am elected." Are there data which show that this admission by the fictional "Candordate" bears resemblance to truth?

10. Mark Twain wrote, of course, before women were granted the right to vote. But in "Female Suffrage" he raises points that 100 years later are still being asked about female involvement in politics. Twain says female candidates would "go straight after each other's private moral character." Is this a part of

political campaigning for male *or* female? When Geraldine Ferraro ran for vice president in 1980, reporters raised questions about her husband's business ethics. Is any member of a candidate's family safe from moral scrutiny?

11. Twain says if women were elected to legislatures they would "start a thousand societies, and cram them full of salaried offices." Have men already set an example for them in this regard? How?

12. Twain worries that if women are given full political rights they "will proceed to run for every confounded office. . . ." Has this indeed happened? There are women governors, representatives, and senators, but is the percentage of women officeholders roughly equal to women's proportion of the population? Why do you think this is the case?

REFERENCES

Bierce, Ambrose. *The Devil's Dictionary.* New York: Thomas Crowell, 1911.

Buchwald, Art. "Ask Not," in *I Never Danced At The White House.* New York: G. P. Putnam's Sons, 1973. 57–58.

Goode, William J. *Principles of Sociology.* New York: McGraw-Hill, 1977.

Chapter Eleven

Religion

READINGS

O ur forebears came to this country for many reasons, but certainly primary among them was the search for religious freedom: the right to worship God as they saw fit. When it came time to write the Constitution, they wrote into the Bill of Rights that Congress would not establish any state church. Church and state were to be separate—forever. Those who wished to worship were free to do so. Those who did *not* with to worship God were free from any coercion to do so. The churches which were founded were voluntary in nature, and this principle has been jealously guarded throughout our history.

One consequence of voluntary churches was that any group who wished to get together and establish a church could do so. The results have been, in one sense, amazing. In addition to the major denominations such as Roman Catholicism, the various major Protestant bodies, and the Jewish synagogues, there are literally hundreds of other groups which are often referred to as sects or cults. The exact number is not known, but more than a thousand different groups can be identified. (cf. Melton, 1979) If one wishes to worship God there are a variety of possibilities. In recent years there has been a significant increase in the number of "new" religions, such as the Hare Krishna movement, the Unification Church (commonly known as the "Moonies"), the Children of God, Zen Buddhism, and numerous others. The "new" aspect of these religions applies primarily to their prominence in the United States. Some are older than Christianity but have only recently become highly visible in this country.

Membership in either the major denominations or the "new" religions is very high. In 1975 the Gallup poll asked a sample of the American population, "Do you happen to be a member of a church or synagogue, or not?" and 71% replied "yes." (*The Gallup Opinion Index*, Report 130, 1975). This was down from 77% in 1936. Actual membership is probably less than this percentage but, nevertheless, a large majority of Americans do belong to some church. Americans attend church: the 21-year average from 1955 to 1975 was 44% reporting church attendance during an average week. A large percentage reported belief in God and Jesus Christ and other doctrinal matters. Finally, Americans support churches financially. Construction of new churches involves millions of dollars annually, and giving for all types of charities, including churches, reaches billions of dollars each year.

However, in the midst of widespread membership and participation in the churches there is genuine concern among leaders and laity alike that the United States is becoming a "secular" society, one in which the influence of religion is waning. The nature of this argument is very complex, but proponents of secularism argue that membership and attendance are wholly inadequate indices of religiosity. Belonging to a church may have only social significance. People may report belief in God or Jesus Christ, but this belief varies widely among those belonging to churches. Glock and Start (1968) found that 99% of Southern Baptists but only 41% of Congregationalists "know God really exists." Figures for other denominations ranged between these two extremes. Belief in some traditional tenets, such as "Jesus was born of a virgin" or "there is a life beyond death," ranged, respectively, from highs of 99% and 97% for Southern Baptists to lows of 21% and 36% for Congregationalists. Conservatives continue to hold traditional beliefs but more liberal bodies have largely abandoned them.

In the late 1960s the idea that "God is dead" attracted much attention among theologians. Some pronounced that God was indeed dead and we had entered a religionless era. While the intensity of this debate has subsided it has by no means disappeared. Certainly the changes in the Roman Catholic Church in recent years have given support to those who argue that religious influence in our society has declined. The changes in the mass, the decline in enrollment in seminaries, and the increasing number of Roman Catholics who choose not to abide by church teachings in such matters as the use of birth control and divorce point to, at the least, marked departures from early eras when the Church could largely dictate adherence to its position on given matters.

On the other hand, there has been a surge in fundamentalist religious groups in this society who urge return to "biblical" morality. The Moral Majority may not be a majority, but its efforts to sway political decisions cannot be lightly dismissed. Fundamentalist religious groups affirm traditional patterns of morality—particularly in the areas of family and sexuality. They may be the only religious groups which still preach against personal "sins"—which they define as sex outside of marriage, drug usage, divorce, etc.

There are, as there always have been, a few who argue that the eventual disappearance of religion is certain. Few data support this position. Changes affect religion as they do all societal institutions. Religion is changing and will continue to do so. But the continued search for the ultimate meaning of life, one of the major questions which religion seeks to answer, suggests that it will persist.

The "God is dead" debate is examined in the selection from Avery Corman's novel, *Oh, God!* The interview between God and the central character of the novel, a writer-reporter, occurs because God himself is concerned that people are going about saying that he is dead, or worse, that he never existed.

Art Buchwald asks the question, "Should Churches Stay Open?" If churches have services on Christmas Day, won't this interfere with efforts to make Christmas into a wholly secular and commercial holiday?

Some Christians continue to believe that Jesus was born of a virgin. In "Miss Higginbotham Declines," Don Marquis relates an account of God's trying to have a second virgin birth in our time and the problems he encounters in securing the cooperation of a virgin to help him.

Nachman, in "Six Semi-Deadly Sins," says that "depravity is so commonplace today that a fellow hardly knows what to do anymore if he wants to feel especially evil...." He offers some contemporary versions of gluttony and other perversions designed to make you feel evil.

 AVERY CORMAN

Is God Dead?

"I'LL TELL you why I'm doing this," He said. "They've been going around saying I'm dead or worse."

"What's worse?"

"That I never was, or what I was was gas or *shmutz*."

"*Shmutz*?"

"You know, particles. With the big bang theories and the little bang theories. When you're God, it's insulting."

He was confiding in me!

"Let's stop right here. I really think you should be talking to somebody higher up. The Pope maybe."

"No, I looked into this. And you're my fella."

I'm His fella! What if I don't ask the right questions? What if I misquote Him? A misquote here has cosmic significance.

"Excuse me. What do I call you?"

"Call me God."

"God, I think I should have a tape recorder."

"Forget it. It wouldn't work."

"Why?"

"My voice—it wouldn't come out on the tape."

"I don't understand."

"I can't go into it. It's very complex. It's like . . . what would you understand? Ghosts. You know how they used to say a ghost was not supposed to cast a shadow? Well, it's like that. You can't record God's voice."

"I really don't understand."

"*Oy-oy-oy*," He said. "Because it's not my real voice. I'm just making this up for you, so you can hear it. I mean, I'm God over everybody, but I'm not speaking Chinese, am I?"

"Actually you sound a little Jewish."

"What then? You're a little Jewish, aren't you?"

"Yes."

"So like I'm telling you, I'm doing this for you. By the way, I was at your Bar Mitzvah. It didn't knock me out."

"You were there?"

"I'm there for everything—prayers, weddings, Bar Mitzvahs, funerals, baptisms—you name it. 'The Pledge of Allegiance' to the flag with that *under God* thing in it—I'm there. A fella stubs his toe and says 'goddammit'—I'm there. Kate Smith sings 'God Bless America'—I'm there."

"For everything? Everywhere on earth, any time anyone invokes the name of God . . . ?"

"I'm there. I got to cover a lot of territory in my work."

"That's an incredible concept. That's something Man has wanted to know for centuries. Are prayers heard? Does God listen?"

"Who says I listen? I only said I'm there. After a while, who can listen?"

"Then God *doesn't* care."

"I care. I care plenty. But what can I do?"

"But you're God!"

"Only for The Big Picture."

"What?"

"I don't get into details."

"Why?"

"It's better that I shouldn't meddle. What am I going to do—get into favorites? So I come up with the concepts, the big ideas—the details can take care of themselves."

"Then the way things happen on earth...."

"They happen. Don't look at me."

"And there's no plan, no scheme that controls our destinies?"

"A lot of it is luck. Luck and who you know."

I was staggered. He just went zipping along.

"Looking back, of course I made a few mistakes. Giraffes. It was a good thought, but it really didn't work out. Avocados—on that I made the pit too big. Then there are things that worked pretty good. Photosynthesis is a big favorite of mine. Spring is nice. Tomatoes are cute. Also raccoons."

"But what about *Man*?" I was trying to rise to the responsibility. "What about his future? The future of the planet?"

"It's a good question."

"And?"

"I couldn't tell you."

"Don't you know?"

"Well, like I say, I don't get into that. Of course I hope you make it. I mean, I'm a real fan. But it's like in a ball game. If you're in the stands, you can root, but that's about all."

"You're God. You can protect our future, alleviate suffering, work miracles!"

"I don't do miracles. They're too flashy and they upset the natural balance. Oh, maybe I'll do a miracle now and then, just for fun—if it's not too important. The last miracle I did was the 1969 Mets and before that the 1914 Boston Braves and before that I think you have to go back to the Red Sea."

"But, as God, you have the power to intervene, to help us in emergencies."

"So where do I draw the line? Say a fella is going to eat a hamburger that's not 100 percent beef. What do I do, knock it out of his hand? How would you like to live with Divine Hands popping out of the sky all the time? It would make people crazy."

"But I'm talking about wars and poverty and health. That's not on the level of hamburgers."

"That depends on where you sit."

"So you've decided to just let us stumble along, and never do a thing to help?"

"You got to understand, I went through my manipulative, controlling stage. You know what I mean from manipulative? It was back in the Ten Commandments days. Now I had it in mind there should be about five thousand commandments, to cover every eventuality. Things like: Thou Shalt Pick Up the Trash from the Picnic Areas. Thou Shalt Help Old Ladies to Cross the Road, Unless You're an Old Lady, in Which Case You Should Watch Good. Like that. Then I changed my mind and did a rewrite. I got it down to about eight hundred commandments. But even that was a little cumbersome. So I rewrote again and got it down to a hundred. Then all the way down to fifteen. Only Moses told me, 'They'll never sit still for fifteen commandments, make it eight.' And I said twelve. And he said nine. And I said ten. And he said *sold*. But he was wrong anyway. They don't even sit still for ten."

"Well, you may think we've disappointed you, but you've disappointed us." Imagine me coming on to Him that way, but somehow I found the nerve and I had to say it. "How can you permit the suffering that goes on in the world?"

"I don't. You do," He said.

"You're not involved."

"Listen—I keep up. I know what's going on. Of course, I don't read enough. I mean nonfiction I never read because, after all, I know everything. Fiction I could read more of. But mostly I prefer television."

"You watch television?"

"The news I don't watch because nothing on the news is news to me. Flip Wilson I like. He puts on a zippy show. Sports I watch. Except baseball I don't like too much on television. It's better in the ball park."

"I'm having a lot of trouble focusing on what it is you do."

"That's just it. Most of what I do, I did. I created the world, which is something. In six days. I work very fast. But now I just sort of watch over it. I guess you can say in a sense I'm retired."

"Right. Exactly what a lot of people feel today. God is retired, absent, dead. The same thing."

"It's not. Retired means I'm around, only I'm not as active. Look at it this way. In the old days, I had a lot more to do, setting things up. That's why I put in so many more appearances back then. Now I sit, I watch, I take a walk."

"You take a walk?"

"In the metaphysical sense. Don't try to understand it. But I see everything. I listen to everything. Even the new music. I can't get no-o satis-fac-tion. Also while I'm on this topic, there was one popular song a while back about believing that for every drop of rain that falls, a flower grows. Well, I want to straighten that out while I'm here. There is some rain that just falls. It just falls. It has nothing to do with flowers."

I was in way over my head—was I ever!—but I was trying to organize in my mind what He was saying.

"Well, it seems to me, if you're not as active as you once were, maybe that's why people are losing faith."

"So that's why I'm here. I'm a little worried. People today, they'll worship, who knows what? Like I used to think maybe they'd end up worshiping a car. God would be the 1940 Lincoln Continental. Now I sometimes think it could be an experience, like flying first-class to Hawaii, eating a steak and watching a movie. That could be a God-thing."

"Yes, but looking at it from our standpoint, frankly, how much more are you offering?"

"Listen to him. I got myself a real ipsy-pipsy here."

"What I mean is—God finally reveals Himself in our time and what is His message? I'm not too active, so why don't you stumble along? I hope you make it."

"Such a smart fella and you missed the point. Now write this down, word for word, so nobody else should miss it. The thing is—to use the expression—God lives! This is important. If God was dead or never was, *then* you should be plenty worried because you wouldn't know if what you got can even work. But God is here and He's giving you a guarantee. I'm telling you that I set all this up for you and made it so it *can* work. Only the deal is *you* have to work at it and you shouldn't look to me to do it for you. So? That's not hopeful?"

"Possibly."

"Possibly he gives me. Go. Tell them what I said. God says they got everything they need—it's all built in, and on that I give my word."

I wrote it down word for word.

"And make sure the story gets placed good, so lots of people will read it," He said.

It was apparent the interview was over. I didn't know what was appropriate to say. Do you say "Amen?" I said, "Thank you."

"That's all right. I'll tell you what. You been such a good fella, I'll give you a little personal advice. Your last play. It's not bad, but you got third act trouble. If you cut a little from Act II and combine it with Act III and make it a two act play, you'll have something good. Listen to me. I know from this."

OH, GOD! from the novel by Avery Corman. Copyright (c) by the author.

ART BUCHWALD

Should Churches Stay Open?

One of the big questions confronting the country is "Should the churches be allowed to remain open on Christmas Day?"

A group of citizens have banned together to protest the way churches are trying to turn Christmas into a religious holiday.

Wendell Wankel, their spokesman, said, "If we allow the churches to do business on Christmas Day, the holiday will lose all its commercial meaning.

"We believe that Christmas is a time for gift giving and eating and television watching, and anything that interferes should be forbidden."

"But," I protested, "there are some people who would like to go to church on Christmas Day. Surely you don't want to interfere with that?"

"They can go to church on Sunday or during the week. Why do they insist on going the one day of the year when people should stay home and enjoy the fruits of our great economy?"

"Maybe they want to thank God for all the good things He has brought them," I suggested.

"That's not enough of a reason to keep the churches open," Wankel said. "Look at all the traffic congestion it causes. The church bells wake up people who are trying to sleep late. Besides, why shouldn't priests and ministers have a day off like everybody else?"

"Maybe they like to work on Christmas."

"That's not the point," Wankel said. "If you keep the churches open, you detract from the great materialistic fervor in this country. We say religion has its place, but not at Christmas."

"But," I said, "Christmas *once* was a religious holiday."

"When?" Wankel asked.

"Quite a few years ago. I read a book that said at one time the religious aspect of Christmas was more important than the exchanging of gifts."

"I don't believe you," Wankel said.

"It's true. The original idea of Christmas was to celebrate the birth of Christ."

"You read that in a book?" he asked disbelievingly.

"Yup. Serious gift giving didn't take place in this country until the department stores got into it. Before that, people gave their children toys and went to church. In some communities going to church was the highlight of Christmas Day."

"I'd like to see that book," Wankel said suspiciously. "Anyway that was another era, and we're dealing with *today*. Our main point is that if you keep churches open, people will feel a temptation to go to them. Entire families may wind up there, and this could hurt the ski-resort business very badly."

"I respect your feelings about Christmas, Wankel," I said, "but I don't think any group in the United States should dictate to any other group what houses of worship must remain open or closed on Christmas."

Wankel replied, "Too much time, money, and advertising have gone into Christmas to have a small minority spoil it by going to church. We're not against churches per se. We're just against churches remaining open on the one day of the year that is sacred to our gross national product."

"Suppose, in spite of your protests, the churches still remain open on Christmas Day. What will you do?"

Wankel smiled. "God will show us a way."

Reprinted with permission of the author.

DON MARQUIS

Miss Higginbotham Declines

"I *wish* everybody would be good," murmured Jehovah, a little plaintively, as he stroked his neat beard and stared out the club window.

And then he fell to considering all the devices he had employed in the last few thousand years in order to persuade, or to compel, people to be good. And after some thought, it occurred to him that the one which had been, on the whole, the most successful had been sending his Only Begotten Son to this planet to give human beings an example of a life lived in consonance with the highest ideals.

Of course, Jesus hadn't been altogether understood. He had been crucified. But the ideas that he had promulgated had, to a very considerable extent, survived his crucifixion; and they had influenced millions of persons throughout several centuries in the most beneficent way. It was true that vast tracts of territory inhabited by enormous populations had never been appreciably influenced by the doctrines known as Christian; and in Christendom itself there was a good deal of lip-loyalty to Jesus that had nothing whatever behind it. The thing certainly hadn't been a complete success, in the sense of inspiring the whole population of the planet to an imitation of Jesus's idealism.

And yet, hadn't it been more of a success than anything else he had ever tried—in the way of spreading notions of kindliness, with here and there some rather notable results in the field of human conduct?

Suddenly Jehovah caught the idea he had been groping for— why not send *another* Begotten Son? It seemed so simple, now that he had thought of it, that he wondered it had not come to him sooner.

And should this one be born of a virgin, also? Jehovah pondered, and decided: Yes. Yes—people were, used to that; they would accept it, therefore, the more readily.

But *what* virgin?

He thought of the very woman; and taking his light overcoat and hat and his carved malacca stick, he left the club at once. For with him, to think was to act.

"Washington Square," he told his driver, and entered the limousine which was waiting for him at the corner. And in a few minutes the car drew up at the curb in front of one of the good old houses which still stand on the north side of the Square; one of the few private residences still remaining in that block.

A Miss Higginbotham lived in the house; and she would live there until she died, no matter what might happen to the rest of the neighborhood, because she had been born there. She was a person who abhorred change of any sort, and for the most part she ignored it. Her ancestors had come to America in the *Mayflower* and had conspicuously helped in shaping the life of New England. Miss Higginbotham's father had been the first of the line to leave New England. Or, rather, he had attempted to bring as much of New England as he might with him to New York City; he did this because he felt it to be his duty, just as one of his brothers had gone as a missionary to the heathen of India.

Miss Higginbotham, needless to say, had no sympathy whatever with the notions professed by many of the younger women of New York today; but there was very little she could do to combat them— very little except to live her own sort of life with a more determined intensity. And she was upheld by her feeling that her kind of existence tallied with the ideals of many millions throughout America who contrive to make the quality of their puritanism heard and felt in spite of all the flagrant iniquity of the era.

Jehovah was ushered into a bright and sunny sitting room on the second floor at the front of the house, overlooking the Square. And he noticed with satisfaction the evidences of an exquisitely refined taste in the sparseness and chastity of the furnishing and decoration. Not that the mood was bleakly Lacedaemonian; on the contrary, one felt in it what one felt in the woman herself: a delicate selection of the objects upon which it might be worth while to glance and touch with the white flame of puritanism.

Jehovah proceeded at once to state the object of his visit.

Miss Higginbotham lifted to him a puzzled brow, and it was evident from the perplexity which clouded the clarity of her deep gray eyes that she did not really comprehend.

She had known Jehovah instantly; her perceptions were too keen to permit her to believe that any imposture was being attempted; and, indeed, there emanated from the presence of Jehovah a majesty and sincerity which made doubt impossible to anyone. It was plain to him that Miss Higginbotham's perplexity arose from the fact that she could not reconcile such a request with her habitual ideas of deity.

"It is an honor which I intend for you; you are to be rewarded above all other women of your place and time because of your purity and devotion," said Jehovah.

"Honored?" said Miss Higginbotham. And there was the faintest trace of asperity in the tone of her voice and upon her regularly beautiful features.

Jehovah thought he saw her difficulty.

"When I speak of another Begotten Son," said Jehovah, reassuringly, "I do not mean to imply the necessity of any such communication as is usual between husband and wife. Do you understand me?"

Her blush showed that Miss Higginbotham had understood.

"This matter," continued Jehovah, "can be kept entirely an affair of the spirit."

"I do not see," replied Miss Higginbotham with a tremor of indignation, "that that makes the slightest difference!"

Jehovah regarded her with something like amazement, if it is proper to say that a deity can be amazed.

"Do you mean to say," he inquired, "that you *refuse*, Miss Higginbotham?"

"I mean to say," she replied, "that I consider myself most outrageously insulted!"

"But——" began Jehovah.

"Coming from you," she interrupted with a wail. "Oh, from *you!*" And she burst into tears.

He waited until she had returned to something like her former calm, and then he suggested gently: "You certainly do not think, Miss Higginbotham, that I would *deliberately* insult you?"

"Then," said she, steadying her voice, "why come to me at all with such a terrible proposal?"

"Let us comprehend one another, Miss Higginbotham," he said. "Am I to understand that you have declined the honor for which I destined you because of some obscure moral inhibition?"

"I should think," said Miss Higginbotham, poised and firm and chastely beautiful, "that you would be the last person in the universe to refer to my motive as *obscure!*"

Then she added, with the sublime simplicity of her traditions: "I am a lady."

"I would be the last to doubt it," said Jehovah, with an old-world courtliness. "And," he continued, "it is precisely the fine fragrance of your maiden ladyhood, the rare essence of your pure morality, which I require in making this experiment."

Jehovah tried another tack.

"Miss Higginbotham," he said, briskly, "I shall permit you to assume, for the sake of argument, that your ideas of right and wrong are superior to mine. They aren't, Miss Higginbotham—but I am in a lenient mood today, and I am not going to force into your consciousness any conception that might have a suddenly shattering effect upon your ego. As you are now, I shall permit you to remain, until the process of natural growth makes you something other. So, keep on thinking that you are right.

"You are right—for the sake of argument—you are right. Let us go on from there. Let me ask a sacrifice of you. Will you not swerve from your rightness for the sake of saving a world? Will you not be wrong once so that millions of others may be led to righteousness? Will you not permit your morality, and your sense of what is due yourself and your morality, to go by the board, in order that vast numbers of the population of this struggling earth may be led to the joys and securities of salvation?"

They looked at each other in silence for a moment with this thought between them. Presently Jehovah remarked:

"There are a great many things in the cosmos which seem to be utterly paradoxical to human beings, but which are quite simple to deity because deity has, after all, an opportunity for a broader and more reconciling outlook. I wish you would take my word for it that what I am asking of you will never be counted against you as a sin but rather to your glory. Can't you trust in the breadth of my vision?"

"You have pointed out to me a number of times," said Miss Higginbotham, "that I do not have your breadth of vision. That is the whole point. I must act according to the vision which has been vouchsafed to me. If I am narrow, then I am narrow. If you wanted me broader, you should have made me broader."

"But," said Jehovah, "isn't there any warmth springing up in your bosom at the thought of a divine mothership?"

"Not," replied Miss Higginbotham, compressing the beautiful contour of her lips into a firm straight line, "not at the thought of motherhood out of wedlock. I am respectable."

Jehovah arose and made her a most dignified and gracious bow. "Madam," he said, "permit me to offer myself in marriage to you."

Miss Higginbotham looked at him gratefully. Her self-respect seemed to be somewhat restored by this courtly gesture. Her lips parted; it seemed as if a syllable of eager assent quivered upon them.

And then her lips closed tightly again while the old troubled look came back into her eyes. Slowly she shook her head from side to side. Finally she said: "I do not approve of polygamy."

"Polygamy?" Jehovah seemed genuinely puzzled.

"If your union with the mother of your first son was quite regular," said Miss Higginbotham, "and still exists, it is obvious that another union of the sort must be essentially polygamous."

"Oh, I see what you mean," murmured Jehovah.

"If, on the other hand," continued Miss Higginbotham, "your union was *not* regular, I could not consider uniting myself in matrimony with a person whose past did not conform to my own standards of propriety."

Jehovah sat down again and meditated.

Possibly he was a little displeased. He made a rather impatient movement and plucked somewhat irritably at his beard. Perhaps more of his omnipotence than he intended escaped from him in his passing irritation. For a seismic shock was felt throughout Manhattan Island. The great towers such as the Woolworth Building vibrated and quivered throughout their steel frameworks.

"Am I to understand," he asked, "that you do not approve, Miss Higginbotham, of the former virgin birth?"

"It was all right for those times," said Miss Higginbotham, "but I do hope we have made *some* progress morally in the last 1900 years!"

There was another interval of silence. In the sunny sitting room Jehovah once more considered the situation. His charm, as he had already determined, he would not use; he would employ no arts wherewith to fascinate this woman. Persuasion had failed. He might use compulsion if he chose, but he had a distaste for that method.

He did not even remind Miss Higginbotham that compulsion would be easy to him, that he had but to will the thing which he requested and it would be instantly accomplished. For he was certain that if he spoke to her in this manner she would reply that she "*preferred death to disgrace*." And he had had about all he could stand of that kind of talk for one day; all that any self-respecting deity could reasonably be expected to listen to and pardon in a mere human being. More than this, he was aware that Miss Higginbotham, with the candor of her nature, relied on him to play the part of a gentleman and respect her motives; he would not disappoint her in this.

And with this willingness to allow the beautiful and resolute virgin her victory there came also the thought that perhaps after all she might not be exactly the ideal character to mother a new saviour of the world. He arose with dignity.

"Miss Higginbotham," he said to her, "I bid you good-afternoon. You have met Jehovah face to face and given him something to think about. I wish also to leave a thought with you—not by way of criticism but merely as a stimulus to possible spiritual growth. You must consider whether the quality of your chastity does not somewhat resemble a spiritual sterility."

With that he left the room. The neatly dressed maid who showed him to the street door on the floor below, a red-lipped, common person with an appealing liquidity of the eye, could not help but think as she glanced at him: "What a splendid-looking man! I wish——"

But she checked the thought. Nevertheless, Jehovah had caught it. He turned and gazed upon her from the doorstep, long and smilingly, and an ecstatic thrill pervaded the vital creature.

Within a year she gave birth to a son, and this child may be somewhere in the world now, and it is possible that great, saintly things are to be expected of him.

GERALD NACHMAN

Six Semi-Deadly Sins

Depravity is so commonplace today that a fellow hardly knows what to do anymore if he wants to feel especially evil—hence, new taboos must be found to make the ordinary man feel as crummy and low-down as he used to when the seven deadly sins were less dull.

Murder, rape, torture, terrorism—they've all been done to death.

After discussing the problem with some master criminals, I came up with a few suggested vices for the modern citizen who desires to feel properly wretched, reprehensible acts highly recommended by professional big-time sinners.

Watching a Rerun of "Love Boat" on a Monday Afternoon:

This is unusually wicked, since Monday is the one day not to be squandered on major silliness. Simply switching on a TV set at 3:30 p.m. creates immediate intense feelings of guilt, which are then multiplied by purposely tuning in to the shabbiest third-rate show available at an hour when all decent, law-abiding people are busily engaged in meaningful pursuits.

Going Out at Midnight, Buying a Large Pepperoni Pizza, Bringing It Home and Wolfing It Down All by Yourself:

To achieve this state of exquisite squalor, you have to be at an extremely low point in your life; if not, this will hurry it along. The very thought of such a despicable act makes one writhe with self-loathing. Many experienced evildoers, asked if they'd ever performed such a rotten deed, could scarcely hide their disgust. "It's unthinkable and inexcusable," said one man on death row. "I mean, it's repulsive enough to consume a pizza all alone, but in your very own living room? How gross!"

Going to a Horrible Movie on Your Lunch Hour:

Businessmen were once able to feel fairly scummy by attending an X-rated film at noontime, but even this old thrill has now sadly degenerated into accepted practice. Rather than ducking into a porno house, therefore, today's ne'er-do-well might consider seeing just a plain lousy G-rated movie-*Herbie Goes to Monte Carlo*, say. To increase his feelings of filth tenfold, he must lunch on a large sack of popcorn, a giant Coke and a big Baby Ruth bar. (Once, I snuck off by myself to a Wednesday matinee of a Broadway musical and felt unclean for weeks. I didn't dare confess to it, but my wife eventually pulled the truth out of me.)

Passing Through a Town You Once Lived in and Stopping at a Telephone Booth to Look Up the Number of an Old Girlfriend:

You need not actually call her at home—and probably won't—to be overcome by waves of wickedness. It's quite degenerate enough merely to thumb through the phone book as devious little fantasies race around your mind. Among 218 death row thugs, only two would own up to ever having committed this ghastly perversion.

Checking into a Ritzy Hotel and Immediately Dialing Room Service:

This is a decadent binge favored by people on expense accounts and junkets, but that takes all of the indecency out of it, alas. If you really want to feel guilt pangs, the thing to do is dial room service when *you're* paying the bill and order a sirloin steak and strawberry shortcake the minute you check in.

Fixing Yourself a Dinner Consisting Entirely of 283 Crackers with Butter and Jam, Topped Off by a Dozen or So Hostess Chocolate Donuts and a Side of Cool Whip:

If you plan to try anything as naughty as this—a dieter's descent into hell—you must first shut all the doors tightly and pull the shades so nobody can witness the senseless carnage going on inside your kitchen.

"Six Semi-Deadly Sins" from OUT ON A WHIM by Gerald Nachman. Copyright (c) 1983 by Gerald Nachman. Reprinted by permission of Doubleday & Co., Inc.

QUESTIONS FOR DISCUSSION

1. In a humorous fashion Avery Corman raises some profound questions. Does God perform miracles today? Is God in control of our destinies? Does God have the power to intervene in emergencies? How do you think members of conservative religious groups would answer these questions? How would liberal churches answer the same questions? How do you answer them?

2. One sociologist states that "the assumption that the supernatural exists raises a new question. *What does the supernatural want or expect from us?*" (Stark, 1985:311–12) Based on the conception of God presented in *Oh, God!* what is the answer to this question?

3. The hero of Corman's *Oh, God!* says, "I'm having a lot of trouble focusing on what you do." Is this statement characteristic of the religious era in which we live? God replies, "That's just it. Most of what I do, I did." What religious groups in our society would strongly disagree with this interpretation of God's activity in our world?

4. In 1983 the American Civil Liberties Union (ACLU) filed suit against Pawtucket, R. I., seeking to prevent it from displaying a Christian Nativity scene. The argument was that the Nativity scene was an endorsement of religion. The suit reached the U.S. Supreme Court which upheld the city. The Nativity scene has since, however, been turned over to a private group for display. (*Harrisburg Patriot*, Oct. 3, 1983) School districts

across the country have had protests from groups about singing the familiar Christmas carols. Are these events a part of
the larger picture which Buckwald is discussing when he asks
if the churches should be allowed to stay open on Christmas?
How is it related to the debate over secularism?

5. Is Wankel right when he says that Christmas is more a materialistic celebration of "our great economy" than it is a religious holiday?

6. Christmas periodically occurs on a Sunday. Do you know
   whether or not attendance is up, or down, when Christmas
   occurs on Sunday? If it is down, what does this suggest about
   the spiritual nature of the Christmas celebration?

7. Wankel says that if churches were open on Christmas it
   "could hurt the ski-resort business very badly." Are churches
   able to compete effectively with Sunday activities of a commercial nature? Is it only nonchurch members who participate
   in these other activities?

8. Miss Higginbotham declines Jehovah's offer of motherhood
   with the reply: "I am a lady." If we are to believe sociological
   studies of extramarital activities and instructions such as Miss
   Manners (Chapter 9) finds it necessary to offer, are there any
   "ladies" left in the 1980s?

9. Faced with Miss Higginbotham's refusal Jehovah says "he
   might use compulsion if he chose, but he had a distaste for
   that method." Is this the same conception of God which
   Corman presents in the selection, *Oh, God?* Is our conception
   of God and the use of force associated, perhaps, with patterns
   of criminal justice in the United States?

10. In our day if a woman reported that she has been impregnat-
    ed by the Holy Spirit, as Mary reported in the New Testa-
    ment, what do you think the reaction would be? If some
    Christians no longer believe in the virgin birth of Jesus, is this
    a measure of secularization? What about Southern Baptists
    and others who continue to believe this—are they not secular?

11. Nachman says that "simply switching on a TV set at 3:30 P.M.
    creates immediate intense feelings of guilt" since "law-abiding
    people are busily engaged in meaningful pursuits" at this time
    of the day. Do college students, some at any rate, struggle

with feelings of guilt about watching day-time soaps when they might be studying? What, if any, behavior (to the best of your knowledge) creates a sense of guilt among college students?

12. Dieting is widespread in our society. Do you think wolfing down a large pepperoni pizza at midnight would create a sense of guilt among those on a diet?

13. One might not feel a sense of guilt at going to a G-rated movie, but is it not true that young people tend to avoid G-rated movies? Is this out of a sense of embarrassment? What else might cause this behavior?

14. Nachman suggests that conventional sins such as "murder, rape, torture, and terrorism" have all been "done to death." What behavior, other than these conventional acts, is considered "sinful" today?

REFERENCES

Glock, Charles Y., and Stark, Rodney. *American Piety: The Nature of Religious Commitment.* Berkeley: Univ. of California Press, 1968.

Melton, J. Gordon. *Encyclopedia of American Religions.* Gaithersburg, Md.: Consortium Books, 1979.

Stark, Rodney. *Sociology.* Belmont, Calif.: Wadsworth Publishing Company, 1975.

VII

SOCIAL CHANGE

Chapter Twelve

Changing Sexual Norms

READINGS

We come to sex. If there is a topic of widespread interest in our society today it is sexual behavior. A parody on the popular television commercial for Rolaids asks the question: "How do you spell relief? I spell it S–E–X." Ours is not the first society to have an interest in sex, but it may be the first to acknowledge it so openly. Profound social changes have swept the western world in the past 30 years. We have become highly industrialized and then, swiftly, passed into a post-industrial era. As noted in the last chapter, religion has experienced such changes that some consider ours a secular society in which religion has minimal influence. In the midst of these changes sex, too, has undergone a revolution. There can be little doubt that the attitudes and behavior of people regarding their sexual nature have changed dramatically from 30 years ago.

In 1948 Kinsey and his associates published a massive research study on *Sexuality in the Human Male.* (Kinsey, et. al., 1948) This was followed in 1953 by a report on female sexual activity. (Kinsey, et. al., 1953) The Kinsey studies were pioneering efforts to bring sexual study "out of the closet." There had been much research on sexual behavior prior to them, but for a variety of reasons, the Kinsey studies were, literally, front page news in many of the nation's major newspapers. Since their publication the studies have been widely cited by later sex researchers. This is true even though they have serious methodological deficiencies which have been repeatedly criticized. They were not, for example, representative of either the male or female population in this country. All the subjects were white males or females, some were prison inmates, too many were midwesterners, and too many were young or Jewish to be representative of the nation's population. Despite these shortcomings the findings were a major breakthrough in efforts to understand this important area of human behavior.

Since the Kinsey studies social scientists have continued to conduct extensive and significant research in this area. One major finding of this research is that there are a variety of perspectives which people have concerning their sexual nature. David Schulz (1979) has succinctly summarized seven basic ways in which sex is regarded in our society.

First, sex is, of course, understood as the means of reproduction. For centuries the Christian church in the western world taught that this was the only purpose of sex. Sex as pleasure was not perceived as the reason couples would engage in this activity. However, sex as pleasure has now come to be the second dominant understanding in our society of sexual activity. Reproduction may occur when sex is engaged in for pleasure, but sex as an end in itself is widely accepted today as a legitimate expression of the emotion men and women may feel for each other. This can occur both within and outside of marriage. Most religious groups today recognize the legitimacy of sex as pleasure within marriage. A few are willing to discuss, at least, the possibility that the pleasure of sex outside marriage is not always "sinful." Of course, many of the more fundamentalist religious churches will not consider this possibility at all.

There is also a view of "dirty" or obscene sex which is widespread in our society. Pornography does not cover all forms of obscene sex, but our literature, movies, and television channels regularly offer what many define as obscene sex. As Schulz notes: "nonreproductive sexual behavior such as masturbation, intercourse with animals, oral–genital, and anal–genital sex between persons of the same or opposite sex are commonly considered 'perverted' or obscene in part as a result of the long-established tradition that sex is essentially baby-making." (1979:9) Legal efforts to define obscenity have proved to be largely unsuccessful due to widespread differences of opinion.

For some, the important aspect of sex is its playful nature. Schulz refers to this as "casual" sex. It is the "playboy" philosophy made popular among some segments of the population by the magazine of the same name. Those who adopt this view are referred to by some as *promiscuous*. What is notable is the freedom which exists today to acknowledge noncommittal relationships of a sexual nature—as illustrated by many couples who cohabit but make little effort to disguise this relationship.

Sex also may be viewed as sacred. Some religious worship, particular forms of Tantric yoga, for example, consider sexual intercourse as an aspect of worship. There are biblical accounts of near eastern religions where temple prostitutes were used as adjuncts to worship (and condemned by Jewish law, cf. Deut. 23:17). In the western religious heritage sex as sacred was not a view which prevailed. Sex was more likely to be denounced as one of the sins of the flesh to be avoided by those seeking salvation.

The sixth kind of sex is commercial or criminal sex, which exists today as it has for centuries. Prostitution, rape, child molestation, and homosexuality are still forms of sex which may lead to arrest and imprisonment. Much debate centers around homosexuality between consenting partners. Laud Humphreys' work (1970) documents the existence of oral sex among all class levels in society and the legal debates over this practice. The political and religious conservatism of the late 1980's has drawn particular societal attention to this sixth type of sexual activity.

Finally, sex may be viewed from a clinical perspective. A major expression of this viewpoint is found in the scores of sex manuals published in our society and in the sex education courses in schools. Sex therapy adopts the position that many forms of sexual expression previously considered "perversions," e.g., oral sex and masturbation, should be considered simply variations on traditional heterosexual intercourse. Kinsey's work, previously noted, and more recent studies by such well-known clinicians as Masters and Johnson (1966) support this view of sexual behavior.

Given the existence of a pluralistic view of sex in our society it is important to ask the simple question: which is the dominant view of sex? Are there normative sexual patterns from which others may be considered departures? Few would argue that sex as reproduction is the attitude of a majority of the population. Some would readily assert that casual sex represents a majority opinion—especially among the younger generation. Schulz, for one, disagrees: "Casual sex is [a] part of the college scene for a very small percentage of students who are commonly called promiscuous. The dominant code on campus, however, is still probably abstinence from intercourse." (1979:13) Many would strongly take exception to Schulz's conclusion. Some sociologists and public health workers such as psychiatrists believe, however, that we are witnessing a retrenchment from the sexual revolution of the 1960s and 1970s. Dr. Shirley Zussman, a Manhattan sex therapist, says that "many men and women in their 30's who were in the forefront of the sexual revolution in the 1960's are beginning to question whether casual sex and the life style that goes with it is really as exciting as it has been made out to be. Many of these people, particularly women, began to see casual sex as a sign of an empty life, and the addition of the herpes scare gave them added pause to examine their sex lives." (*New York Times*, October 4, 1983) It may be that the current conservative philosophy in both the politics and religion of the 1980s is having an effect upon other areas of behavior as well.

One indirect measure of sexual attitudes in America is revealed in the manner in which humorists treat the subject. Thurber's now classic *Is Sex Necessary?*, published in 1919, is tame compared to much sexual humor being published today in popular magazines such as the *National Lampoon*. Indeed, much of the content of such publications as the *National Lampoon* simply could not have been published for open distribution when Thurber wrote. The same would be true for some of the material in the first selection by Judith Wax, "They Don't Make Sex Like They Used To," which addresses many of the current issues of sexual behavior today: sex manuals, sex orgies, single motherhood, and sex for older people. She bemoans the fact that "even if I *had* been born in time for the Sexual Revolution [my] parents wouldn't have let me go to it anyway. Not, at least, if it were being held in the summer; I was never allowed to go *anywhere* in polio season."

In the selection, "A Few Words About Breasts," Nora Ephron discusses one of the central issues faced by young females coming to puberty in our society. With what some have described as an "obsession" or a "fixation" on the female breast in today's sexual culture, how do females with small breasts adjust to the image of the "ideal" female breast?

The final selection, "Positions" by Vernard Eller, is a parody on the importance of various sexual positions in intercourse described in sex manuals. Eller's essay represents a part of the conservative opposition to such emphasis on sex in our society.

 JUDITH WAX

They Don't Make Sex Like They Used To

When Shel and I decided the world would be a better place once we contributed our issue to it, I experimented with the body temperature method to pinpoint the fertile days. The first time I tried it, though, I got scared and called my friend Sheila, who had put me onto the technique in the first place. "What do you do if the thermometer breaks in there?" I asked her. "Isn't the mercury dangerous?"

"In *where*?" Sheila said, and straightened me out when I told her. I'd imagined you had to regulate your temperature *in situ*, like preheating an oven. Doing a headstand afterward was my own fecundity ritual and meant to direct sperm traffic—like some wee dumb Chinooks—properly upstream.

Over the years, I did manage to become a lot more familiar with the body's terrain; when you're a short person, there's less to memorize. My friends tell similar stories of bodily incompetence (which a lot of us saw as good manners), and—happily—it would be hard to find our counterparts in naiveté among young women today. But occasionally I get an uneasy feeling that in the great leap forward, some of the excitement of discovery got trampled to death. You can take such a clinical, direct, and no-nonsense approach to sex that it's also no-fun. And though it's true that the mainstream of sexual advice runs to "relax, enjoy, and don't count orgasms" counsel, an impression lingers on of some ghostly expert standing by the bed with a digital computer.

There's no doubt that my generation as well as my mother's could have benefited vastly from today's general loosening up and availability of information. There are sexual self-help articles in nearly every magazine at nearly every checkout counter, and they're often written with such how-to-proceed clarity that they make the diagram in a box of tampons look like directions for making DNA at home. The catch with some of these articles is that in their fondness for terms of instruction like "doing your homework" (masturbation) and "the next assignment" (enlisting someone to rub you with baby oil) they can give you a feeling you're learning more about pant-by-numbers than ecstasy. For instance, I came across one self-help piece that charted a day-by-day, week-by-week plan for heightening sexual response through familiarity with your own body. It was meant to help women overcome problems of orgasmic dysfunction, a worthy goal and who would quarrel with it? But reading those instructions, you can get the disquieting feeling that if getting to know yourself isn't a little more fun than that, maybe you'd rather not be introduced.

This was basic Week One strategy: every day, for one week, look at your genitals in a mirror. For one hour each day. Now there's no question that she who considers her genitals repulsive, shameful, or second-class members needs attitudinal alteration, or maybe a bath. (I believe bidets ought to be an everyday American plumbing option, even though the one woman I know who owns a bidet—hers is red porphyry like Napoleon's tomb—only uses it to wash her feet.) Many women of my age can be grateful to younger ones for leading the way toward self-acceptance, even though most of us will never feel really relaxed with such refinements as the speculum buddy system. A lot of women learned late that what they grew up uneasily calling "down there" is really a nice place. Shakespeare's term was "a nest of spices," and a freshman I once interviewed said proudly, "The vagina is self-cleaning, you know." (She apparently had the same fixation on oven imagery I did twenty-three years earlier with my "fertility thermometer.")

Back to the Plan for Week One, however, and the daily crotch watch. Now heightened sensuality and correcting orgasmic reluctance are first-rate objectives. But one hour every day of mandatory staring could make you feel you were eight years old again and told to sit quietly through *The March of Time* because it would do you worlds of good. I think when you get the hang of staring (there could be an honor system) by whatever day it took, they should let you get up and read Colette or Nadine Gordimer or Jean Rhys to learn some other things about being a woman, or at least be dismissed early so you can go downstairs and start the soup.

Or why not just begin Week Two before the other pupils? Though that was the week you moved on to basic masturbating, again for the requisite one hour every day for seven days, there were still no concessions to the quick study. There wasn't even a hint about what to do in case *you're* finished before the hour is. In *Life Signs*, a sad and funny novel by the late Johanna Davis, the protagonist says that she's ashamed to admit to her psychiatrist that she has never masturbated. She's not, she confesses, even quite certain where to find her own clitoris, an oversight she ascribes to never having had "to do anything for herself which somebody else could be found to do for her." Now I can really identify with that; it's the reason I've never learned to change my own typewriter ribbon.

Still, it's obvious that character and I both need to unjell our mind-sets, so on to Week Three. There's danger by this time (the article didn't mention it) that if you've been following the previous weeks' schedule, you may have been locked in your room for so long people have forgotten you. But if you can still scare one up, this is the week for a partner to get into the act. Or acts. The problem is I can't remember exactly what they *are* or what the instructions were beyond this point (and for all I know I'm the last woman in this country who can't play the marimba with a dildo). I stopped reading, not because I couldn't use erotic instruction. No, indeed. It's just that if there's one thing I've always hated, it's knowing exactly where I'm going to *be* every day.

As for America's vibrator explosion, I'm not much of a reporter on that front, either. I don't even know anybody who uses one—or who talks about it, anyway. But then I didn't have much chance for ecstasy *ex machina*; my mother still warns me that people get electrocuted if they bathe during a lightning storm. Or keep the radio on.

When your own experience is limited, sometimes you have to rely on the testimony of strangers, such as the gentleman who wrote to a magazine's letters column to share his discovery of bliss beyond vibrator. He and his wife, he reported, had found something much better, and not only did the earth move, their whole condominium trembled when he stuffed the lady with scarves (he recommended top-quality silk ones) and slowly disengaged them. Perhaps when the scarves weren't in play for peak sex, she tied them into that little sling for one's bottom certain stylish ladies began wearing over skirts and slacks a few seasons ago.

It's hard to judge that couple's standing on the scale of looniness without knowing how old they were. Sexual perceptions, like so many other things, often depend on generational vantage point, and while we may perform the same acts (forget scarf tricks) with comparable, if older, equipment, we sometimes invest those acts with different meanings. A friend who is my age and a late-starting playwright was dazed by such perception differences when she went to a read-through of one of her plays. She is a gentle soul and her play, its wit, and its heroine (who exclaims, "Oh, fiddle!" as her creator sometimes does) are all gentle, too. But the acting troupe getting the feel of my friend's comedy to "see how it plays" was accustomed to stark, very contemporary confrontation drama and the director and cast were considerably younger than she was.

The main communication problem centered on a goat, whose dramatic significance—other than as laugh getter—was to point up the heroine's kindhearted vagueness. The animal had followed her home, and rather than confess having given it asylum in their basement, she explains the occasional offstage bleatings to her stuffy husband as "trouble with the furnace, dear."

During the run-through, my friend began squirming when it became apparent that the young woman playing the *Voice of the Turtle*—ish heroine was interpreting the character as though she'd sprung from the head of Albee. But the actress was conscientious about her craft, and afterward, in pursuit of motivational purity, she cornered the gentle, middle-aged playwright. "Is the woman I play actually making it with the goat?" the young actress inquired. "Or is she just bringing him off by hand?"

Though it's possible to share a great deal with a younger friend, even an age difference that seems inconsequential can suddenly become a chasm that leaves you standing on either side of it, staring at each other. A younger friend of mine is unmarried by choice and elected, in her thirties, to have and raise the baby when she became pregnant. ("It's now or never," she said, "and I don't want to miss the experience of motherhood.") I wouldn't presume to judge the wisdom of that, but I was pleased to be invited to a large shower given a few weeks after the baby was born, and flattered to be included among so many younger women who must have recognized (I told myself) my "young attitude," my flexibility. I was not, it turned out, flexible enough to jump the gap. I understood perfectly well the huge problems she faced in raising and supporting a child by herself and as an unmarried career woman/mother in a society not yet geared for such an arrangement. But as I watched her opening that undiminishing pyramid of baby gifts, the increasing worry I felt for her had nothing to do with the realities of her life and everything to do with what I'd once learned were the essential issues. Luckily, everyone at the shower thought my question was meant to be funny. "How will you *ever* manage to cope," I asked nervously, "with all the thank-you notes?"

Once Shel, too, nearly got a hernia trying to leap the age chasm. It happened the summer afternoon we were the only middle-aged couple invited to a party a group of younger married couples whom we barely knew gave at a farm they'd rented in the country. We congratulated ourselves (I'd blacked out the lesson of the shower) on being so noticeably young in spirit we'd been included in this gathering of our juniors. I suppose I will die with the still-fresh remembrance of Shel's struggle for composure when our young hostess greeted us as naked as the collection of children frolicking round her comely bottom. The only time I've seen my decorous husband so determined at facial control was at a dinner where he was seated next to a jolly, motherly-looking lady with a bristling, Jerry Colonna walrus mustache (its luxuriance not to be confused with standard superfluous hair). He knew he mustn't look, but his eyeballs wouldn't listen; above all, he felt he must fight his urge to *tell* the lady what had invaded her upper lip and to recite ancient

Burma Shave roadside jingles. And at the summer lawn fete where the hostess greeted him in radiant nakedness (a fact not one guest ever remarked upon, then or later), though he admired the weather as well as the chick-pea dip and addressed himself with great seriousness to this nation's foreign policy, I knew with what vein-popping restraint he was choking back, "Excuse me, young lady, but YOU DON'T HAVE ANY CLOTHES ON!"

Another middle-aged couple we know were chatting amiably at a party of younger couples when—at some mysterious signal—everyone shucked their clothes and leaped into the host's pool. The woman elected to sit it out poolside and think lofty thoughts, not easy for her when she saw her fifty-three-year-old husband throw caution, clothes, and everything except his Fruit of the Looms to the suburban wind and join the young swimmers, an "I do this all the time" look of non-chalance on his face, and his boxer shorts ballooning with water like some strange striped-cotton life preserver.

Neither that couple, nor my playwright friend the goat lady, nor Shel and I are closed to change and innovation; we simply need our glasses sometimes for the fine points. I like to think I'm as eager to learn about new things as I was in my Girl Scout days. I've even been known to experiment. Which is how it happened a few years ago that I (onetime wearer of boned, long-line Merry Widows) ventured into the world bravely braless. I'd recklessly bought a backless gown for some event, and there was no hiding place beneath it for underwear. A friend took an oath on her husband's life that I looked okay, however, and the halter straps that tied around my neck seemed to give just the proper little hoist I hoped might let me get away with it.

Yet while I think most young women look lovely with their nice protuberances perking through soft fabrics, I wasn't so addled as to think it was the right look for *me*, and that's where I drew the line. Or rather, drew on the adhesive bandage strips. The idea came from the saleswoman who sold me the gown, after I told her that though I loved it, I was worried I might embarrass myself if I got chilly when I wore it. Just stick the little one-inch strips on, she advised; *lots* of her customers did that and found there was no need to worry about pop-ups.

It worked! I felt comfortable, dashingly contemporary, moderately alluring—yet not aggressive. But though I may have pulled that off, retribution came in a different sort of pull-off. The little adhesive strips, this consumer can report, had never been nipple-tested when they were promoted as "ouchless." Many people claim that my screams were heard in Detroit, and the person who shares my life—

that sunshine husband—locked himself into the bathroom and cowered there till the all-clear.

If the Girl Scouts of America hadn't failed me when I turned to them, I might have worked out some of this stuff on a reasonable schedule. It's also possible I wouldn't have accepted quite so many article assignments (and asked all those nosy questions) concerning sexual attitudes among women of all ages had I not been curious still about what other people are really doing. Or maybe things would have been different if the age of sensual enlightenment had been courteous enough to dawn a little earlier. But the truth is, it probably wouldn't have changed things at all, even if I *had* been born in time for the Sexual Revolution. My parents wouldn't have let me go to it anyway. Not, at least, if it were being held in the summer; I was never allowed to go *anywhere* in polio season. And in the winter, they made me wear leggings.

From STARTING IN THE MIDDLE by Judith Wax. Copyright (c) 1979 by Judith Wax. Reprinted by permission of Henry Holt & Co., Inc.

NORA EPHRON

A Few Words About Breasts

I have to begin with a few words about androgyny. In grammar school, in the fifth and sixth grades, we were all tyrannized by a rigid set of rules that supposedly determined whether we were boys or girls. The episode in *Huckleberry Finn* where Huck is disguised as a girl and gives himself away by the way he threads a needle and catches a ball—that kind of thing. We learned that the way you sat, crossed your legs, held a cigarette, and looked at your nails—the way you did these things instinctively was absolute proof of your sex. Now obviously most children did not take this literally, but I did. I thought that just one slip, just one incorrect cross of my legs or flick of an imaginary cigarette ash would turn me from whatever I was into the other thing; that would be all it took, really. Even though I was outwardly a girl and had many of the trappings generally associated with girldom—a girl's name, for example, and dresses, my own telephone, an autograph book—I spent the early years of my adolescence absolutely certain that I might at any point gum it up. I did not feel at all like a girl. I was boyish. I was athletic, ambitious, outspoken, competitive, noisy, rambunctious. I had scabs on my knees and my socks slid into my loafers and I could throw a football. I wanted desperately not to be that way, not to be a mixture of both things, but instead just one, a girl, a definite indisputable girl. As soft and as pink as a nursery. And nothing would do that for me, I felt, but breasts.

I was about six months younger than everyone else in my class, and so for about six months after it began, for six months after my friends had begun to develop (that was the word we used, develop), I was not particularly worried. I would sit in the bathtub and look down at my breasts and know that any day now, any second now, they would start growing like everyone else's. They didn't. "I want to buy a bra," I said to my mother one night. "What for?" she said. My mother was really hateful about bras, and by the time my third sister had gotten to the point where she was ready to want one, my mother had worked the whole business into a comedy routine. "Why not use a Band-Aid instead?" she would say. It was a source of great pride to my mother that she had never even had to wear a brassiere until she had her fourth child, and then only because her gynecologist made her. It was incomprehensible to me that anyone could ever be proud of something like that. It was the 1950s, for God's sake. Jane Russell. Cashmere sweaters. Couldn't my mother see that? *"I am too old to wear an undershirt."* Screaming. Weeping. Shouting. "Then don't wear an undershirt," said my mother. "But I want to buy a bra." "What for?"

I suppose that for most girls, breasts, brassieres, that entire thing, has more trauma, more to do with the coming of adolescence, with becoming a woman, than anything else. Certainly more than getting your period, although that, too, was traumatic, symbolic. But you could see breasts; they were there; they were visible. Whereas a girl could claim to have her period for months before she actually got it and nobody would ever know the difference. Which is exactly what I did. All you had to do was make a great fuss over having enough nickels for the Kotex machine and walk around clutching your stomach and moaning for three to five days a month about The Curse and you could convince anybody. There is a school of thought somewhere in the women's lib/women's mag/gynecology establishment that claims that menstrual cramps are purely psychological, and I lean toward it. Not that I didn't have them finally. Agonizing cramps, heating-pad cramps, go-down-to-the-school-nurse-and-lie-on-the-cot cramps. But, unlike any pain I had ever suffered, I adored the pain of cramps, welcomed it, wallowed in it, bragged about it. "I can't go. I have cramps." "I can't do that. I have cramps." And most of all, gigglingly, blushingly: "I can't swim. I have cramps." Nobody ever used the hard-core word. Menstruation. God, what an awful word. Never that. "I have cramps."

The morning I first got my period, I went into my mother's bedroom to tell her. And my mother, my utterly-hateful-about-bras mother, burst into tears. It was really a lovely moment, and I remember it so clearly not just because it was one of the two times I ever saw my mother cry on my account (the other was when I was caught being a six-year-old kleptomaniac), but also because the incident did not mean to me what it meant to her. Her little girl, her firstborn, had finally become a woman. That was what she was crying about. My reaction to the event, however, was that I might well be a woman in some scientific, textbook sense (and could at least stop faking every month and stop wasting all those nickels). But in another sense—in a visible sense—I was as androgynous and as liable to tip over into boyhood as ever.

I started with a 28 AA bra. I don't think they made them any smaller in those days, although I gather that now you can buy bras for five-year-olds that don't have any cups whatsoever in them; trainer bras they are called. My first brassiere came from Robinson's Department Store in Beverly Hills. I went there alone, shaking, positive they would look me over and smile and tell me to come back next year. An actual fitter took me into the dressing room and stood over me while I took off my blouse and tried the first one on. The little puffs stood out on my chest. "Lean over," said the fitter. (To this day, I am not sure what fitters in bra departments do except to tell you to lean over.) I leaned over, with the fleeting hope that my breasts would miraculously fall out of my body and into the puffs. Nothing.

"Don't worry about it," said my friend Libby some months later, when things had not improved. "You'll get them after you're married."

"What are you talking about?" I said.

"When you get married," Libby explained, "your husband will touch your breasts and rub them and kiss them and they'll grow."

That was the killer. Necking I could deal with. Intercourse I could deal with. But it had never crossed my mind that a man was going to touch my breasts, that breasts **had** something to do with all that, petting, my God, they never mentioned petting in my little sex manual about the fertilization of the ovum. I became dizzy. For I knew instantly—as naïve as I had been only a moment before—that only part of what she was saying was true: the touching, rubbing, kissing part, not the growing part. And I knew that no one would ever want to marry me. I had no breasts. I would never have breasts.

My best friend in school was Diana Raskob. She lived a block from me in a house full of wonders. English muffins, for instance. The Raskobs were the first people in Beverly Hills to have English muffins for breakfast. They also had an apricot tree in the back, and a badminton court, and a subscription to *Seventeen* magazine, and hundreds of games, like Sorry and Parcheesi and Treasure Hunt and Anagrams. Diana and I spent three or four afternoons a week in their den reading and playing and eating. Diana's mother's kitchen was full of the most colossal assortment of junk food I have ever been exposed to. My house was full of apples and peaches and milk and homemade chocolate-chip cookies—which were nice, and good for you, but-not-right-before-dinner-or-you'll-spoil-your-appetite. Diana's house had nothing in it that was good for you, and what's more, you could stuff it in right up until dinner and nobody cared. Bar-B-Q potato chips (they were the first in them, too), giant bottles of ginger ale, fresh popcorn with melted butter, hot fudge sauce on Baskin-Robbins jamoca ice cream, powdered-sugar doughnuts from Van de Kamp's. Diana and I had been best friends since we were seven; we were about equally popular in school (which is to say, not particularly), we had about the same success with boys (extremely intermittent), and we looked much the same. Dark. Tall. Gangly.

It is September, just before school begins. I am eleven years old, about to enter the seventh grade, and Diana and I have not seen each other all summer. I have been to camp and she has been somewhere like Banff with her parents. We are meeting, as we often do, on the street midway between our two houses, and we will walk back to Diana's and eat junk and talk about what has happened to each of us that summer. I am walking down Walden Drive in my jeans and my father's shirt hanging out and my old red loafers with the socks falling into them and coming toward me is . . . I take a deep breath . . . a young woman. Diana. Her hair is curled and she has a waist and hips and a bust and she is wearing a straight skirt, an article of clothing I have been repeatedly told I will be unable to wear until I have the hips to hold it up. My jaw drops, and suddenly I am crying, crying hysterically, can't catch my breath sobbing. My best friend has betrayed me. She has gone ahead without me and done it. She has shaped up.

Here are some things I did to help:

Bought a Mark Eden Bust Developer.

Slept on my back for four years.

Splashed cold water on them every night because some French actress said in *Life* magazine that that was what *she* did for her perfect bustline.

Ultimately, I resigned myself to a bad toss and began to wear padded bras. I think about them now, think about all those years in high school I went around in them, my three padded bras, every single one of them with different-sized breasts. Each time I changed bras I changed sizes: one week nice perky but not too obtrusive breasts, the next medium-sized slightly pointy ones, the next week knockers, true knockers; all the time, whatever size I was, carrying around this rubberized appendage on my chest that occasionally crashed into a wall and was poked inward and had to be poked outward—I think about all that and wonder how anyone kept a straight face through it. My parents, who normally had no restraints about needling me—why did they say nothing as they watched my chest go up and down? My friends, who would periodically inspect my breasts for signs of growth and reassure me—why didn't they at least counsel consistency?

And the bathing suits. I die when I think about the bathing suits. That was the era when you could lay an uninhabited bathing suit on the beach and someone would make a pass at it. I would put one on, an absurd swimsuit with its enormous bust built into it, the bones from the suit stabbing me in the rib cage and leaving little red welts on my body, and there I would be, my chest plunging straight downward absolutely vertically from my collarbone to the top of my suit and then suddenly, wham, out came all that padding and material and wiring absolutely horizontally.

Buster Klepper was the first boy who ever touched them. He was my boyfriend my senior year of high school. There is a picture of him in my high-school yearbook that makes him look quite attractive in a Jewish, horn-rimmed-glasses sort of way, but the picture does not show the pimples, which were air-brushed out, or the dumbness. Well, that isn't really fair. He wasn't dumb. He just wasn't terribly bright. His mother refused to accept it, refused to accept the relentlessly average report cards, refused to deal with her son's inevitable destiny in some junior college or other. "He was tested," she would say to me, apropos of nothing, "and it came out a hundred and forty-five. That's near-genius." Had the word "underachiever" been coined, she probably would have lobbed that one at me, too. Anyway, Buster was really very sweet—which is, I know, damning with faint praise, but there it is. I was the editor of the front page of the high-school newspaper and he was editor of the back page; we had to work together, side by side, in the print shop, and that was how it started. On our first date, we went to see *April Love*, starring Pat Boone. Then we started going together. Buster had a green coupe, a 1950 Ford with an engine he had hand-chromed until it shone, dazzled, reflected the image of anyone who looked into it, anyone usually being Buster polishing it or the gas-station attendants he constantly asked to check the oil in order for them to be overwhelmed by the sparkle on the valves. The car also had a boot stretched over the back seat for reasons I never understood; hanging from the rearview mirror, as was the custom, was a pair of angora dice. A previous girl friend named Solange, who was famous throughout Beverly Hills High School for having no pigment in her right eyebrow, had knitted them for him. Buster and I would ride around town, the two of us seated to the left of the steering wheel. I would shift gears. It was nice.

There was necking. Terrific necking. First in the car, overlooking Los Angeles from what is now the Trousdale Estates. Then on the bed of his parents' cabana at Ocean House. Incredibly wonderful, frustrating necking, I loved it, really, but no further than necking, please don't, please, because there I was absolutely terrified of the general implications of going-a-step-further with a near-dummy and also terrified of his finding out there was next to nothing there (which he knew, of course; he wasn't that dumb).

I broke up with him at one point. I think we were apart for about two weeks. At the end of that time, I drove down to see a friend at a boarding school in Palos Verdes Estates and a disc jockey played "April Love" on the radio four times during the trip. I took it as a sign. I drove straight back to Griffith Park to a golf tournament Buster was playing in (he was the sixth-seeded teen-age golf player in southern California) and presented myself back to him on the green of the 18th hole. It was all very dramatic. That night we went to a drive-in and I let him get his hand under my protuberances and onto my breasts. He really didn't seem to mind at all.

"Do you want to marry my son?" the woman asked me.
"Yes," I said.

I was nineteen years old, a virgin, going with this woman's son, this big strange woman who was married to a Lutheran minister in New Hampshire and pretended she was gentile and had this son, by her first husband, this total fool of a son who ran the hero-sandwich concession at Harvard Business School and whom for one moment one December in New Hampshire I said—as much out of politeness as anything else—that I wanted to marry.

"Fine," she said. "Now, here's what you do. Always make sure you're on top of him so you won't seem so small. My bust is very large, you see, so I always lie on my back to make it look smaller, but you'll have to be on top most of the time."

I nodded. "Thank you," I said.

"I have a book for you to read," she went on. "Take it with you when you leave. Keep it." She went to the bookshelf, found it, and gave it to me. It was a book on frigidity.

"Thank you," I said.

That is a true story. Everything in this article is a true story, but I feel I have to point out that that story in particular is true. It happened on December 30, 1960. I think about it often. When it first happened, I naturally assumed that the woman's son, my boyfriend, was responsible. I invented a scenario where he had had a little heart-to-heart with his mother and had confessed that his only objection to me was that my breasts were small; his mother then took it upon herself to help out. Now I think I was wrong about the incident. The mother was acting on her own, I think: that was her way of being cruel and competitive under the guise of being helpful and maternal. You have small breasts, she was saying; therefore you will never make him as happy as I have. Or you have small breasts; therefore you will doubtless have sexual problems. Or you have small breasts; therefore you are less woman than I am. She was, as it happens, only the first of what seems to me to be a never-ending string of women who have made competitive remarks to me about breast size. "I would love to wear a dress like that," my friend Emily says to me, "but my bust is too big." Like that. Why do women say these things to me? Do I attract these remarks the way other women attract married men or alcoholics or homosexuals? This summer, for example. I am at a party in East Hampton and I am introduced to a woman from Washington. She is a minor celebrity, very pretty and Southern and blond and outspoken, and I am flattered because she has read something I have written. We are talking animatedly, we have been talking no more than five minutes, when a man comes up to join us. "Look at the two of us," the woman says to the man, indicating me and her. "The two of us together couldn't fill an A cup." Why does she say that? It isn't even true, dammit, so why? Is she even more addled than I am on this subject? Does she honestly believe there is something wrong with her size breasts, which, it seems to me, now that I look hard at them, are just right? Do I unconsciously bring out competitiveness in women? In that form? What did I do to deserve it?

As for men.

There were men who minded and let me know that they minded. There were men who did not mind. In any case, I always minded.

And even now, now that I have been countlessly reassured that my figure is a good one, now that I am grown-up enough to understand that most of my feelings have very little to do with the reality of my shape, I am nonetheless obsessed by breasts. I cannot help it. I grew up in the terrible fifties—with rigid stereotypical sex roles, the insistence that men be men and dress like men and women be women and dress like women, the intolerance of androgyny—and I cannot shake it, cannot shake my feelings of inadequacy. Well, that time is gone, right? All those exaggerated examples of breast worship are gone, right? Those women were freaks, right? I know all that. And yet here I am, stuck with the psychological remains of it all, stuck with my own peculiar version of breast worship. You probably think I am crazy to go on like this: here I have set out to write a confession that is meant to hit you with the shock of recognition, and instead you are sitting there thinking I am thoroughly warped. Well, what can I tell you? If I had had them, I would have been a completely different person. I honestly believe that.

After I went into therapy, a process that made it possible for me to tell total strangers at cocktail parties that breasts were the hang-up of my life, I was often told that I was insane to have been bothered by my condition. I was also frequently told, by close friends, that I was extremely boring on the subject. And my girl friends, the ones with nice big breasts, would go on endlessly about how their lives had been far more miserable than mine. Their bra straps were snapped in class. They couldn't sleep on their stomachs. They were stared at whenever the word "mountain" cropped up in geography. And *Evangeline*, good God what they went through every time someone had to stand up and recite the Prologue to Longfellow's *Evangeline*: ". . . stand like druids of eld . . . With beards that rest on their bosoms." It was much worse for them, they tell me. They had a terrible time of it, they assure me. I don't know how lucky I was, they say . . .

I have thought about their remarks, tried to put myself in their place, considered their point of view. I think they are full of shit.

 **VERNARD ELLER**

Positions

Hoo, boy! This is the chapter where most marriage manuals really let themselves go—because it lends itself to such interesting illustrations and photographs, I suppose. Also, the positions of the partners—their accumbency, acclivity, accessibility, acrobativity, actuation, acceleration, acumination, and accuracy—this is the easiest aspect of the sexual experience to vary, diversify, and experiment with.

So whenever sex goes sick, the thing to try is a new position. "I'm sorry, dear, but we've come to the last one in the book, a Spanish invention called *el posturo ludicrusioso*, plate 101 on page 934. I know you had to go to the chiropractor last time; this could be different. But we've just got to find *something* that makes it!"

It is interesting that books of this sort—although more so in the past than now—were called "*marriage* manuals." "Unmarriage manual" would be nearer the truth of the matter. For one thing, when the relationship between a man and wife has come to the place that items of sex technique are a primary concern, it usually is obvious that the factors which truly are important for marriage already are long gone. For another, the chances of saving a marriage by introducing innovative interminglings for instant idyllics is about the same as for saving suicides who jump from the Golden Gate Bridge by painting the bridge a different color.

And yet ... and yet in suggesting that one's position *vis-à-vis* hisorher partner is *the* key to sexual fulfillment, the manuals are just exactly right—or would be if they weren't so just exactly wrong.

("*Vis-à-vis*" is a French term meaning "face-to-face." However, we do not intend it to suggest any limits regarding the positions involved but use it in the broad sense of "in relation to." "Hisorher," on the other hand, is an Ellerian term designed to bring both sexes under one umbrella and keep this book bisexual, as it were—our modest contribution to women's lib.)

The manuals, which are mostly propaganda pieces for today's sex kick, are wrong in suggesting that *physical* posture is normally a critical factor in great and good sex. After all, millions upon millions of people managed to become competent copulators before sex manuals even were invented; and even today millions make it without the help of manuals. If these books were purchased only by people who actually need instruction in positional technique and whose relationship truly is improved through use of a book, my guess is that the publishers would go broke.

For the truth is that learning the mutual operations of anthropological sex equipage is not the same sort of problem as learning to drive an automobile. For one thing, it is a two-man rather than a one-man job (here using "man" in the sense that embraces woman). It employs (or should employ) only union labor. There is (or should be) much better communication between operator and equipment. The equipment is (or should be) much more responsive and cooperative than is the case with most automobiles. And above all, human beings have been made for each other in a way that cars and drivers simply were not; there have been provided instincts which can be counted upon to get the job done one way or another. And whether or not it has been well done is entirely for the participants to say; the opinion of experts has nothing to do with the matter.

Thus, in all but the most exceptional cases, the manuals with their position papers are superfluous. On the other hand, they are positively harmful if they disturb contented people into thinking that some sort of sexual paradise lies just beyond them, attainable if only they can find the magic posture, grip, and swing (or, more often than not, the magic *partner*). But really, the surest way to spoil the fun of sex is to all the time be straining after something that most likely doesn't even exist. This is a transform play into work, fun into fear, and frolic into failure. It is the same sickness that plagues us elsewhere, but in this case it is known as "keeping up with the Johnson and Masters."

However, be that as it may, if "posture" is taken to signify, not the physical arrangement of the players, but how they are mentally, emotionally, and spiritually positioned toward each other, then posture is indeed the very pivot upon which sexual success turns.

Even so, when we make this change in the definition of "positions," we radically change the nature of the problem as well. Rearranging physical positions is easy, because the alignment of bodies is all that needs to be changed; the partners can go on being their normal, twisted, old selves. But finding new positions *vis-à-vis* each other as *persons* means that the partners themselves will need to be changed. ("Partners themselves being changed" is not at all the same thing as "a change of partners"—that last is a too-easy ploy which usually fails to accomplish anything except to shuffle the frustrated and compound their frustration.)

Moreover, when the question is that of physical correlation, there are any number of positions couples can assume and still be "right." If a position works, it is correct; and the manuals would indicate that the possibilities are amazing in scope and number. But when speaking of *human* correlation, there is only one position that is proper and that can be depended upon to work under all conditions, vine, verse, and adverse.

This one and only position is identified as "marriage." (Yes, we *are* going to go through all that again; after all, some readers may not catch on as fast as you do.)

Recall that marriage is not everything that the state has licensed or the church blessed as being such. It is precisely nothing more nor less than a particular position that a man and a woman can take *vis-à-vis* each other (and the stance is in every sense a *sexual* one, too). This relational posture is indeed a profound and subtle one, too fine and complex to be photographed as the other sex positions are— and thus not providing much in the way of exciting resources for illustrated manuals. Oh, certainly it is true that married people can be photographed; but photos of married people also can be posed, just as photos of other sex positions are. (Likewise, married people have been known to pose as unmarried.) But marriage itself is something that definitely cannot be posed. Posed marriages (of which our society is full) are actually no marriages at all.

Many details of the marriage posture can, of course, be varied at will; but the basic elements of the stance are invariable. The fundamental feature is mutual commitment, his making her welfare his own and her making his hers. This commitment is connected to fidelity; fidelity is connected to trust; trust is connected to letting oneself go; and letting oneself go is connected to *getting* all of himorher; and it all is connected to de head bone. "Now hear de word of de Lawd!" (namely: "Therefore a man . . . cleaves to his wife, and they become one flesh" [Genesis 2:24]).

And hear this real good too: In spite of all manuals that imply otherwise, this authoritative Puritan manual is ready to proclaim that such a marriage posture is *the* position for sex.

That statement is correct but perhaps slightly misleading; it implies that the position is one thing and the sex something else that takes place out of and sequential to the position. But not so; the very *position* of marriage is a sexual relationship and would be so even if for some reason the act of physical intercourse could not take place. That is, it is a relationship based upon and made possible by the fact that he is a male and she is a female. The bump and boin-n-ng constitute simply one aspect (and not necessarily even the central aspect) of this larger and immensely grander sex act called "marriage."

It follows truly that intercourse apart from the context of marriage is a truncated and frustrated sex act. It may not be *coitus interruptus*, but it certainly can be described as *sexus interruptus*—and with many of the drawbacks of the former.

Buy all the manuals you can find, try all the positions they suggest and invent some of your own; you won't find anything that even remotely approaches the thrill and bliss of the marriage posture. Conversely, once you get going on the marriage posture, you can throw the manuals away; in the great majority of instances questions of physical position naturally will answer themselves. Likewise, if you now are doing it more but enjoying it less (or doing it less because you aren't enjoying it anymore), you would be smart to try improving positions. But the one to work on is the marital rather than the coital.

From THE SEX MANUAL FOR PURITANS by Vernard Eller. Copyright (c) 1971 by Abingdon Press. Used by permission.

QUESTIONS FOR DISCUSSION

1. Judith Wax discusses the availability of sexual information for young people in this generation. Nevertheless, some literature, e.g., how to overcome the problem of orgasmic dysfunctions for women, is less helpful than she thought. For those of you who are female, do you agree with Wax's disenchantment with such literature?

2. Wax says that she and many of her friends suffered from "bodily incompetence (which a lot of us saw as good manners)." Some feminists argue that a woman must know, as well as have control over her own body. What does Wax mean when she equates "bodily incompetence" with "good manners"?

3. "As for America's vibrator explosion ... I don't even know anybody who uses one—or who talks about it, anyway." Is there a suggestion here that minority sexual practices are often presented in the media as if they were normative? Are letters to magazines' representative of sexual behavior of men and women?

4. Referring to the man who "stuffed [his wife] with scarves" Wax says that "it's hard to judge that couple's standing on the scale of looniness without knowing how old they were." She adds that "sexual perceptions, like so many other things, often depend on generational vantage point...." Does this imply that sexual behavior of the young is likely always to be seen as suspect, if not "wrong," by those of another generation—especially one's parents?

5. At the baby shower Wax was laughed at when she asked the unmarried career mother "How will you *ever* manage to cope ... with all the thank-you notes?" Such matters Wax defines as the "essential issues" of life. Is there a perspective here which comes only from a "generational vantage point"?

6. Nora Ephron felt that nothing would make her feel like a girl except developed breasts and a bra. Which specific aspects of our culture imprint such an attitude on young girls?

7. Among women, as well as men, Ephron seemed to be constantly reminded of her small breasts. It was suggested to her, "you have small breasts; therefore you are less woman than I am." Or, "you have small breasts; therefore you will doubtless have sexual problems." Hollywood has emphasized the female breast as much as any part of our culture. But, are there female Hollywood superstars whose breast size has been negligible? Are they perceived as "less woman"? Is there any evidence that they have had sexual problems due to their small breasts? How do you account for this?

8. Ephron asks, "What can I tell you? If I had had them, I would have been a completely different person. I honestly believe that." She went into therapy and was able to tell strangers at cocktail parties that "breasts were the hang-up of my life...." Is Ephron simply a deviant in this matter? Or is she a totally honest woman willing to share what most women with similar concerns never would?

9. In "Positions" Eller argues that "when the relationship between a man and wife has come to the place that items of sex technique are a primary concern, it usually is obvious that the factors which truly are important for marriage already are long gone." Eller doesn't say, but what factors do research data suggest are more important to marriage than sexual technique?

10. If Eller is right that "millions upon millions of people managed to become competent copulators before sex manuals even were invented," how do you account for the widespread popularity of such manuals and sexual counselors? Are there data to support that this generation is more sexually incompetent than previous ones?

11. Eller argues that the only correct sexual position "is identified as 'marriage.'" Do you think most college students you know would agree with Eller, or would they argue that "casual" sex, as discussed by Schulz, is the correct sexual position?

REFERENCES

Humphreys, Laud. "Tearoom Trade: Impersonal Sex in Public Places." *Transaction* 7, 3 (1970), 10–14.

Kinsey, Alfred C., et. al. *Sexual Behavior in the Human Male.* Philadelphia: W. B. Saunders, 1948.

———. *Sexual Behavior in the Human Female.* Philadelphia: W. B. Saunders, 1953.

Masters, William, and Johnson, Virginia. *Human Sexual Response.* Boston: Little, Brown, 1966.

Schulz, David. *Human Sexuality.* Englewood Cliffs, N.J.: Prentice-Hall, 1979.

Chapter Thirteen

Gender and Sex Roles

*A*ll societies have allocated work tasks by sex since the beginning of recorded history. Men have done some work; women have done other jobs. Certain work came to be associated with men, such as hunting, fishing, lumbering, and boatbuilding. Women traditionally spun, cooked, and fetched water. (cf. Murdock and Provost, 1973) With the advent of the industrial revolution in the western world, many women were brought into the urban areas to work in mills and were no longer exclusively tied to nonpaying jobs in the home. As industrialism became the dominant form of the western world's occupational activity, women found themselves unemployable except for restricted activities such as secretarial work. They did not stoke the steel furnaces, drive trucks, or build highways. Their roles were primarily those of housewife and mother. The professions especially were closed to women. In 1872 the Supreme Court, in *Bradwell vs. Illinois*, upheld the refusal of the Illinois Supreme Court to admit women to the practice of law. The Court argued that "the natural and proper timidity and delicacy which belongs to the female sex evidently unfits it for many of the occupations of civil life." While this decision applied only to the practice of law, the choice of words reflected a then widespread view of the "natural" abilities of women vis-à-vis the world of work. Sexual differences between men and women were thought to "unfit" women for work deemed "natural" for men.

More than 100 years later it may seem that sexual differences no longer make a difference. But is this the case? *Are* there differences between men and women which affect their respective positions in society? Of course. Some of the differences are sex based; others gender based. Sex is a biological fact and some sexual differences between males and females—the genital organs—are readily observable and functionally important in terms of childbearing. Females menstruate; males do not. As a result, some males argue, women are unreliable and unstable. They are "physically and emotionally handicapped by menstruation, goes the argument, and therefore cannot compete with men." (Delaney, et. al., 1976:2) Other differences are found in the body chemistry of males and females. Females usually have more estrogen and males more testosterone. These hormonal differences are important in the physical development of males and females.

Acknowledged physiological differences between the sexes have given rise to gender based differences. There are gender behaviors which a society typically associates with males or with females. Males and females dress in a manner which enables the observer to identify gender. Females have more latitude in dress than males, but dress is not a casual, take-it-or-leave-it matter. Males who regularly showed up at work in a blouse and skirt, or a dress, would experience difficulties with their employers. And in spite of changes in attitudes which have occurred in the last two decades, women who are employed and give birth to a child are expected to be the parent who takes a leave of absence and stays home with the child—at least for a period of several months. Men are expected to continue at their work, and few companies would grant them a leave of absence for child rearing purposes. Thus, what we call *gender roles* in a society do influence in a dramatic fashion the behavior of both males and female.

No one doubts the existence of gender roles. The question is why do all societies assign some roles to women and others to men? Certainly after birth a child could be cared for by a male as competently as by a female. The woman could continue her work and the man take a leave of absence to care for the newly born. Although both male and female work in our society the females continue to perform the bulk of household duties. Why? Are men unable to cook and wield a vacuum cleaner?

A long-standing answer to the assignment of gender roles is that anatomy is destiny. This perspective holds that women are biologically destined to be nurturing, caring, mothering types: "A woman's place is in the home." Such an interpretation has come under wide criticism in recent years, but the defeat of the Equal Rights Amendment is evidence that this view is still present in American society.

Another sociological position, functionalism, does not argue that a woman's place should be in the home. Instead, it suggests that the division of labor whereby women care for children and men work has come about because of the reproductive role of women. Children are then socialized to later adopt the roles, respectively, of male and female.

An opposing view of gender roles' origin and maintenance comes from conflict sociologists. Conflict theory argues that men dominate women because it is to their advantage economically, politically, and otherwise. Collins notes that "males on the average are bigger and stronger than females, in the human species. Women are also made physically vulnerable by bearing and caring for children. That is to say, resources for social domination are distributed unequally between the sexes in general ... Following the conflict approach, we would then expect that persons take advantage of inequalities in resources...." (1975: 230) Thus, men organize institutions in society which tend to perpetuate their favored positions in society.

Whatever the origins of gender differences, many women have refused to accept the unequal arrangements of sexual activities. In the nineteenth century feminine voices were raised to decry the idea that women were fit only for the roles of mother and wife. The movement toward economic and political emancipation of women, also known as feminism, began. The feminist position has been succinctly stated by Freeman:

> The traditional view of society assumes that men and women are essentially different and should serve different social functions; their diverse roles and statuses simply reflect essential differences. The feminist perspective starts from the premise that women and men are constitutionally equal and share the same human capabilities; observed differences therefore demand a critical analysis of the social institutions that cause them. (1984:553)

There is no single organization representing women and their struggle for equality. The movement consists of hundreds of organizations around the country. Probably the best known of these groups is the National Organization of Women (NOW). Other, and somewhat less well-known groups are the National Women's Political Caucus (NWPC), Federally Employed Women (FEW), and the Women's International Terrorist Conspiracy from Hell (WITCH). While these groups vary in their methods for reaching different goals, it is possible, nevertheless, to identify specific goals which are common to all groups.

The most basic concern of the feminist movement is probably about its opposition to assignment of tasks on the basis of gender alone. Other than obviously biologically determined roles—only women can bear children—the movement argues that roles should be assigned on the basis of individual ability. Feminists point to the fact that we have yet to elect a female for president as a prime example of gender role bias. The United States, of course, lags behind other countries—Israel, India, and Great Britain—who have elected women to their highest political office.

In 1984 the Democratic party did nominate Geraldine Ferraro for vice president. While this was hailed as a victory for the feminist cause at the time, later political commentators have revealed, once again, the difficulties women face in achieving equal standing in political affairs:

> ... the Democrats do not have a woman who deserves a place on the 1988 ticket because of her own national stature. In fact, with all due respect to Geraldine Ferraro, they didn't have one in 1984 either. Mrs. Ferraro was chosen to run for Vice President because the democratic nominee, Walter Mondale, desperately needed an innovative stroke to pick up his lagging campaign; and the outcome is not likely to encourage another such gamble. (Wicker, 1986)

Tom Wicker, the political columnist who wrote the above statement did, however, go on to point out that in his judgment there are several Republican women who would make good potential vice presidential candidates. None is mentioned as a presidential possibility.

Job training is a prime issue for the feminist movement. NOW is vigorous in its pursuit of this goal. Equal rights laws do exist, but, in practice, many women experience subtle forms of discrimination in securing training for all jobs.

Closely related to the equality of job training is the effort to change women's self-image. Many groups stress "consciousness raising" as the primary need of women. Women must see themselves as equal to men. The traditional image of women as passive, dainty, and submissive is still prevalent in children's literature, textbooks, and the general socialization of girls from infancy on. (cf. Weitzman, et. al., 1972; Weitzman and Rizzo, 1974)

This passive image of women is still encouraged in male-dominated families. Thus, some groups feel that the family as it is constituted must be radically changed. The more radical feminists attack the family directly and argue that it is a primary source of women's problems. Others argue that it is not the family per se, but the structure of the family which is the issue. The radical arm of the movement has attracted much media attention in its attacks upon the family. When some opponents of the feminist movement argue strongly against it they are, more often than not, attacking what constitutes only a small minority of all feminists. NOW, for example, certainly does not call for the abolition of the family.

Abortion is probably the most controversial issue in the feminist movement, and again, is the focus of much media attention. The "pro-life" and the "pro-choice" groups have engaged in bitter, acrimonious debate over this issue. The position on abortion of the nation's largest religious group, the Roman Catholic Church, has been a source of concern to all groups within the feminist movement. In addition to abortion, feminists take issue with the Roman Catholic Church's refusal to ordain women to the priesthood—a matter resolved by several of the major Protestant bodies who now will ordain women.

What some outside the movement consider a minor issue is the matter of sexist language. The relationship of language and culture (see Chapter 3) supports the argument that language does help to shape our ideas and behavior. Thus, the substitution of *chairperson* for *chairman*, or the use of "he/she" and other variations upon the traditionally exclusive use of the male pronoun in writing, are indicative of the struggles in this area. Recently, the National Council of Churches offered a new lectionary of the Bible which seeks to eliminate all sexist language. In the creation story, for example, instead of saying that God formed "man of dust from the ground" the new version reads: "formed a human creature of dust." Other changes seek to point to the femininity as well as masculinity of God. In one familiar passage where Jesus appears to the disciples after the Resurrection, he says: "Peace be with you. As God the Mother and Father has sent me, even so I send you." Not all religious groups support these modifications of traditional scripture passages, but this massive effort on the part of a national religious body indicates the successful efforts of the feminist movement to bring about such changes in language.

Finally, equal treatment in the enforcement of the law is a prime concern of the feminist movement. Feminists deplore the fact that the female prostitute is arrested, but her male accomplice is not subject to any penalties. And female victims of rape are often accorded treatment in examinations by attending officers which suggests that the victim may have behaved in a fashion which led the rapist to his act of violence.

The feminist movement has not achieved all the goals discussed here, but the appointment of Sandra Day O'Connor to the Supreme Court, the nomination of Geraldine Ferraro as vice president in 1984 and the awareness of other potential candidates, the election of several female governors to state houses, and the growing representation of women in the professions and other occupations all suggest that progress is likely to continue. On the other hand, the defeat of the ERA is sufficient evidence that the struggle continues. Not all women support the movement and many men are reluctant to grant women full equality. If the study of power relationships in sociology has demonstrated anything, it is that those in power do not freely relinquish it.

The feminist movement has generated much humor. Male humorists have had a field day satirizing the movement. Female humorists have, however, used humor to point to the absurdities of male conceptions of females, gender-based roles, and other aspects of male–female relationships. In the first selection, "The Human-Not-Quite-Human," Dorothy Sayers wonders what would happen to males' self-image if they were constantly reminded of their "biological function". Why are there no books such as "Males of the Bible"? Or newspaper features such as the "Men's Corner"? And, certainly, no *man* should trouble his "handsome little head about politics." Probably few, if any, males have entertained the ideas Sayers vigorously puts forward in this piece.

In the second selection Gloria Steinem wonders what would happen "If Men Could Menstruate" (and women could not). While women are generally (especially by men) defined as being incapacitated by menstruation, men would, no doubt, turn this into a male symbol of strength and uniqueness. For example, only men would be eligible for service in the Army: "you have to give blood to take blood." Religious authorities would turn the present conception of uncleanliness around. Rabbis would argue that "without the monthly loss of impurities, women remain unclean." In short, men would, again, justify their positions in terms of biological properties not possessed by females.

The third selection, by Roy Blount, examines "Women in the Locker Room!" Note the exclamation point used by Blount in his title. Exclamation points are often used to convey protests, or complaints. Certainly there is on the part of some male sportswriters a protest against the recent admission of women into male locker rooms following sports activities. Why any objection? Are female sportswriters not entitled to the same privileges as male sportswriters? Sure, but, well, males run around *naked* in locker rooms, don't they? (Answer: yes, many do.) And, of course, if females are admitted to male locker rooms doesn't this mean that males must be admitted to female rooms? It is a new day, a day of consciousness-raising.

DOROTHY SAYERS

The Human-Not-Quite-Human

Probably no man has ever troubled to imagine how strange his life would appear to himself if it were unrelentingly assessed in terms of his maleness; if everything he wore, said, or did had to be justified by reference to female approval; if he were compelled to regard himself, day in day out, not as a member of society, but merely (*salvâ reverentiâ*) as a virile member of society. If the centre of his dress-consciousness were the cod-piece, his education directed to making him a spirited lover and meek pater-familias; his interests held to be natural only in so far as they were sexual. If from school and lecture-room, Press and pulpit, he heard the persistent outpouring of a shrill and scolding voice, bidding him remember his biological function. If he were vexed by continual advice how to add a rough male touch to his typing, how to be learned without losing his masculine appeal, how to combine chemical research with seduction, how to play bridge without incurring the suspicion of impotence. If, instead of allowing with a smile that "women prefer cave-men," he felt the unrelenting pressure of a whole social structure forcing him to order all his goings in conformity with that pronouncement.

In any book on sociology he would find, after the main portion dealing with human needs and rights, a supplementary chapter devoted to "The Position of the Male in the Perfect State." His newspaper would assist him with a "Men's Corner," telling him how, by the expenditure of a good deal of money and a couple of hours a day, he could attract the girls and retain his wife's affection; and when he had succeeded in capturing a mate, his name would be taken from him, and society would present him with a special title to proclaim his achievement. People would write books called, "History of the Male," or "Males of the Bible," or "The Psychology of the Male," and he would be regaled daily with headlines, such as "Gentleman-Doctor's Discovery," "Male-Secretary Wins Calcutta Sweep," "Men-Artists at the Academy." If he gave an interview to a reporter, or performed any unusual exploit, he would find it recorded in such terms as these: "Professor Bract, although a distinguished botanist, is not in any way an unmanly man. He has, in fact, a wife and seven children. Tall and burly, the hands with which he handles his delicate specimens are as gnarled and powerful as those of a Canadian lumberjack, and when I swilled beer with him in his laboratory, he bawled his conclusions at me in a strong, gruff voice that implemented the promise of his swaggering moustache." Or: "There is nothing in the least feminine about the home surroundings of Mr. Focus, the famous children's photographer. His 'den' is panelled in teak and decorated with rude sculptures from Easter Island; over his austere iron bedstead hangs a fine reproduction of the Rape of the Sabines." Or: "I asked M. Sapristi, the renowned chef, whether kitchen-cult was not a rather unusual occupation for a man. 'Not a bit of it!' he replied, bluffly. 'It is the genius that counts, not the sex. As they say in *la belle Ecosse*, a man's a man for a' that'— and his gusty, manly guffaw blew three small patty pans from the dresser."

He would be edified by solemn discussions about "Should Men serve in Drapery Establishments?" and acrimonious ones about "Tea-Drinking Men"; by cross-shots of public affairs "from the masculine angle," and by irritable correspondence about men who expose their anatomy on beaches (so masculine of them), conceal it in dressing-gowns (too feminine of them), think about nothing but women, pretend an unnatural indifference to women, exploit their sex to get jobs, lower the tone of the office by their sexless appearance, and generally fail to please a public opinion which demands the incompatible. And at dinner-parties he would hear the wheedling, unctuous, predatory female voice demand: "And why should you trouble your handsome little head about politics?"

If, after a few centuries of this kind of treatment, the male was a little self-conscious, a little on the defensive, and a little bewildered about what was required of him, I should not blame him. If he traded a little upon his sex, I could forgive him. If he presented the world with a major social problem, I should scarcely be surprised. It would be more surprising if he retained any rag of sanity and self-respect.

Dorothy L. Sayers, UNPOPULAR OPINIONS. New York: Harcourt, Brace and Company, 1947. Copyright (c) 1947 by Dorothy L. Sayers.

GLORIA STEINEM

If Men Could Menstruate

Living in India made me understand that a white minority of the world has spent centuries conning us into thinking a white skin makes people superior, even though the only thing it really does is make them more subject to ultraviolet rays and wrinkles.

Reading Freud made me just as skeptical about penis envy. The power of giving birth makes "womb envy" more logical, and an organ as external and unprotected as the penis makes men very vulnerable indeed.

But listening recently to a woman describe the unexpected arrival of her menstrual period (a red stain had spread on her dress as she argued heatedly on the public stage) still made me cringe with embarrassment. That is, until she explained that, when finally informed in whispers of the obvious event, she had said to the all-male audience, "and you should be *proud* to have a menstruating woman on your stage. It's probably the first real thing that's happened to this group in years!"

Laughter. Relief. She had turned a negative into a positive. Somehow her story merged with India and Freud to make me finally understand the power of positive thinking. Whatever a "superior" group has will be used to justify its superiority, and whatever an "inferior" group has will be used to justify its plight. Black men were given poorly paid jobs because they were said to be "stronger" than white men, while all women were relegated to poorly paid jobs because they were said to be "weaker." As the little boy said when asked if he wanted to be a lawyer like his mother, "Oh no, that's women's work." Logic has nothing to do with oppression.

So what would happen if suddenly, magically, men could menstruate and women could not?

Clearly, menstruation would become an enviable, boast-worthy, masculine event:

Men would brag about how long and how much.

Young boys would talk about it as the envied beginning of manhood. Gifts, religious ceremonies, family dinners, and stag parties would mark the day.

To prevent monthly work loss among the powerful, Congress would fund a National Institute of Dysmenorrhea. Doctors would research little about heart attacks, from which men were hormonally protected, but everything about cramps.

Sanitary supplies would be federally funded and free. Of course, some men would still pay for the prestige of such commercial brands as Paul Newman Tampons, Muhammad Ali's Rope-a-Dope Pads, John Wayne Maxi Pads, and Joe Namath Jock Shields—"For Those Light Bachelor Days."

Statistical surveys would show that men did better in sports and won more Olympic medals during their periods.

Generals, right-wing politicians, and religious fundamentalists would cite menstruation (*"men-*struation") as proof that only men could serve God and country in combat ("You have to give blood to take blood"), occupy high political office ("Can women be properly fierce without a monthly cycle governed by the planet Mars?"), be priests, ministers, God Himself ("He gave this blood for our sins"), or rabbis ("Without a monthly purge of impurities, women are unclean").

Male liberals or radicals, however, would insist that women are equal, just different; and that any woman could join their ranks if only she were willing to recognize the primacy of menstrual rights ("Everything else is a single issue") or self-inflict a major wound every month ("You *must* give blood for the revolution").

Street guys would invent slang ("He's a three-pad man") and "give fives" on the corner with some exchange like, "Man, you lookin' *good!*"

"Yeah, man, I'm on the rag!"

TV shows would treat the subject openly. (*Happy Days*: Richie and Potsie try to convince Fonzie that he is still "The Fonz," though he has missed two periods in a row. *Hill Street Blues*: The whole precinct hits the same cycle.) So would newspapers. (SUMMER SHARK SCARE THREATENS MENSTRUATING MEN. JUDGE CITES MONTHLIES IN PARDONING RAPIST.) And so would movies. (Newman and Redford in *Blood Brothers!*)

Men would convince women that sex was *more* pleasurable at "that time of the month." Lesbians would be said to fear blood and therefore life itself, though all they needed was a good menstruating man.

Medical schools would limit women's entry ("they might faint at the sight of blood").

Of course, intellectuals would offer the most moral and logical arguments. Without that biological gift for measuring the cycles of the moon and planets, how could a woman master any discipline that demanded a sense of time, space, mathematics—or the ability to measure anything at all? In philosophy and religion, how could women compensate for being disconnected from the rhythm of the universe? Or for their lack of symbolic death and resurrection every month?

Menopause would be celebrated as a positive event, the symbol that men had accumulated enough years of cyclical wisdom to need no more.

Liberal males in every field would try to be kind. The fact that "these people" have no gift for measuring life, the liberals would explain, should be punishment enough.

And how would women be trained to react? One can imagine right-wing women agreeing to all these arguments with a staunch and smiling masochism. ("The ERA would force housewives to wound themselves every month": Phyllis Schlafly. "Your husband's blood is as sacred as that of Jesus—and so sexy, too!": Marabel Morgan.) Reformers and Queen Bees would adjust their lives to the cycles of the men around them. Feminists would explain endlessly that men, too, needed to be liberated from the false idea of Martian aggressiveness, just as women needed to escape the bonds of "menses-envy." Radical feminists would add that the oppression of the nonmenstrual was the pattern for all other oppressions. ("Vampires were our first freedom fighters!") Cultural feminists would exalt a female bloodless imagery in art and literature. Socialist feminists would insist that, once capitalism and imperialism were overthrown, women would menstruate, too. ("If women aren't yet menstruating in Russia," they would explain, "it's only because true socialism can't exist within capitalist encirclement.")

In short, we would discover, as we should already guess, that logic is in the eye of the logician. (For instance, here's an idea for theorists and logicians: If women are supposed to be less rational and more emotional at the beginning of our menstrual cycle when the female hormone is at its lowest level, then why isn't it logical to say that, in those few days, women behave the most like the way men behave all month long? I leave further improvisations up to you.) *

The truth is that, if men could menstruate, the power justifications would go on and on.

If we let them.

* With thanks to Stan Pottinger for many of the improvisations already here.

ROY BLOUNT, JR.

Women in the Locker Room!

I'll tell you who—if he were with us in this hour—would be the ideal dressing-room reporter.

Undrape! you are not guilty to me, nor stale nor discarded,
I see through the broadcloth and gingham whether or no,
And am around, tenacious, acquisitive, tireless, and cannot
be shaken away.

Walt Whitman. If you read it right, "Song of Myself" is all about sportswriting.

Blacksmiths with grimed and hairy chests environ the anvil,

Each has his main-sledge, they are all out, there is a great
heat in the fire.

From the cinder-strew'd threshold I follow their movements,

The lithe sheer of their waists plays even with their massive
arms,

Overhand the hammers swing, overhand so slow, overhand
so sure,

They do not hasten, each man hits in his place.

Wouldn't Walt be hell rhapsodizing on batting practice? His sensitivities are masculine enough, so to speak, that he can really get into hammering, and feminine enough, so to speak, that he can be turned on by men's waists. We don't have any Whitmans among the locker-room-invading press today, but we do have women.

These women face the same deadlines and inside-flavor requirements that men reporters do. So why should they be forced to wait outside, in the hall or in a special interview room, while their male competitors walk right in and grill the players in the act of taking their pants off one leg at a time? It is not uncommon today to see Lois Lane in the phone booth with supermen of nearly every team sport—partly because of a lawsuit filed against Major League Baseball in 1977 by Melissa Ludtke and her then employer, *Sports Illustrated.*

"If those broads don't watch it, they're going to get us all thrown out," a prominent male scribe exclaimed at the time.

"Bowie Kuhn really screwed up," Ludtke said of the baseball commissioner, whose denial of her application for World Series locker-room credentials led to her sex-discrimination suit. "He opened up a can of worms across the board. He could have worked something out. But now if we win, there won't be any way a woman can be kept out by åny club down to the high-school level, really, which is ridiculous." Barbara Walters surrounded by slack-jawed naked Murfreesboro Blue Devils—she's trying to get them to be serious, they're popping her with towels . . . That has not yet come to pass, alas.

A couple of years ago, I was sitting next to Stephanie Salter, who used to cover sports for the *San Francisco Examiner*, when she was ejected—"We'll call a cop!"—from the New York Baseball Writers' annual dinner for not being a stag. Because I would generally rather eat with a friend of mine who has been tossed out of somewhere than with someone who has done the tossing, I walked out with her; but I hated missing Casey Stengel's postdinner remarks.

The previous year, Stengel had laid down an ageless boyish sports guideline when he said of one of his stauncher explayers, "When it came time to piss in the road, he pissed harder than anybody." It was to preserve speakers' freedom to say such things, I suppose, that women were excluded. I doubt that Stengel, then around eighty and as full of strange music as *Finnegans Wake*, would have been inhibited by a woman's presence, or by anything short of a fire bomb, but there does seem to be an issue there somewhere. Men may suspect that a woman will regard pissing hard in the road as something quaintly obstreperous, something that only a man who "has to prove himself" would care about. My wife says she doesn't think women feel this way. My wife has been in the dressing room of the Pittsburgh Pirates. I have told her I don't want to hear about it.

But colleges have coed dorms, don't they? Olympic athletes have to take sex tests, don't they? And at least one World Team Tennis team was known to make do with a single dressing room for its men and women players. Strictly speaking, a dressing room with self-respecting men reporters in it is not a stag affair anyway, because self-respecting reporters are going to report some of the proceedings to readers, including women. Most of the really fun stuff that goes on in dressing rooms, like running nude and landing seated in a teammate's birthday cake, goes on when reporters of all sexes are absent.

I can't claim to have felt like a woman in a men's dressing room, but I have been made to feel rather . . . chirpy, and like a second-class citizen, by male players who didn't like sharing their scene with Clark Kent. An interviewee may have no towel around his waist yet still have one around his mind. On the other hand, the first time I brought my young son into the locker room of the Pittsburgh Steelers, we were received like two of the boys (somebody even threw a little piece of soap at us), and it was the zenith of my credibility as a father.

Which reminds me: Former Steeler Bruce Van Dyke's son was a toddler when Van Dyke brought him into the dressing room for the first time. Van Dyke looked away for a moment, and when he turned back, the lad had gotten so thoroughly into the spirit of the place that he was naked.

"People won't believe that nakedness is not the problem," said Ludtke, after having been into basketball dressing rooms as well as baseball clubhouses. Like the other women reporters who first penetrated these sancta, she was interviewed in newspapers and on the radio all over the country. "I was on a call-in show in Pittsburgh for an hour," she said, "and all anybody wanted to talk about was nakedness. Every subject would be turned around to nakedness. There were grandmothers worried about their grandsons facing this onslaught of women, and there were other women who just didn't think it was right. Before I went into this business, I wouldn't have seen the necessity of it either. But the players can use a towel if they want to. And when you're interviewing somebody, it's eye-to-eye and mouth to-notebook-and-pen sort of contact. I don't just sit there *looking*."

The dressing rooms that admit women reporters have done so only after the players have voted their approval, and for the most part, players seem to have adjusted to the onslaught pretty well, though with ethnic differences. Generally, young black players have been the least self-conscious, I am told. Lawrie Mifflin, who covered hockey and soccer for the *New York Daily News*, told me there is a New York Cosmo from Italy who always wears a bathrobe in the clubhouse, women or no. Everybody does in Italian clubhouses.

Jane Gross of the *New York Times*, a pioneer woman in NBA dressing rooms, has written about finding in the locker room "a kind of caring for each other you don't see often in groups of women."

"The dressing room is a place where I don't feel I belong," said Salter, speaking more as a press person than as a woman, "but the players have gotten used to me. In fact, sometimes they talk to me because it's harder to tell a woman to go away." Kareem Abdul-Jabbar did ask her to please get her knee off his stool, but that could have happened to Grantland Rice (assuming he was limber enough to reach Jabbar's stool with his knee). Another superstar embarrassed Salter the same way he would any male reporter who pinned him down. "He was complaining about 'not being a part of the offense.'" she said, "and I asked him if he was saying that he was pissed off because his teammates weren't getting him the ball. He started yelling in front of everybody, 'That's exactly the kind of question—that's exactly what the press gets wrong!' And then he flounced off to the john. Later I sat down with him and got him to explain what he meant. Essentially, it was that he was pissed off because his teammates weren't getting him the ball."

Lawrie Mifflin said she felt quite comfortable in locker rooms because she grew up in them, as an interscholastic field-hockey player. "In my school the cheerleaders were the strange ones, who couldn't make the team," she said. She added that she was close to her brothers and belonged to the first coeducational class at Yale—as did the *New York Times*'s Robin Herman at Princeton.

"The first time I walked into a dressing room," said Herman, "there were about fifty men in suits in the middle of the room, and then the athletes undressing in a ring around them. I thought, 'I'll just melt into this group of clothed people ...' Of course it didn't work out that way. Cameras started flashing, and people were asking *me* questions. It *is* a strange setting. Where else in life do people talk to people while they're dressing? Unless it's a husband or a wife or your children. Even your parents don't talk to you while you're dressing. You notice all kinds of things in the dressing room. Like people who put on their shoes and socks before their undershirt. Things you don't really want to know." But she and Mifflin were for a while the only reporters traveling with the New York Rangers, and Herman said she eventually became convinced the players had "forgotten we're women."

The only way her exposure to dressing rooms had affected her feelings toward men, Herman said, was that "I'm really spoiled now in favor of men who take care of their bodies. I don't think I could go out with a skinny guy who gets sand kicked in his face." Some women reporters rule out romance with players, and some don't. One says players never ask her out until after they've left the dressing room. "I guess undressed is a very vulnerable state to be rejected in. I could say, 'Why would I go out with you? Look at you!'"

After all, these reporters are women, and their slants are somewhat different from men's. Maybe they will dispel some of the stale cigar smoke that suffuses the sportswriting profession. Not that all such smoke should go, from the press box or from the stands, but it is refreshing to hear a sportswriter say that a player "flounced" or that jockeys "just chattered and chattered until they got on their horses and rode off," as Salter did, or that the New York Islanders "are still kind of skittish," as Herman did. It is also interesting, though odd, to hear a woman reporter say that a certain veteran player "is beginning to look like a saggy old woman."

She was not going to put that in the paper. But one reason why anybody who covers a team should have access to the dressing room is that the bodies are such a big part of the story.

"Sure, it's interesting, to look at their chests and shoulders," said Mifflin. "But if I say that, then people will say, 'See, they claim it's not sexual, but she's been looking at their bodies!'"

"I have no apologies to make," said Herman. "I know why I'm looking and what I'm looking for. Seeing the way they're built helps you understand the way they play. But I feel like I'm treading on dangerous ground now, talking about it."

Exactly the kind of ground Walt Whitman liked. Let us have wide, nonprurient male and female eyes in the dressing room, because significant bodies ought to be witnessed. The most remarkable one I ever saw was Satchel Paige's. His huge feet were completely archless, spread across the floor, with all the toes bent sharply to the right for some reason, and his lower legs were heavily scarred and as straight as Popeye's upper arms. And yet dressed, as he said himself, he looked "like a young doctor."

I like to see players in the flesh because I never cease to entertain, as a point of reference, the eternal sportswriter's question: "Why is this guy getting paid to play ball and not me?" I have seen players whose bodies immediately implied every foot-pound their games must require, which is more oomph than I can imagine commanding. I have seen a *few* players whose bodies looked less prepossessing than mine. Then there are the scars and bent limbs.

So, you're going to ask next, should men reporters be allowed in women's locker rooms? Well, I'm going to reply in a measured tone, we generally don't need to yet, because those women's sports, such as tennis, that are heavily reported are not really team sports, and it's possible to catch all the principals before they go off to dress. Women's basketball, however, thanks to recent strides toward equality in funding of women's intercollegiate sports, has been attracting more and more deadline-pressure coverage. Male reporters have, in fact, been in women's basketball locker rooms after games already, but the players have kept their uniforms on until the press left. I'm told it looks strange, a dressing room full of people with no dressing going on. Presumably there would be too much ogling if a lot of male scribes were to barge into a functioning sanctum of women. But women can wear towels too, and a band of athletes has a corporate air that discourages even optical barging. Wouldn't any sincere nonsexist student of sport take a respectful interest in what a woman strong-forward's chest and shoulders look like? I know Walt Whitman would have—he who asked all the crucial sportswriting questions:

> *Who goes there? hankering, gross, mystical, nude;*
> *How is it I extract strength from the beef I eat?*
>
> *What is a man anyhow? what am I? what are you?*

From WHAT MEN DON'T TELL WOMEN by Roy Blount, Jr. Copyright (c) 1984 by Roy Blount, Jr. By permission of Little, Brown & Company in association with The Atlantic Monthly Press.

QUESTIONS FOR DISCUSSION

1. Sayers wonders what would happen to a man if he felt the "unrelenting pressure of a whole social structure forcing him to order all his goings...." What specific behaviors of females are pressured by the society in which we live today? Do such pressures operate unequally on women of different social classes?

2. When women refuse to behave as the social structure dictates, as many do today, what pressures are then brought to bear upon them?

3. Are not men, also, constrained by the society to behave in a given fashion? What evidence can you offer that this is more the case with women than with men?

4. Sayers suggests that women are urged to be learned without losing their feminine appeal. Some would argue this is no longer the case. Based on your own experiences as college students, would you agree with Sayers? Are there data to support your position?

5. The media often use a sexual designation when referring to women in particular occupations, e.g., "female astronauts." Some maintain that this is necessary so that young females

will have role models whose accomplishments will encourage them to break out of preconceived roles. Do you agree? Who was Geraldine Ferraro's role model when she ran for vice president?

6. Does the fact that women have now entered some previously all-male bastions, the service academies, for example, mean that males in general do perceive women as equals?

7. Steinem, like Sayers, speculates upon role-reversal for males and females. Is her conclusion that men would turn menstruation into a sign of male superiority just whimsy, or does it seem to follow logically from other traits which males currently see as making them superior to women? What are these traits?

8. Steinem says that "male intellectuals would offer the most moral and logical arguments" about the abilities of women who do not menstruate. They could not master mathematics, for example, "without that in-built gift for measuring the cycles of the moon and planets." What biological argument is used today to "prove" that women are not as competent as men in math? Are there any areas of intellectual accomplishments where females are under-represented? If so, is the explanation biological or cultural in nature?

9. Both Sayers and Steinem seem to suggest that women derive a large part of their self-image from men. If this is the case, why do women derive their self-image from men and not vice versa?

10. Steinem notes that not all within women's groups are supporters of the ERA and other concerns of the women's liberation movement. How do you account for differences among women in this respect?

11. Blount says of Walt Whitman that "his sensitivities are masculine enough ... and feminine enough...." Would feminists agree that there are masculine and feminine sensitivities? How do you respond to this?

12. Blount suggests that there is a language used by females different from that used by males: "a player 'flounced' " or "jockeys 'just chattered and chattered.' " Is this a sexist idea about language use?

13. Stephanie Salter was thrown out of the New York Baseball Writer's annual dinner in part, apparently, to preserve the right to say things like "pissed" at the meetings. Yet later on Salter herself is quoted as saying, "I asked him if he was saying he was pissed off...." Based on your own experiences would you argue that there are female–male differences in the use of off-color language?

14. Melissa Ludtke, who filed the lawsuit which resulted in women being admitted to male lockerrooms, said, "People won't believe that nakedness is not the problem." If nakedness is not, then what *is* the problem?

15. If, on the other hand, Ludtke is correct, then why is there any reluctance to admit male reporters to female lockerrooms? Blount says that "presumably there would be too much ogling...." Does this mean that males are less able than females to be only professionally interested in a naked body?

REFERENCES

Bradwell vs. *Illinois*, 83 U.S. (16 Wallace), 130 (1872).

Collins, Randall. *Conflict Sociology.* New York: Academic Press, 1975.

Delaney, Janice, Lupton, Mary Jane, and Toth, Emily. *The Curse.* New York: E. P. Dutton, Inc., 1976.

Freeman, Jo. "The Women's Liberation Movement: Its Origins, Structure, Activities, and Ideas," in *Women: A Feminist Perspective.* Freeman, Jo, ed. Palo Alto, Calif.: The Mayfield Publishing Co., 1984. 543–56.

Murdock, G. P., and Provost, C. "Factors in the Division of Labor by Sex." *Ethnology* 12, 2 (April, 1973).

Weitzman, L. J., et. al. "Sex Role Socialization in Picture Books for Preschool Children." *American Journal of Sociology* 77 (May, 1972), 1125–50.

Weitzman, L. J., and Rizzo, D. *Biased Textbooks: A Research Perspective.* Washington, D.C.: The Resource Center on Sex Roles in Education, The National Foundation for the Improvement of Education, 1974.

Wicker, Tom. "Women and the G.O.P." *New York Times*, April 25, 1986. A-35.

Chapter Fourteen

Population

READINGS

*P*sychologists call it selective perception. In the midst of a configuration of objects we tend to see what we want to see. Thus, if you are looking for a specific individual in a crowded room you will tend not to see the many others who are there; you will concentrate your efforts on locating the one individual for whom you are looking. Something of a related nature applies when we discuss the world population situation. If we look around in the United States we do not see cities teeming with millions of people who are unhoused, ill-fed, and lacking job opportunities. We tend to see bustling cities where a majority are employed and able to enjoy the amenities of life. Yet, in many cities of the world such a situation does indeed exist. Some of our cities are crowded, housing is a problem for many lower-class families especially, and many people are unemployed. In discussing population growth, then, it is important to keep in mind the sometimes dramatic differences between what we in the United States are experiencing and what is happening in other parts of the world—particularly the developing countries. In addition, we must consider the implications of population growth and decline on individual communities and different sections of the country. Some communities in the United States are losing population and others are growing rapidly. Obviously, the impact of population change is not the same for these types of communities. The Northeast is not growing, but the Southwest is experiencing significant growth. Again, the consequences of population change are different for these two sections.

We might assume that with population changes having such important meaning for the lives of individuals and communities, the United States would have some kind of national population policy to help guide governmental action in this area. Such is not the case. The personal right of a couple to have or not have children, or the number of children to have, is jealously guarded in our society. (This is not true everywhere—China, for example.) The right of individuals or families to migrate from one section of the country to another is also free from any governmental restrictions. This is not true in all countries. An important reason why we, at this time, see no reason to put restrictions upon population growth or free movement is that there are those who do not believe the United States has a population problem.

Norman Ryder, Office of Population Research at Princeton University, has stated, for example, that

> The kind of population growth that now seems likely poses no major problem that I can see. We have a host of problems in this country. But population seems to me to be a relatively minor component. (1976)

Many would strongly oppose such a statement. And certainly all, including Ryder, agree that the impact of rapid population growth on individual communities can be severe.

Whether or not one feels that the United States has a population problem, we have entered an era where we are forced to consider the implications of continued and unrestricted population growth. Baldassare notes that

> The mood of the American public today also differs sharply from that of previous times ... Open conflicts about the limits of freedom and the importance of further economic development, especially on a local level, are more numerous. Residents are also more likely to question the rights of developers and newcomers to disrupt the present size and composition of their community. The promise that economic growth and population growth will lead to a better standard of living for all in the locality is now viewed cautiously, and even skeptically. A central theme in today's debates about growth, hardly as well articulated in the past, is whether population change will maintain or improve the "quality of life" in a given residential area. Localities once took pride in statistics on population size, economic growth, or industrial capacity. Now they more frequently turn to social indicators and public opinion polls which measure residential quality and evaluations of housing, government, local services, facilities, and overall well-being. (1981)

The debate over our population growth is occurring in the midst of a decline in the United States birth rate, on the one hand, and the continuing growth of our population on the other hand. Until the 1980s the United States had experienced for two decades a rather sharp decline in its birth rate. In 1960 the birth rate was 23.7 per 1000. By 1970 this had dropped to an all-time low of 14.8. There has been an upturn in recent years—reaching 16.0 in 1982. Our death rate continues to decline (9.4 per 1000 in 1970; 8.7 in 1980). If we have a population problem, one aspect of it is the increasing number of the aged in our society—those 65 years and older. The proportion of the population aged 65 and older increased significantly in the past two decades, growing by

54%. The implications of a "graying" society are not to be minimized. More older people will put increased strains on the Social Security system, which is already having financial difficulties. A larger proportion of the population in the retirement years means that there is a smaller proportion in the work force paying into the Social Security system. Medical care for the aged requires increasing amounts of the funds available for social services. These must be balanced against other demands on the tax dollar.

An additional concern about our rate of growth is the fact that the birth rate varies among the several nationality groups in the United States. While the overall birth rate in 1979 was 15.9, there were some significant differences among the white, black, and Hispanic-American groups in the society. The black birth rate was 50% higher than that of whites, and Hispanic-American rates of reproduction were more than 70% higher than the white birth rate. In addition, blacks and Hispanics are not evenly dispersed in the society. Blacks are disproportionately concentrated in the cities and Hispanics are found primarily in California, New York, Florida, and the Southwest. Blacks and Hispanic-Americans have, on average, lower incomes than other groups, and concentrations in few areas result in strains on the provisions of social services and the overall infrastructure.

Our population concerns, on a comparative basis, are far fewer than those in the developing countries. Overcrowding of cities, lack of employment opportunities, and continuing high birth rates characterize many countries in Latin America and Africa. Unsettled political conditions and fewer economic opportunities have contributed in recent years to an increased flow of illegal immigrants into the United States. World population problems affect all countries—not just those where the problems are immediate.

Efforts to resolve the growth of population are often, simplistically, put in Malthusian terms. Thomas Malthus, in 1798, published an *Essay on the Principle of Population*. Malthus argued that population growth inevitably outruns the ability of people to grow enough food to sustain themselves. When there are too many people to feed certain factors, "war, pestilence, and famine" occur to reduce the population to manageable means. Malthus foresaw this cycle being repeated over and over, resulting in human misery, starvation, and poverty. Malthus was, in his day and ever since, the source of much controversy. Those who oppose the Malthusian argument point to the advances in food production and the development of increasingly efficient means of contraception. Some argue that the problem is not the production of food but the inefficient distribution of it, due to political and other factors. In specific areas of the world Malthus' predictions have unfortunately proven to be the case: too many people and too few food resources. Furthermore, Malthus could not have foreseen the rapid advancement in medical technologies which have helped to reduce the death rate in developing countries while birth rates have remained at a very high level.

Recently there has been an encouraging slowdown in the world's rate of birth. Former predictions of a world with 6 billion people by the year 2000 have now been reduced to around 5.5 billion, with some expectations that the population will, at least for the foreseeable future, stabilize around this figure. Just how many people the world can accommodate we do not know, but most are in agreement that there can be no letup in efforts to bring population and resources into balance.

In the first selection in this chapter, Arthur Hoppe offers "A Proven System" for birth control. Recognizing that family sizes are much smaller in the upper classes than in the lower classes, he attributes this to different sleeping quarters for the various classes. The population explosion, he argues, "boils down to a question of opportunity."

In a humorous fashion Arthur Hoppe deals with serious constitutional matters in "Family Planning." What are the constitutional rights of the unborn? Usually the "unborn" refers to a fetus in some stage of development. Hoppe carries the question back farther: what about the unfertilized egg? What about the rights of the millions of spermatozoa? The newly organized Fair Play for Spermatozoa Committee is working on these matters.

A major problem in controlling population has always been the availability of an inexpensive and reliable means of contraception. In *"Through the Tube Darkly ... Telecontraception,"* Margaret Bennett thinks she has found the answer. Lying on the floor watching television exposes the sex glands to radiation which can result in sterility. Bennett argues for more, not less, levels of radiation emanating from our television sets. This way we could, in one generation, reduce the reproduction of "the glazed-eyed, slack-jawed perpetual viewers of roller derbies and Westerns and Gomer Pyle reruns...." At the same time "the readers, the thinkers, and the doers of the world's work would reproduce." In the end, "television will at last have become, in every sense of the word, the sterile medium."

Jonathan Swift was born in Dublin, Ireland, in 1667. He was a political activist, a priest in the Church of Ireland, a political satirist, and an acclaimed Irish patriot. He both loved and despaired of his Irish compatriots, fighting continually on their behalf against the oppressive rule of England, which he felt was primarily responsible for Ireland's extreme poverty in the seventeenth century. He also felt that Irish landlords were a cause of Irish pain and suffering. In vain, he advanced many proposals over the years to lift Ireland up from its desperate state. It is in this context that he offered yet another "Modest Proposal," the last selection in this chapter, for helping Ireland to improve itself and its economy.

 ARTHUR HOPPE

A Proven System

Hats off to the Upper Classes. They generally have separate bedrooms built into their houses. I think this will solve the population explosion. I'm not, heaven forbid, prying into anyone's personal affairs. I only wish to salute them for helping popularize the only proven-safe, easily understood, guaranteed-effective method of Planned Parenthood. It's what we experts in the field refer to as Geographical Birth Control.

Actually, up to now, it's been a matter of economics. The richer you get, the farther away from your wife you get. The poor, as you know, sleep in double beds. The middle class, in twins. While the rich enjoy separate bedrooms, separate cabanas and separate vacations. This explains why we have so many poor people in the world. And so few rich. So hats off again to our social leaders, I say. For pointing the way through Geographical Birth Control.

For the population explosion, let's face facts, boils down to a question of opportunity. Statistics bear this out irrefutably. The poor, who sleep in double beds, average a shocking 7.2 children per household. Now a few sociologists hold this is due to the lack of outdoorsy leisure-time activities. Such as water polo and quoits. But the double bed's essential responsibility cannot be ignored.

Take the middle class in its twin beds. A far more admirable average of only 2.4 children per household. More quoit players, you say? Perhaps. But the prime factor is that opportunity has been withdrawn a good yard. Or, as Rotarian speakers invariably put it, "Seizing opportunity requires get-up-and-go." But to date the problem has been solved satisfactorily only by the rich. I doubt any more effective method will ever be devised than having to get up on a cold night, fumble in the closet for one's bathrobe and slippers, stumble down a drafty hall and knock three times on a closed door. Only to find she's off someplace on a separate vacation. The very thought quells the spirit of romance. Thus it is no surprise that the Idle Rich, as we call them, average a distinguished 1.2 children. A goal for us all to shoot at.

If the Government wishes to enter the field of birth control, logic dictates that it should promote the only perfect method. And let our battle cry then be: "Separate Bedrooms for the Poor!" With perhaps a few quoits thrown in.

Meanwhile, it is up to us as individuals. Join the Geographical Birth Control League today. Do your part to save the world by stamping out Togetherness.

 ARTHUR HOPPE

Family Planning

So family planning, one way or another, is now *de rigueur*. Unfortunately, the government appears determined to make it more difficult than ever. I had thought that if the government stepped into the field of family planning, it would license parents. The government dearly loves licensing people to do things. It licenses them to drive cars, fly airplanes, and go fishing. Surely motherhood requires as much, if not more skill than hooking a small-mouth bass. Yet as matters stand, any unskilled, ill-equipped, untrained, accident-prone couple can willy-nilly help shape the next generation without so much as a by-your-leave. No wonder the nation's in a mess. But, no, instead of licensing parents, our lawmakers appear bound and determined to confer the full rights of the United States Constitution on fertilized eggs, all of which would enjoy the blessings of American citizenship as long as they were, needless to say, American. And that's a problem right there. For if children born on American soil of foreign parents are automatically American, surely eggs fertilized on American soil are equally American. And what is to prevent hordes of foreigners from honeymooning in America so that in later life their fertilized eggs can swarm through our immigration barriers? The very thought of America being overrun by alien-looking fertilized eggs would churn the stomach of any patriot.

That's the conservative view. For the liberal view of such legislation. I refer you to Minerva Hibbins, author of *Sex and the Single Egg*. "It's all well and good to provide Constitutional protection to the fertilized egg," says the noted feminist, "but what about the unfertilized egg? Surely she, too, is alive. And surely, if her mother is an American, she, too, is an American. Should she be deprived of her American citizenship simply because she hasn't mated?"

In *Sex and the Single Egg*, Ms. Hibbins outlines the cruel fate awaiting her heroine, Eva the Ovum: Born in the warm depths of the ovarian bower, Eva shyly ventures forth to hide coyly in the soft folds of the fallopian tube, there to await the arrival of her eager swain. Monogamous to the core, she seeks no casual relationships or one-night stands; she will mate only in holy union for life. But what happens to Eva in these barbarous times when she is unprotected by the majesty of the law? Millions of suitors may set forth to woo this precious jewel, only to be fouly murdered—every single one of them—in the attempt, thereby leaving Eva to expire, alone and unfulfilled, her all-too-brief life wasted in cold spinsterhood. Or, worse, poor Eva may become a hapless victim of the Pill, condemned to spend her days imprisoned within the ovarian bower, subject to no habeus corpus proceedings, arbitrarily denied the right to travel—a right enjoyed today even by avowed Communists. Once Americans are aware of Eva's plight, Ms. Hibbins says, there can be no question that their sense of justice will drive them to support vociferously the Equal Rights for Eggs Amendment.

But what, you may well ask, about the swain? We have already seen them perishing in a slaughter unequaled in the annals of human genocide. Does no one speak for them? Rest assured that where there are innocent victims, from the harp seals to the frobish lousewort, tender human hearts will come to their rescue with an organization. Thus was born the Fair Play for Spermatozoa Committee. We members of the Committee are fully aware that hitherto there has been little clamor to provide Constitutional protection for these little fellows. It is all too true that their numbers are legion and their mission virtually impossible. No wonder our society has always held their lives cheap. Yet their dedication, their determination, and their indomitable grit should be held aloft to one and all as Americanism at its finest. We need but to make the nation cognizant of their heart-stirring story.

Consider, then, the apocryphal history of but one of these unborn countrymen of ours. Let us, for the sake of identification, call him Harold. For his first ninety days, tiny Harold lies idly about, growing daily, gathering strength, practicing swimming, and mustering resolve. At last, looking like a cuddly tadpole, he is deemed mature enough for The Quest. His single-minded goal: to seek out, too, and win Eva the Ovum. No knight vowing to free a princess imprisoned in a tower was ever endowed with more chastity, felicity, and nobleness of purpose. Tada! Ta-da! With eighty million or so of his fellows, each equally determined, Harold bravely sets forth on his mission, a mission far more hazardous than faced by the heroes of the Light Brigade. His little tail flailing away, he struggles onward, ever onward. Excelsior! One by one, to the left and right of him, his companions fall by the wayside. At last he and he alone wins through to his soulmate. They are joined as the Good Lord decreed, and with His blessings, they go forth together to the sanctity of the womb where they will flourish and multiply.

Isn't that a beautiful story? *But that's not the way it is.* In these decadent times, this is the way it usually is: No sooner has Harold set forth on his glorious Quest than he and his companions run into an impenetrable elastic barrier. Time and again, they butt their little heads against this unyielding wall with all the force at their command—to no avail. They hurl themselves forward and rebound over and over, knowing no other course, until at last they collapse and expire from sheer frustration. Or, even more poignant, they find their way clear. With hopes high, they dash forward—only to plunge blindly into a sea of noxious, lethal poisons from which there is no escape. Or, most cruel of all, Eva's mother is a feminist on the Pill or a Catholic on the rhythm method. It is then that Harold struggles ever onward, overcoming insuperable odds, triumphantly winning through in the end to the silken fallopian folds, which he eagerly parts—only to discover that no one's home. Is it any wonder that he succumbs to a broken heart?

Some masculinists argue that they have the right to do what they wish with their own spermatozoa. "Keep your laws off our bodies," they say. But surely an end must be put to this vicious practice of spermatocide. If a fertilized egg can be sheltered by the Constitution, surely these doughty little battlers also deserve the fruits of American citizenship. I have done my best to enlist the support of my dear wife, Glynda, in this crusade to give every spermatozoa a chance. You know what she said? She said, "Go lay an egg."

 MARGARET BENNETT

Through the Tube Darkly ... Telecontraception

Today most sentient beings agree that overpopulation is the greatest threat to the continuation of life as we know it. But even though the problem is recognized, it has thus far been impossible to solve. Everyone refuses to have his most intimate right restricted. Politicians are unwilling to get involved with the sensitive area of population control for fear of losing votes. The tragic result is that usually the more intelligent persons practice birth control and limit the size of their families, while the average and subaverage citizens continue to breed wantonly.

What we need, therefore, is a natural-selection process to insure the survival of the fittest and the elimination of the unfit. But in this modern age when we are so far removed from the regulating forces of nature, where will we find such a process? Simple. It is right in front of our noses. I refer to the television set.

For years there have been intermittent warnings about radiation from TV sets. We have all been cautioned not to sit too close. And we have been particularly warned not to let children watch television lying on their backs on the floor in front of the TV exposing their sex glands to the rays, lest sterility result.

Let me repeat that. Lest sterility result.

Now, recently we have been told that manufacturers have managed to reduce the radiation to a harmless level. This is unconscionable. Instead of cutting down radiation, they should do exactly the opposite. They should increase it to the point that anyone watching television in excess of four hours a day would, in the course of a year, become permanently, irrevocably sterile. We would then have telecontraception—the perfect birth-control device—inexpensive, effective for either sex, requiring no forethought or manual or mental dexterity on the part of the user, causing no diminishment of sexual pleasure, and unobjectionable on religious grounds.

Think of the wonders of telecontraception. In only one generation the population would fall dramatically in quantity and rise dramatically in quality. The readers, the thinkers, the doers of the world's work would reproduce. The glazed-eyed, slack-jawed perpetual viewers of roller derbies and Westerns and Gomer Pyle reruns would not. The robust outdoor-playing children whose indoor hours are devoted to reading and doing homework would arrive at puberty with healthy, functioning sex glands. The pasty-faced, hollow-chested ones who spent their childhood glued to the TV would not.

There would, of course, have to be some provision for viewers of educational channels. This would be a simple matter to arrange. UHF programs could be transmitted in such a way as to cut off radiation. Children could watch Mister Rogers and Sesame Street without damage, and adults could learn to speak Italian or play the guitar or understand foreign policy with impunity.

Telecontraception very quickly could solve our horrendous welfare problem. After only a year of sitting in front of the TV with a can of beer, a chronically out-of-work man would cease to father more dependent children. This would immediately allow irate taxpayers to drop another of their major complaints: "Look at that, Marge! They're living in that shack and they're on welfare, but they can still afford a television—and on our money." As a matter of fact, each person who goes on welfare could, as standard policy, be given a TV set with his first check.

Not only would telecontraception eliminate overpopulation, it would also strengthen the faltering family unit. No longer would parents use the TV as a baby-sitter and a method of ignoring their children—not if they wanted to be grandparents. Consequently, the homes of America would no longer echo with the phrase, "Shut up and go watch TV."

The constant battles between husbands and wives over televised sporting events would also end. Wives could immediately command their husbands' attention with, "Go ahead and watch the Super Bowl, if you want to be sterile." Then again, perhaps the wives wouldn't say a word, and the men could forever watch their games in peace.

As with any scheme for human betterment, there will be detractors. Many will scream that this is nothing but blatant "boobicide" and that we would be wiping out the backbone of the nation, those individuals who, with their undiscriminating consumption, have made America what it is today. Used-car dealers and manufacturers of breakfast cereals, headache pills, deodorants, and mouthwash all will claim that their source of livelihood will die out and that the economic repercussions will undermine the country. And it is only to be expected that every politician in the nation will do all in his power to stop telecontraception, since not one could get into office without the votes of brainwashed TV addicts.

But all men of conscience will have to agree that the long-range benefits of telecontraception would outweigh any short-range problems. Let us therefore band together to demand increased radiation standards in TV sets. Let us work concertedly toward that utopian day when the Pill has given way to the box, and television will at last have become, in every sense of the word, the sterile medium.

 **JONATHAN SWIFT**

A Modest Proposal

It is a melancholly Object to those, who walk through this great Town or travel in the Country, when they see the Streets, the Roads and Cabbin-doors crowded with Beggers of the Female Sex, followed by three, four, or six Children, all in Rags, and importuning every Passenger for an Alms. These Mothers instead of being able to work for their honest livelyhood, are forced to employ all their time in Stroling to beg Sustenance for their helpless Infants, who, as they grow up, either turn Thieves for want of Work, or leave their dear Native Country, to fight for the Pretender in Spain, or sell themselves to the Barbadoes.

I think it is agreed by all Parties, that this prodigious number of Children in the Arms, or on the Backs, or at the Heels of their Mothers, and frequently of their Fathers, is in the present deplorable state of the Kingdom, a very great additional grievance; and therefore whoever could find out a fair, cheap and easy method of making these Children sound and useful Members of the Commonwealth, would deserve so well of the publick, as to have his Statue set up for a Preserver of the Nation.

But my Intention is very far from being confined to provide only for the Children of professed Beggers, it is of a much greater Extent, and shall take in the whole Number of Infants at a certain Age, who are born of Parents in effect as little able to support them, as those who demand our Charity in the Streets.

As to my own part, having turned my Thoughts, for many Years, upon this important Subject, and maturely weighed the several Schemes of other Projectors, I have always found them grossly mistaken in their computation. It is true, a Child just dropt from its Dam, may be supported by her Milk, for a Solar Year with little other Nourishment, at most not above the Value of two Shillings, which the Mother may certainly get, or the Value in Scraps, by her lawful Occupation of Begging; and it is exactly at one Year Old that I propose to provide for them in such a manner, as, instead of being a Charge upon their Parents, or the Parish, or wanting Food and Raiment for the rest of their Lives, they shall, on the Contrary, contribute to the Feeding and partly to the Cloathing of many Thousands.

There is likewise another great Advantage in my Scheme, that it will prevent those voluntary Abortions, and that horrid practice of Women murdering their Bastard Children, alas! too frequent among us, Sacrificing the poor innocent Babes, I doubt, more to avoid the Expence than the Shame, which would move Tears and Pity in the most Savage and inhuman breast.

The number of Souls in this Kingdom being usually reckoned one Million and a half, Of these I calculate there may be about two hundred thousand Couple whose Wives are Breeders; from which number I substract thirty Thousand Couples, who are able to maintain their own Children, although I apprehend there cannot be so many, under the present Distresses of the Kingdom; but this being granted, there will remain an hundred and seventy thousand Breeders. I again Substract fifty Thousand, for those Women who miscarry, or whose Children die by accident, or disease within the Year. There only remain an hundred and twenty thousand Children of poor Parents annually born: The question therefore is, How this number shall be reared, and provided for? which, as I have already said, under the present Situation of Affairs, is utterly impossible by all the Methods hitherto proposed; for we can neither employ them in Handicraft or Agriculture; we neither build Houses, (I mean in the Country) nor cultivate Land: They can very seldom pick up a Livelihood by Stealing till they arrive at six years Old; except where they are of towardly parts; although, I confess, they learn the Rudiments much earlier; during which time they can however be properly looked upon only as Probationers; as I have been informed by a principal Gentleman in the County of Cavan, who protested to me, that he never knew above one or two Instances under the Age of six, even in a part of the Kingdom so renowned for the quickest proficiency in that Art.

I am assured by our Merchants, that a Boy or a Girl before twelve years Old, is no saleable Commodity, and even when they come to this Age, they will not yield above three Pounds, or three Pounds and half a Crown at most, on the Exchange; which cannot turn to Account either to the Parents or Kingdom, the Charge of Nutriment and Rags having been at least four times that Value.

I shall now therefore humbly propose my own Thoughts, which I hope will not be liable to the least Objection.

I have been assured by a very knowing American of my acquaintance in London, that a young healthy Child well Nursed is at a year Old a most delicious nourishing and wholesome Food, whether Stewed, Roasted, Baked, or Boiled; and I make no doubt that it will equally serve in a Fricasie, or a Ragoust.

I do therefore humbly offer it to publick consideration, that of the Hundred and twenty thousand Children, already computed, twenty thousand may be reserved for Breed, whereof only one fourth part to be Males; which is more than we allow to Sheep, black Cattle, or Swine, and my Reason is, that these Children are seldom the Fruits of Marriage, a Circumstance not much regarded by our Savages, therefore, one Male will be sufficient to serve four Females. That the remaining Hundred thousand may at a year Old be offered in Sale to the Persons of Quality and Fortune, through the Kingdom, always advising the Mother to let them Suck plentifully in the last Month, so as to render them Plump, and Fat for a good Table. A Child will make two Dishes at an Entertainment for Friends, and when the Family dines alone, the fore or hind Quarter will make a reasonable Dish, and seasoned with a little Pepper or Salt will be very good Boiled on the fourth Day, especially in Winter.

I have reckoned upon a Medium, that a Child just born will weigh 12 pounds, and in a solar Year, if tolerably nursed, encreaseth to 28 Pounds.

I grant this food will be somewhat dear, and therefore very proper for Landlords, who, as they have already devoured most of the Parents seem to have the best Title to the Children.

Infant's flesh will be in Season throughout the Year, but more plentiful in March, and a little before and after; for we are told by a grave Author an eminent French Physician, that Fish being a prolifick Dyet, there are more Children born in Roman Catholick Countries about nine Months after Lent, than at any other Season; therefore reckoning a Year after Lent, the Markets will be more glutted than usual, because the Number of Popish Infants, is at least three to one in this Kingdom, and therefore it will have one other Collateral advantage, by lessening the Number of Papists among us.

I have already computed the Charge of nursing a Begger's Child (in which List I reckon all Cottagers, Labourers, and four fifths of the Farmers) to be about two Shillings per Annum, Rags included; and I believe no Gentleman would repine to give Ten Shillings for the Carcass of a good fat Child, which, as I have said will make four Dishes of excellent Nutritive Meat, when he hath only some particular Friend, or his own Family to dine with him. Thus the Squire will learn to be a good Landlord, and grow popular among his Tenants, the Mother will have Eight Shillings neat Profit, and be fit for Work till she produces another Child.

Those who are more thrifty (as I must confess the Times require) may flay the Carcass; the Skin of which, Artificially dressed, will make admirable Gloves for Ladies, and Summer Boots for fine Gentlemen.

As to our City of Dublin, Shambles may be appointed for this purpose, in the most convenient parts of it, and Butchers we may be assured will not be wanting; although I rather recommend buying the Children alive, and dressing them hot from the Knife, as we do roasting Pigs.

A very worthy Person, a true Lover of his Country, and whose Virtues I highly esteem, was lately pleased, in discoursing on this matter, to offer a refinement upon my Scheme. He said, that many Gentlemen of this Kingdom, having of late destroyed their Deer, he conceived that the Want of Venison might be well supply'd by the Bodies of young Lads and Maidens, not exceeding fourteen Years of Age, nor under twelve; so great a Number of both Sexes in every Country being now ready to Starve, for want of Work and Service: And these to be disposed of by their Parents if alive, or otherwise by their nearest Relations. But with due deference to so excellent a Friend, and so deserving a Patroit, I cannot be altogether in his Sentiments; for as to the Males, my American acquaintance assured me from frequent Experience, that their Flesh was generally Tough and Lean, like that of our Schoolboys, by continual exercise, and their Taste disagreeable, and to fatten them would not answer the Charge. Then as to the Females, it would, I think with humble Submission, be a Loss to the Publick, because they soon would become Breeders themselves: And besides it is not improbable that some scrupulous People might be apt to Censure such a Practice, (although indeed very unjustly) as a little bordering upon Cruelty, which, I confess, hath always been with me the strongest Objection against any Project, how well soever intended.

But in order to justify my Friend, he confessed, that this expedient was put into his Head by the famous Sallmanaazor, a Native of the Island Formosa, who came from thence to London, above twenty Years ago, and in Conversation told my Friend, that in his Country when any young Person happened to be put to Death, the Executioner sold the Carcass to Persons of Quality, as a prime Dainty, and that, in his Time, the Body of a plump Girl of fifteen, who was crucified for an attempt to poison the Emperor, was sold to his Imperial Majesty's prime Minister of State, and other great Mandarins of the Court, in Joints from the Gibbet, at four hundred Crowns. Neither indeed can I deny, that if the same Use were made of several plump young Girls in this Town, who, without one single Groat to their Fortunes, cannot stir abroad without a Chair, and appear at a Play-house, and Assemblies in Foreign fineries, which they never will pay for; the Kingdom would not be the worse.

Some Persons of a desponding Spirit are in great concern about that vast Number of poor People, who are Aged, Diseased, or Maimed, and I have been desired to imploy my Thoughts what Course may be taken, to ease the Nation of so grievous an Incumbrance. But I am not in the least Pain upon that matter, because it is very well known, that they are every Day dying, and rotting, by cold and famine, and filth, and vermin, as fast as can be reasonably expected. And as to the younger Labourers, they are now in almost as hopeful a Condition. They cannot get Work, and consequently pine away for want of Nourishment, to a degree, that if at any Time they are accidentally hired to common Labour, they have not Strength to perform it, and thus the Country and themselves are happily delivered from the Evils to come.

I have too long digressed, and therefore shall return to my Subject. I think the Advantages by the Proposal which I have made are obvious and many, as well as of the highest Importance.

For *First*, as I have already observed, it would greatly lessen the Number of Papists, with whom we are Yearly over-run, being the principal Breeders of the Nation, as well as our most dangerous Enemies, and who stay at home on purpose with a Design to deliver the Kingdom to the Pretender, hoping to take their Advantage by the Absence of so many good Protestants, who have chosen rather to leave their Country, than stay at home, and pay Tithes against their Conscience, to an Episcopal Curate.

Secondly, The poorer Tenants will have something valuable of their own which by Law may be made lyable to Distress, and help to pay their Landlord's Rent, their Corn and Cattle being already seized, and Money a Thing unknown.

Thirdly, Whereas the Maintenance of an hundred thousand Children, from two Years old, and upwards, cannot be computed at less than Ten Shillings a Piece per Annum, the Nation's Stock will be thereby increased fifty thousand Pounds per Annum, besides the Profit of a new Dish, introduced to the Tables of all Gentlemen of Fortune in the Kingdom, who have any Refinement in Taste, and the Money will circulate among our Selves, the Goods being entirely of our own Growth and Manufacture.

Fourthly, The constant Breeders, besides the gain of eight Shillings Sterling per Annum, by the Sale of their Children, will be rid of the Charge of maintaining them after the first Year.

Fifthly, This Food would likewise bring great Custom to Taverns, where the Vintners will certainly be so prudent as to procure the best Receipts for dressing it to Perfection; and consequently have their Houses frequented by all the fine Gentlemen, who justly value themselves upon their Knowledge in good Eating; and a skilful Cook, who understands how to oblige his Guests, will contrive to make it as expensive as they please.

Sixthly, This would be a great Inducement to Marriage, which all wise Nations have either encouraged by Rewards, or enforced by Laws and Penalties. It would encrease the Care and Tenderness of

Mothers towards their Children, when they were sure of a Settlement for Life, to the poor Babes, provided in some Sort by the Publick, to their annual Profit instead of Expence; we should soon see an honest Emulation among the married Women, which of them could bring the fattest Child to the Market. Men would become as fond of their Wives, during the Time of their Pregnancy, as they are now of their Mares in Foal, their Cows in Calf, or Sows when they are ready to farrow, nor offer to beat or kick them (as is too frequent a Practice) for fear of a Miscarriage.

Many other Advantages might be enumerated. For Instance, the Addition of some thousand Carcasses in our Exportation of Barrel'd Beef: The Propagation of Swine's Flesh, and Improvement in the Art of making good Bacon, so much wanted among us by the great Destruction of Pigs, too frequent at our Tables, which are no way comparable in Taste, or Magnificence to a well grown, fat yearling Child, which roasted whole will make a considerable Figure at a Lord Mayor's Feast, or any other Publick Entertainment. But this, and many others, I omit, being studious of Brevity.

Supposing that one thousand Families in this City, would be constant Customers for Infant's Flesh, besides others who might have it at merry Meetings, particularly at Weddings and Christenings, I compute that Dublin would take off Annually about twenty thousand Carcasses, and the rest of the Kingdom (where probably they will be sold somewhat cheaper) the remaining eighty Thousand.

I can think of no one Objection, that will possibly be raised against this Proposal, unless it should be urged, that the Number of People will be thereby much lessened in the Kingdom. This I freely own, and 'twas indeed one principal Design in offering it to the World. I desire the Reader will observe, that I calculate my Remedy for this one individual Kingdom of Ireland, and for no Other that ever was, is, or, I think, ever can be upon Earth. Therefore let no man talk to me of other Expedients: Of taxing our Absentees at five Shillings a Pound: Of using neither Cloaths, nor Household Furniture, except what is of our own Growth and Manufacture: Of utterly rejecting the Materials and Instruments that promote Foreign Luxury: Of curing the Expensiveness of Pride, Vanity, Idleness, and Gaming in our Women: Of introducing a Vein of Parcimony, Prudence and Temperance: Of learning to love our Country, wherein we differ even from Laplanders, and the Inhabitants of Topinamboo: Of quitting our Animosities, and Factions, nor act any longer like the Jews, who were murdering one another at the very Moment their

City was taken: Of being a little cautious not to sell our Country and Consciences for nothing: Of teaching Landlords to have at least one Degree of Mercy towards their Tenants. Lastly, Of putting a Spirit of Honesty, Industry, and Skill into our Shop-keepers, who, if a Resolution could now be taken to buy only our Native Goods, would immediately unite to cheat and exact upon us in the Price, the Measure, and the Goodness, nor could ever yet be brought to make one fair Proposal of just Dealing, though often and earnestly invited to it.

Therefore I repeat, let no Man talk to me of these and the like Expedients, till he hath at least some Glimpse of Hope, that there will ever be some hearty and sincere Attempt to put them in Practice.

But as to my self, having been wearied out for many Years with offering vain, idle, visionary Thoughts, and at length utterly despairing of Success, I fortunately fell upon this Proposal, which as it is wholly new, so it hath something Solid and Real, of no Expense and little Trouble, full in our own Power, and whereby we can incur no Danger in disobliging England. For this kind of Commodity will not bear Exportation, the Flesh being of too tender a Consistence, to admit a long Continuance in Salt, although perhaps I cou'd name a Country, which wou'd be glad to eat up our whole Nation without it.

After all, I am not so violently bent upon my own Opinion, as to reject any Offer, proposed by wise Men, which shall be found equally Innocent, Cheap, Easy, and Effectual. But before something of that Kind shall be advanced in Contradiction to my Scheme, and offering a better, I desire the Author or Authors, will be pleased maturely to consider two Points. *First*, As Things now stand, how they will be able to find Food and Raiment for a hundred Thousand useless Mouths and Backs. And *Secondly*, There being a round Million of Creatures in Human Figure, throughout this Kingdom, whose whole Subsistence put into a common Stock, would leave them in Debt two Millions of Pounds Sterling, adding those, who are Beggers by Profession, to the Bulk of Farmers, Cottagers and Labourers, with their Wives and Children, who are Beggers in Effect; I desire those Politicians, who dislike my Overture, and may perhaps be so bold to attempt an Answer, that they will first ask the Parents of these Mortals, Whether they would not at this Day think it a great Happiness to have been sold for Food at a Year Old, in the manner I prescribe, and thereby have avoided such a perpetual Scene of Misfortunes, as they have since gone through, by the Oppression of Landlords, the Impossibility of paying Rent without Money or

Trade, the Want of common Sustenance, with neither House nor Cloaths to cover them from the Inclemencies of the Weather, and the most inevitable Prospect of intailing the like, or greater Miseries, upon their Breed for ever.

I profess in the Sincerity of my Heart, that I have not the least Personal Interest in endeavouring to promote this necessary Work, having no other Motive than the Publick Good of my Country, by advancing our Trade, providing for Infants, relieving the Poor, and giving some Pleasure to the Rich. I have no Children, by which I can propose to get a single Penny; the youngest being nine Years Old, and my Wife past Child-bearing.

QUESTIONS FOR DISCUSSION

1. The poor do have higher birthrates than the middle and up-per class and they do live in more crowded housing. This is particularly true in the newly developing countries. Is there, thus, some truth to Hoppe's whimsical argument in *"A Proven System"*?

2. "Telecontraception" is not likely to come about. If, however, a very inexpensive means of contraception were made readily available to the "glazed-eyed, slack-jawed perpetual viewers" of TV, what political problems would be encountered in re-quiring, or even urging, its use by this segment of the popula-tion?

3. Any successful method of birth control—"boobicide" or what-have-you—does restrict population growth. Some economists argue that there is more truth than fiction (or humor) in the argument that more people = more consumption = a pros-perous economy. Is this a valid argument?

4. Is our "horrendous welfare problem" a function of the repro-ductive habits of the chronically out-of-work? Or is unemploy-ment not associated with size of family?

5. Hoppe says that "as matters stand, any unskilled, ill-equipped, untrained, accident-prone couple can willy-nilly shape the next generation. . . ." Would it infringe upon the rights of cit-

izens for government to require some type of standards for parenthood?

6. For most of our history the government did, in a sense, guarantee the right to life for all fetuses in that abortion was illegal in the United States. What attitudinal and legal changes in our culture brought about legal abortion?

7. Children born in the United States of foreigners are legal citizens of the United States. In the political era in which we live, is it ridiculous to think that lawyers might claim that if a woman conceived in the United States the fetus which results should have a claim to citizenship?

8. Hoppe says that little Harold at last is joined with Eva "as the Good Lord decreed...." Do some pro-life advocates argue, in all seriousness, that the joining of Harold and Eva is exactly what the good Lord decreed?

9. "Some masculinists argue that they have the right to do what they wish with their own spermatozoa." No one needs to be told who is being parodied here. But, what rights does the father of a fetus have if a woman wishes to have an abortion? Do you know what the Supreme Court ruling is in this matter?

10. Among other things, "A Modest Proposal" tends to dehumanize persons and treat them as an economic commodity. Where is this spelled out in the "Proposal"?

11. Drawing directly upon Swift's "A Modest Proposal," a 1986 British television program called the "Spiting Image" portrays a puppet caricature of Prime Minister Margaret Thatcher and her problems with unemployment in Britain:

> Where Swift proposed that poor children be eaten, the Thatcher puppet—speaking in tones of moral certitude and a voice that seemed a near-perfect imitation of the Prime Minister's—declared that the solution to the problem of unemployment was for the unemployed to "learn to eat their own flesh." (*New York Times*, April 10, 1986)

Do such proposals, seemingly disgusting, represent an effort to overcome the impersonality of unemployment statistics and make such a condition more personal?

12. Swift says "let no man talk to me of other expedients" of solving Ireland's problems. They had not worked. What ways of dealing with population and poverty have we tried which have not worked? Is the number of truly poor increasing or decreasing in our society today? What "modest proposals" are being offered to relieve their condition?

13. One commentator on Swift's satire says that "since there was no earthly chance of his previous remedies being applied, why not adopt that simplest and most radical of all: of reducing the population by profitable euthanasia?" (Murry, 1955) If we could reduce the growing cost—especially medical—of sustaining the life of the elderly by adopting a policy of euthanasia, what do you think would be the public response to such a proposal?

REFERENCES

Baldassare, Mark. *The Growth Dilemma.* Berkeley: Univ. of California Press, 1981.

Malthus, Thomas R. *An Essay on the Principle of Population.* New York: Random House, 1960.

Murry, John M. *Jonathan Swift.* New York: Farrar, Straus, and Giroux, 1955.

Ryder, Norman. *U.S. News and World Report.* March 22, 1976. 39.

Contributors

Woody Allen

One of America's most acclaimed Oscar-winning film writers; producer; actor; playwright; and winner of the O. Henry Award (1977) and other honors. A serious writer whose mode is humor. Author: *Without Feathers; Getting Even*; contributor to *The New Yorker, Playboy*, others.

Russell Baker

Syndicated columnist for *The New York Times*; since 1962 has written the "Observer," which appears three times a week and examines the foolishness of the human scene in its totality. Author: *Growing Up; Poor Russell's Almanac*; contributor to leading periodicals. "Russell Baker presides over the incongruous with total mastery."—Norman Cousins.

David Barry

Syndicated journalist whose column appears in over 100 newspapers. Author: *Stay Fit and Healthy until You're Dead; Babies and Other Hazards of Sex; Bad Habits; The Taming of the Screw.* Proceeds from the sales of Barry's books benefit the Dave Barry Ferrari Maintenance Fund.

Margaret Bennett

Pen name for Barbara Toohey and Jean Biermann, retired librarians from the Los Angeles Valley College, Van Nuys, California. Currently operate the Sugar Free Clinic for Diabetics in Van Nuys.

Roy Blount

Reporter, sports columnist, editorial writer for various papers; contributor to *Sports Illustrated, The New Yorker, New York Times Magazine*. Author: *About Three Bricks Shy of a Load* (nonfiction); *Not Exactly What I Had in Mind; What Men Don't Tell Women*. Became a journalist because he "couldn't play third base well enough."

Stephanie Brush

Author: *Men: An Owner's Manual*; Contributor to *Viva, Self, Cosmopolitan*. Lives in Greenwich Village and openly acknowledges that she enjoys watching television.

Art Buchwald

Widely syndicated columnist for the *Los Angeles Times* who resides in Washington, D.C. Buchwald is one of the nation's leading political satirists who has offered unsolicited (and unheeded) advice to presidents for a quarter of a century. Author: *You Can Fool All the People All the Time; Laid Back in Washington; Down the Seine and Up the Potomac; I Never Danced at the White House*.

Alice Childress

Actress; writer; lecturer; director of American Negro Theater for 12 years; Obie Award for best original off-Broadway play (1956), *Trouble in Mind*. Author: *Like One of the Family: Conversations from a Domestic's Life; Wine in the Wilderness* (play); *A Hero Ain't Nothing but a Sandwich* (juvenile).

Avery Corman

Novelist, playwright, educational film writer, book collaborator. Author: *Oh, God!; Kramer vs Kramer*. Both novels were made into successful movies. Contributor to *Esquire, Cosmopolitan, McCall's, New York*.

J. P. Donleavy

American author and playwright-in-exile since 1967, when he renounced his citizenship and moved to Ireland. Author: *The Ginger Man; The Unexpurgated Code: A Complete Manual of Survival and Manners; Shultz*; various plays.

Vernard Eller

Clergyman; professor of religion at La Verne College, La Verne, California; contributor to religious periodicals. Author: *His End Up; The Puritan Sex Manual; The MAD Morality.*

Nora Ephron

Columnist-editor for *Esquire*; contributor to *New York, Oui, Mc-Call's, Cosmopolitan.* Author: *Wallflower at the Orgy; Crazy Salad; Heartburn*

Bruce Feirstein

Freelance writer; contributor to *Playboy, New York.* Author: *Real Men Don't Eat Quiche.*

Harry Golden

1902–1981. Journalist, reporter, editor and publisher, *Carolina Israelite.* Lecturer before civic and religious groups; author numerous pamphlets on civil rights, Zionism, socialism. Contributor to major periodicals; author: *Enjoy! Enjoy!; Only in America; For 2¢ Plain.*

Lee Haggerty

Sociologist, Portland State University; specialty—methodology.

Joseph Heller

Author: *Catch-22* (translated into more than a dozen languages; sales of more than 8,000,000 worldwide); *God Knows.* Asked what he does for hobbies: "Nothing. What I *do* like is lying down."

Arthur Hoppe

Syndicated columnist for the *San Francisco Chronicle.* Contributor to leading periodicals including *The New Yorker* and *Harpers.* Author: *The Love Everybody Crusade; Miss Lollipop and the Doom Machine; The Marital Arts.*

Garrison Keillor

Writer; radio broadcaster. Since 1974 producer and host for "A Prairie Home Companion" which features reports from Lake Wobegon where "all the women are strong, all the men are good-looking, and all the children are above average." Winner in 1980 of the George Foster Peabody award for distinguished broadcasting. Contributor to *The New Yorker, Atlan-*

tic Monthly, Los Angeles Times. Author: *Happy to Be Here; Lake Wobegon Days*.

Fran Lebowitz

Writer with previous picturesque jobs in New York including bulk mailing and taxi driving. Columnist for *Mademoiselle, Interview*, and *Changes*. Author: *Metropolitan Life Social Studies*. She considers autographing books the "ultimate human activity."

Don Marquis

1878–1937. Columnist, playwright, poet. Worried that he might be remembered primarily for creating a cockroach (Archy). Author: *The Life and Times of Archy and Mehitabel; The Almost Perfect State; Hermione and Her Little Group of Serious Thinkers; The Old Soak* (play).

Judith Martin

Reporter, *Washington Post*. Author of the syndicated column, "Miss Manners." Member of faculty, George Washington University. Author: *The Name on the White House Floor; Miss Manners' Guide to Rearing Perfect Children; Miss Manners' Guide to Excruciatingly Correct Behavior*. She writes about etiquette because "somebody has to tell everyone how to act."

Gerald Nachman

Syndicated columnist, "The Single Life." Contributor to *Esquire, Newsweek, Penthouse, Saturday Review*. Author: *Playing House; Out on a Whim; Some Very Close Brushes with Life*.

Mike Royko

Chicago news columnist of whom it has been said that he "owns" Chicago. Well known for his caricatures of long-time Chicago mayor, Richard Daley. Author: *Boss: Richard J. Daley of Chicago; Up Against It; I May Be Wrong, But I Doubt It*. Pulitzer Prize, 1972, for commentary.

Dorothy Sayers

1893–1957. English novelist; detective stories; religious dramas; translator of Dante's *Divine Comedy*; social critic. One of the first women to obtain an Oxford degree; early feminist writer. Author: *Murder Must Advertise; The Nine Tailors; Unpopular Opinions*.

Jean Shepherd

Radio and television actor; playwright off-Broadway. Author: *The America of George Ade; In God We Trust, All Others Must Pay Cash; Wanda Hickey's Night of Golden Memories and Other Disasters; A Fistful of Fig Newtons.* Contributor to *Playboy, Car and Driver.*

Gloria Steinem

Television and film writer; editor of *Ms.*; columnist for *New York*; contributor to *Esquire, Vogue, Cosmopolitan.* Activist in the women's movement from 1968 on. Author: *The Thousand Indias; The Beach Book; Outrageous Acts and Everyday Rebellions.*

Jonathan Swift

1667–1745. English satirist; clergyman; champion of liberty for his native Ireland under British rule. Prolific writer, including *Gulliver's Travels.* Many essays, including *A Modest Proposal; An Argument against Abolishing Christianity; A Meditation upon a Broom Stick.*

Mark Twain

1835–1910. Pen name of Samuel Langhorne Clemens. The quintessential American humorist; reporter; novelist; writer of short stories. Probably best known for his pictures of pre-Civil War life along the Mississippi River: *The Adventures of Tom Sawyer; The Adventures of Huckleberry Finn; Life on the Mississippi.*

Bill Vaughan

1915–1977. Editor *Kansas City Star* and author of the nationally syndicated column, "Starbeams." Author: *Half the Battle.*

Kurt Vonnegut, Jr.

One of America's most widely read novelists and off-Broadway playwrights. Contributor to numerous publications including *Saturday Evening Post; McCall's; Playboy; Cosmopolitan.* Author: *Player Piano; Cat's Cradle; Slaughterhouse Five; God Bless You, Mr. Rosewater.*

Judith Wax

1932–1979. Bunny director for Playboy Enterprises; author: "The Watergate Tales" a satirical piece about the Watergate episode; *Starting in the Middle.*